# The Foreign Language Educator in Society
*Toward a Critical Pedagogy*

# The Foreign Language Educator in Society
## Toward a Critical Pedagogy

Timothy G. Reagan
Terry A. Osborn
*The University of Connecticut*

LONDON AND NEW YORK

First published 2002 by
Lawrence Erlbaum Associates, Inc.

Published 2016 by Routledge
2 Park Square, Milton Park, Abingdon, Oxfordshire OX14 4RN
711 Third Avenue, New York, NY 10017

*Routledge is an imprint of the Taylor and Francis Group, an informa business*

First issued in hardback 2015

Copyright © 2002 by Lawrence Erlbaum Associates, Inc.
All rights reserved. No part of this book may be reproduced in any form, by photostat, microform, retrieval system, or any other means, without prior written permission of the publisher.

Cover design by Kathryn Houghtaling Lacey

**Library of Congress Cataloging-in-Publication Data**
Reagan, Timothy G.
The foreign language educator in society : toward a critical pedagogy /
   Timothy G. Reagan, Terry A. Osborn.
      p. cm.

Includes bibliographical references and index.
ISBN 978-0-8058-3592-2 (pbk)
ISBN 978-1-138-13740-0 (hbk)

1. Language and languages—Study and teaching.
   I. Osborn, Terry A., 1966- II. Title.
P51 .R34    2002
418'.0071—dc21                     2001042856
                                                            CIP

*This book is dedicated to those,
both past and present, who have spent their lives
teaching and studying languages*

# Contents

| | | |
|---|---|---|
| | **Preface** | xi |
| 1 | **When Methodology Fails: A Critical Look at Foreign Language Education** | 1 |
| | The Realities of Contemporary Foreign Language Education | 2 |
| | The Ideological Limitations on Foreign Language Education in the United States | 7 |
| | Making the Case for Foreign Language Education | 11 |
| | Questions for Reflection and Discussion | 14 |
| | Focus on the Classroom | 14 |
| | Notes | 15 |
| 2 | **From Reflective Practice to Emancipatory Knowledge in Foreign Language Education** | 17 |
| | The Knowledge Base for the Foreign Language Educator | 18 |
| | The Real-World Tasks of the Teacher | 21 |
| | Reflective Practice in Foreign Language Education | 22 |
| | The Native–Heritage Language Teacher | 26 |
| | Critical Pedagogy and Public Schooling | 27 |
| | Emancipatory Democratic Schooling and the Foreign Language Educator | 29 |
| | Question for Reflection and Discussion | 30 |
| | Focus on the Classroom | 31 |
| | Notes | 31 |

## 3 Whose Language Is Real? Language Variation and Language Legitimacy — 33

- The Concept of Linguistic Legitimacy — 34
- The Debate About African American Vernacular English — 36
- Recognizing American Sign Language — 42
- Esperanto and Other Problems — 46
- Toward a Critique of Linguistic Legitimacy — 48
- Linguistic Legitimacy and the Foreign Language Educator — 50
- Questions for Reflection and Discussion — 51
- Focus on the Classroom — 52
- Notes — 53

## 4 Constructivist Epistemology and Foreign Language Teaching and Learning — 55

- Metaphors in Educational Discourse — 56
- Constructing Constructivism — 58
- Constructivist Teaching — 60
- Constructivism in Foreign Language Pedagogy — 62
- Questions for Reflection and Discussion — 68
- Focus on the Classroom — 68
- Notes — 69

## 5 Critical Curriculum Development in the Foreign Language Classroom — 70

- Problem Posing — 72
- Holism and the Critical Curriculum: The Role of Interdisciplinary Units — 74
- Critical Assessment and Evaluation — 79
- Implications for Foreign Language Pedagogy — 79
- Questions for Reflection and Discussion — 80
- Focus on the Classroom — 81
- Notes — 81

| | | |
|---|---|---|
| **6** | **Foreign Language Teaching as Social Activism** | 83 |
| | Foreignness as Imprimatur | 85 |
| | Curricular Nullification, Revisited | 87 |
| | Toward Practicing Praxis | 89 |
| | Toward a Critical Activism | 91 |
| | Questions for Reflection and Discussion | 91 |
| | Focus on the Classroom | 92 |
| | Notes | 92 |
| | | |
| **7** | **Language Rights as Human Rights: Social and Educational Implications** | 93 |
| | Conceptualizing Language Rights | 95 |
| | Violations of Language Rights | 97 |
| |     The Nonexistence of Kurdish | 97 |
| |     The Case of Post-Soviet Estonia | 98 |
| |     The Case of the United States | 100 |
| |     The Case of the Deaf | 100 |
| | Implications for the Foreign Language Classroom | 102 |
| | Questions for Reflection and Discussion | 103 |
| | Focus on the Classroom | 104 |
| | Notes | 104 |
| | | |
| **8** | **When in Rome (or Pretoria): Language Policy in International Perspective** | 106 |
| | The Nature and Purposes of Language Planning | 107 |
| | Ideologies of Language Policy | 110 |
| | The Language Planning Process | 113 |
| | Evaluating Language Policies | 114 |
| | The Case of Post-Apartheid South Africa | 115 |
| | The Case of Irish | 124 |
| | Language Policy and the Foreign Language Educator | 130 |

|   |   |   |
|---|---|---|
|   | Questions for Reflection and Discussion | 132 |
|   | Focus on the Classroom | 132 |
|   | Notes | 133 |
| **9** | **Toward a Critical Foreign Language Pedagogy** | **134** |
|   | The Metalinguistic Content of the Foreign Language Classroom | 135 |
|   | The Role of Portfolios and Teacher Narratives | 136 |
|   | What Do Two White Guys Know, Anyway? | 137 |
|   | Conclusion | 138 |
|   | Questions for Reflection and Discussion | 139 |
|   | Focus on the Classroom | 139 |
|   | Note | 140 |
|   | **References** | 141 |
|   | **Author Index** | 171 |
|   | **Subject Index** | 181 |

# Preface

> To be bilingual or multilingual is not the aberration supposed by many (particularly, perhaps, by people in Europe and North America who speak a "big" language); it is, rather, a normal and unremarkable necessity for the majority in the world today. A monolingual perspective is often, unfortunately, a consequence of possession of a "language of wider communication," as English, French, German, Spanish and other such languages are sometimes styled. This linguistic myopia is sometimes accompanied by a narrow cultural awareness and is reinforced by state policies which, in the main, elevate only one language to official status.
>
> —*Edwards* (1994, p. 1)

Language is at the core and heart of the human experience. It is not only what makes us unique among our fellow beings on our planet, but it is arguably the single most important tool that we use in maintaining human societies. It is, in fact, the glue that holds virtually everything else that we value together. Without language, there could be little technology, only fairly rudimentary human relationships, and at best incredibly limited cultures. To be sure, one can imagine communication without language—a dog is certainly capable of conveying feelings, needs, desires, affections, and so on, and many species have evolved fairly complex systems for communicating both within the species and between species. Such communication, though, is far more limited and restricted in nature than is human language, and it is with human language that we are concerned here.[1]

The authors of this volume have spent their lives studying, learning, and teaching languages. The love of language runs deep in both of us. As language educators, we have not only an affection for the languages that we study and teach, but also a desire to share that affection with our students, colleagues, and friends. We have found, however, that outside of the fairly small circle of bilingual and multilingual individuals we know in our own society, apathy (and even antipathy) are by far the most common responses among our fellow citizens toward foreign language study. Not only has the study of foreign languages not been a terribly successful or rewarding experience for many, but, the lessons that seem to have been learned about language are problematic. Many, perhaps even most people in our society, have fundamental misconceptions about the nature of language, attributes and characteristics of language, social and cultural functions of language, and the role of language in human society. In our experience, all too often these misconceptions and misunderstandings are found not only among those whose language learning experiences have been unsuccessful, but also ironically, among the smaller group of people who have met with success in language learning. As H. Tonkin (personal communication, 1998) once observed, linguistic chauvinism is by no means necessarily counteracted by bilingualism or even by multilingualism.

This volume then, seeks to address the social context of language, language teaching, and language learning in the United States. Its emphasis is on what teachers, and future teachers, of foreign languages in this country ought to know and understand about language, language attitudes, language practices, language rights, language policy, and related issues. We hope that it will encourage foreign language educators to somewhat broaden their conception of our own discipline, in ways that will make language study both more relevant for students and more critical with respect to its value in the development of the educated person in a democratic society.

## ORGANIZATION OF THE BOOK

*The Foreign Language Educator in Society: Toward a Critical Pedagogy* consists of nine chapters, each of which concludes with a series of questions for reflection and discussion, as well as a set of questions related directly to classroom practice. Chapter 1 sets the stage for the remainder of the volume by asking us to move beyond the typical focus on methodology in foreign language teaching and learning. In this chapter, we explore the practical and ideological realities of foreign language education in contemporary U.S. society, and discuss how one might begin to make a credible case for the relevance of foreign language study in what is in fact, for many of our students, a predominantly monolingual social and cultural context. In chapter 2, we turn our concern to the foreign language educator, seeking to determine both the knowledge base that is necessary for effective foreign language teaching and the nature of reflective practice as a component of critical and democratic schooling. Chapter 3 provides an examination of the concept of linguistic legitimacy: that is, what do people mean when they talk about real languages, and what are the implications of such discourse for education? In this chapter, we explore three specific cases: African American Vernacular English, American Sign Language, and Esperanto. These are all very controversial topics, but they are also issues about which foreign language educators need to be well informed. The role of epistemology in foreign language teaching and learning is the focus of chapter 4, as we attempt to build a case for the relevance and importance of constructivism for foreign language pedagogy. Chapter 5 addresses issues of critical curriculum development in foreign language education, and chapter 6 introduces the concept of the foreign language educator as a social activist. The nature and implications of language rights for foreign language education are explored in chapter 7, and chapter 8 moves us to a broader discussion of the nature, purposes, and evaluation of language planning and language policy around the world. Finally, in chapter 9, we discuss some of the implications of the rest of the volume for foreign language teaching and learning, with an emphasis on the development of metalinguistic awareness as a component of critical language awareness and critical foreign language pedagogy in U.S. education.

## ACKNOWLEDGMENTS

Some material in this volume was published in earlier versions in a variety of academic journals. We wish to thank the editors and publishers of their respective journals for permission to include parts of the following in this book:

- Timothy Reagan (1997). When is a language not a language? Challenges to 'linguistic legitimacy' in educational discourse. *Educational Foundations, 11,* 5–28.
- Timothy Reagan and Terry Osborn (1998). Power, authority, and domination in foreign language education: Toward an analysis of educational failure. *Educational Foundations, 12,* 45–62.
- Timothy Reagan (1999). Constructivist epistemology and second/foreign language pedagogy. *Foreign Language Annals, 32,* 413–425.

In writing this volume, we benefitted from the love and support of our wives, Jo Ann and Dina, and from our children. We are also grateful to our many friends and colleagues at the University of Connecticut for their critical insights and suggestions. Naomi Silverman of Lawrence Erlbaum Associates has, as always, been a wonderful friend and supporter. Finally, we would like to thank the reviewers of this manuscript—Theresa Austin, University of Massachusetts; Joan Kelly Hall, University of Georgia; Frank Nuessel, University of Louisville; Tove Skutnabb-Kangas, University of Roskilde; Lorrie Stoops Verplaetse, University of Southern Connecticut—for their many helpful comments and suggestions.

*—Timothy G. Reagan and Terry A. Osborn*

## NOTE

1. This does not mean that we believe that only human beings as a species (terrestrial or extraterrestrial, for that matter) are capable of creating and using language in the sense intended here. At this point in time, though, promising lines of research notwithstanding, we do not know of another species that uses language as do humans. The discovery of a nonhuman language that functions as do human languages

would create fascinating linguistic issues and questions. Indeed, one could argue that all human languages are simply varieties or dialects of a single Terran or Earthish language. Kalbfleisch, for instance, noted that, "According to Chomsky, a Martian sent to Earth would conclude we speak a variety of dialects with mutually unintelligible vocabularies—but dialects, nonetheless, of a single Earthish tongue" (quoted in Elgin, 2000, p. vii).

# 1

# When Methodology Fails: A Critical Look at Foreign Language Education

> Boys and girls "take" French or Spanish or German ... for three, four, or five years before entering college, only to discover there that they cannot read, speak, or understand it. The word for this type of instruction is not "theoretical" but "hypothetical." Its principle is "If it were possible to learn a foreign language in the way I have been taught, I should now know that language."
>
> —*Jacques Barzun* (1954, p. 119)

As experienced foreign language educators who have spent our personal and professional lives studying, learning, and teaching foreign languages, we find Barzun's criticism of our field all too timely, despite the fact that it was written nearly half a century ago. Far too little has changed since the 1950s in terms of how Americans[1] study and learn (or, more often, do not learn) languages other than English. This is not to say, of course, that there have not been significant changes in the teaching of foreign languages in the United States. Indeed, there have been dramatic changes in many ways. The shift from an essentially grammar-translation approach in language teaching to more communicative approaches (including the earlier popularity of audiolingual methods and more contemporary concerns with communicative language teaching) provides evidence for the claim that foreign language education is a discipline engaged in on-going self-examination and reflection. In fact, although the phrase paradigm shift has been widely overused in the educational literature, there can be little argument that what has taken place in foreign language education over the past century should really count as such an example of fundamental shifts in both the theories and methods used by practitioners. And yet, despite new approaches, theories, and practices, we find that little has changed in terms of the outcomes of foreign language education in our society. Even today, only roughly half of the students in the American public schools are likely to study a language other than English at some point in their education, and relatively few of those who do are likely to develop even a minimal level of competence in the target language.

The challenge that we have set for ourselves in this volume is to try to offer a start for understanding why this situation continues to exist in our society. We take as a given that foreign language education in American public schools is largely unsuccessful at producing individuals competent in second languages. We also take as a given that this lack of success is not due to any particular methodological or pedagogical failure on the part of foreign language teachers. To be sure, some foreign language teachers are better than others, some are more competent in the languages that they teach than others, and some foreign language programs are better designed and implemented than others. These factors alone do not, and cannot, explain the overwhelming nature of our failure to achieve our articulated goals. Rather, to explain why foreign language education is relatively unsuccessful in contemporary American society, we need to look more critically at the social, political, cultural, historical, and economic context in which foreign language education takes place. Only by contextualizing the experience of the foreign language learner, we believe, can one begin to understand both what is taking place in foreign language education and why it is taking place.

It is this contextualization of foreign language education and of the teaching and learning of languages other than English, which we believe is so essential for the foreign language teacher to understand. The classroom teacher of a language other than English must not only have competence in the target language, but must also understand the nature of language writ large, and must be sensitive to the political and sociocultural aspects of language and language use. In other words, the teacher of foreign languages must be able to function in a classroom setting as something of a critical, applied linguist. The role of the foreign language teacher, then, is not merely that of a guide to the target language, but also, and perhaps more importantly, of a mentor and colleague in the students' development of critical language awareness. Our purpose in writing this volume is to help you, as a future or current foreign language teacher, develop your own critical language awareness and sensitivity to linguistic issues that will help you yourself to be such a mentor for your own students.

## THE REALITIES OF CONTEMPORARY FOREIGN LANGUAGE EDUCATION

There are a large number of constraints in the public schools that tend to work against the effectiveness of contemporary foreign language education programs in the United States (see Osborn & Reagan, 1998; Reagan & Osborn, 1998). Among these constraints are the amount of time actually devoted to foreign language teaching and learning, the lack of significant extracurricular institutional support for foreign language learning, institutional and individual biases with respect to which languages are offered and who takes which language, the public justifications for foreign language education, the articulated goals of foreign language education, and finally, what might be termed the social expectation of failure with respect to the learning of languages other than English in the U.S. context.

Although various kinds of programs involving the teaching of foreign languages in the elementary school are gaining popularity in many parts of the United States (see Curtain & Pesola, 1994; Lipton, 1992), for the most part foreign language education still most often begins at either the middle or secondary school level for most students (see Rhodes & Branaman, 1999). This is, of course, counterintuitive at the very least. Although the measurable merits for early foreign language instruction can be debated, there is little doubt that the earlier one begins studying a second language, the better.[2] In societies in which language learning is considered to be an essential component of a child's education, children routinely begin the study of foreign languages very early in their schooling (see Baldauf, 1993; Beardsmore, 1993a, 1993b). Furthermore, when foreign language learning begins is only one part of the broader problem. Perhaps even more important is the amount of time actually devoted to language teaching and learning. Typically in American schools, foreign language classes meet one period a day, allowing in most school districts for a maximum of fewer than 150 hours of language study per year—a maximum that does not, it should be noted, take into account the many factors that inevitably impinge on this total, including teacher and student absences, fire drills, pep rallies, snow days, and so on, all of which reduce the amount of time actually devoted to language learning.

This hypothetical 150 hours of language study is actually very telling because we do know roughly how much time is needed to acquire different levels of competence in different languages (see Liskin-Gasparro, 1982). Using the expected levels of speaking proficiency guidelines from the Foreign Service Institute, we find that in order to achieve a level 1 to 1+ on the 5-point Interagency Language Roundtable (ILR) scale (which basically refers to survival proficiency), students with average aptitude for language learning require a minimum of 240 hours of instruction in French and Spanish, 480 hours for German, and even longer in the cases of most of the "less commonly taught languages," such as Arabic, Chinese, Japanese, and Russian (Hadley, 1993, p. 28; see also Brecht & Walton, 1994; Everson, 1993; Walker, 1989). In other words, given the time required for the acquisition of different languages, the time allocated to foreign language instruction in the schools in effect ensures that students, over the course of two years of study, will have had sufficient exposure to the target language to achieve at best minimal survival levels of competence in the target language, and are in fact very unlikely to achieve even that.

The time-related constraints on foreign language education are illuminating because they so clearly conflict with what is known (both intuitively and empirically) about what is required for successful second language learning. The bottom line here would seem to be that because no one could seriously expect the current approach to foreign language education to succeed, then the system must in fact be expected, at least to some degree, to fail.[3] This is, on its own, an intriguing insight, but it is far from the whole picture.

The time constraints in foreign language education are further exacerbated by the lack of any significant external institutional support for foreign language learning. Voluntary foreign language clubs and the occasional school-sponsored field trip notwithstanding, students of languages other than English in U.S. schools have very few real opportunities to utilize the target language in meaningful ways outside of the classroom context. Content courses (that is, courses in social studies, literature, mathematics, science, and so on) are almost never taught in foreign languages.[4] Even the growing popularity of interdisciplinary approaches in the classroom has had little impact on the foreign language education in many school districts. In short, in the typical middle and secondary school, foreign language education is very much seen by students and non-foreign language educators alike as peripheral to the real school experience.

Both subtle and blatant bias also impact foreign language instruction in the schools. A clear Eurocentric bias continues to be reflected in the languages most commonly offered in U.S. public schools, with the vast majority of students enrolled in French, Spanish, German, and Latin. Furthermore, social class background often affects the student's decision to study a foreign language at all, and folk wisdom about the relative ease and difficulty of particular languages, as well as assumptions about the appropriateness of different languages for particular students, also affect which language the student is likely to chose (or to be advised by school personnel to take). In our experience, Spanish is generally seen as a relatively easy option by students, parents, counselors, and other teachers, whereas German and Latin are seen as more difficult and thus suited to more capable students.[5] Thus, it could be argued that the language offerings of the school are grounded in historic sociopolitical power relationships, and that the selection of the language to be studied by the student is further constrained by his, her, or both social and educational background and expected life outcomes.

Public justifications for the study of foreign languages include three distinct types of arguments: cognitive, cultural, and pragmatic arguments. Cognitive arguments tend to emphasize the effectiveness of language study in promoting critical thinking, providing mental discipline, increasing mental flexibility and creativity, and improving cognitive functioning (see Jarvis, 1980; Keeskes & Papp, 2000). Although the evidence for such benefits is, we believe, quite compelling, it is not at all clear that these arguments have any more than rhetorical force in the arena of educational policy-making. The cultural arguments used to support foreign language study are less strong, and tend to rely largely on personal experience and anecdotal evidence. Beyond this, though, it is also evident that bilingualism all too often accompanies bicultural chauvinism rather than broad cultural tolerance and understanding. Pragmatic arguments, which are those that are grounded in con-

# WHEN METHODOLOGY FAILS

cerns about national security, the economic needs of U.S. society, and the consequences of foreign language study for employment, tend to be the most compelling in the public sphere (see Simon, 1980). Typical of pragmatic arguments is the following passage:

> With a language skill added to your other skills, you might double the chances of getting the job you want. There are openings for an auto mechanic who also speaks Arabic, an electronic radio expert who knows Japanese, a chef (even a woman chef) who understands French. It even could be a foreign language would be more useful to you during the next ten years than a college diploma ... You should weigh the judgment of one executive: "A person who speaks two languages is worth two people." Language is, in fact, your hidden job insurance. (Jarvis, 1980, pp. 31–32)

The basic problem with this type of argument is that while it may have a certain degree of face validity for foreign language educators and our allies, it is not in fact compatible with the life experiences of most students (or, for that matter, with the life experiences of their parents). The United States, regardless of how one personally feels about it, is in fact a profoundly monolingual society ideologically if not empirically, and relatively few students (or parents, teachers, or policy-makers) really believe that second language skills are really necessary for the marketplace. Claims about language skills being "job insurance" are viewed with considerable scepticism in a society in which monolingualism in English is seen as the norm (see Hymes, 1996, pp. 84–85). A final problem with such pragmatic arguments is the issue of competence: The level of language competence required in those jobs that do require language skills are far beyond what students can be expected to learn in a typical foreign language program at the secondary level. Even if a student had been fortunate enough to study Arabic for two or three years at the high school level, for instance, and also had the benefit of appropriate automotive training, it is hardly likely that she, he, or both would be able to function as an Arabic-speaking auto mechanic.

If the justifications commonly offered for studying a foreign language in secondary school are not compelling, then why do students do so? Are they wasting their time? Are they simply ignorant of their own self-interest? The answer is really quite simple: Taking (and passing) foreign language classes often functions as a necessary condition for admission to college. In other words, getting through a couple of years of foreign language classes is simply one of the hurdles that one must endure to get into higher education (which, in turn, is a hurdle that is for the most part required for social class maintenance and upward mobility). It is this function, rarely articulated publicly but commonly recognized by both students and others, that in actual fact would seem to be served by secondary level foreign language classes.

Another problem area in need of consideration here is that of the articulated goals of foreign language education in the United States, especially when placed in contrast to those of bilingual education programs. These two kinds of programs, in general, serve different populations and seek to achieve different ends, although both are concerned with second language acquisition. The difference between the two is perhaps best seen in terms of the kind of language proficiency that is the goal. In the literature on contemporary U.S. bilingual education, a common distinction is made between what are called basic interpersonal communicative skills (BICS) and cognitive academic language proficiency (CALP; see Collier, 1987, 1989; Cummins, 1980, 1981, 1984). BICS refers to the language skills needed for casual conversational use of the target language, while CALP refers to the degree and kind of proficiency needed for intellectual and academic purposes (see Samway & McKeon, 1999). As Cummins (1994) explained:

> Research studies ... suggest that very different time periods are required for students to attain peer-appropriate levels in conversational skills in English as compared to academic skills. Specifically, while there will be major individual differences, conversational skills often approach nativelike levels within about two years of exposure to English, whereas a period of four to nine years ... or five to seven years of school exposure has been reported as necessary for second language students to achieve as well as native speakers in academic aspects of English. (p. 39)

Researchers and bilingual educators have argued, based on these results, that students achieve BICS far sooner than CALP, and that this distinction makes necessary extended transitional programs for non-English-speaking students in the U.S. context. Although the distinction between BICS and CALP may in fact be somewhat questionable (see Martin-Jones & Romaine, 1986; Spolsky, 1989), it is nevertheless an interesting one for discussion purposes here, since the kinds of language proficiency included in BICS probably more than exceed typical expectations for student functioning in the target language in foreign language education programs. Indeed, the kind of proficiency downplayed in bilingual education programs as inadequate would be seen in a foreign language context as quite impressive. It would certainly not, in our view, be out of line to suggest that achieving a good level of BICS would constitute a high level of success in the typical foreign language program.

Finally, the last of the structural and pedagogical constraints against which foreign language education finds itself working is a widespread and general social expectation of failure. This social expectation of failure is in fact the thread that holds together the other structural, institutional, and pedagogical constraints discussed here. Foreign language education in the United States is clearly not successful for most students, nor could it be given the way that it has been, and continues to be, implemented in the schools. Furthermore, it is clear that most students, parents, teachers, and policy-makers do not seriously expect it to succeed. Rather, it serves an important tracking and sorting function in U.S. education—a function quite different from the arguments that foreign language educators sincerely offer for it. The same is, for the most part, true in higher education as well. At the undergraduate level, completion of a certain number of foreign language classes often serves as a requirement for graduation, whereas graduate level programs commonly require the demonstration of reading proficiency in a foreign language, but generally give no credit for course work to satisfy this requirement. In fact, in recent years many institutions have attempted to circumvent the foreign language requirement with the establishment of a cognate field, or even the declaration of computer language or statistics as satisfying the foreign language requirement. Even among the best educated persons in our society, in short, competence in a second language is often seen as irrelevant, except in its limited role of serving to control and restrict access.

Although many of these structural, institutional, and pedagogical constraints might at first appear to be the result of technical and scheduling difficulties, we would suggest that they represent far deeper and more significant features of public education in our society. We turn now to a discussion of the ideological constraints on foreign language education in the United States to allow for the further exploration of this point.

## THE IDEOLOGICAL LIMITATIONS ON FOREIGN LANGUAGE EDUCATION IN THE UNITED STATES

The ideological content of both the formal and hidden curricula is well established and well documented in general terms (see Altbach, Kelly, Petrie, & Weis, 1991; Apple, 1990, 1995; Apple & Weiss, 1983). Extensive scholarly analysis has been done on such areas as social studies, the literary canon in English, sexism and racism in textbooks, and so on (see Luke, 1988; Woodward, Elliott, & Nagel, 1988). As Apple and Christian-Smith (1991) noted, "During the past two decades, a good deal of progress has been made on answering the question of whose knowledge becomes socially legitimate in schools" (p. 1). Although the fundamental issue here is one of epistemology (see Steedman, 1988; Steffe, 1995), normative issues of value and bias also play significant roles in the establishment and maintenance of ideological hegemony in U.S. society (see Beyer & Apple, 1988).

Teachers and other educators have been made very aware of and sensitive to explicit issues of bias in the curriculum, and teacher education students are commonly advised about identifying and rectifying such biases in the curriculum (see, for example, Banks, 1994, pp. 117–121; Gollnick & Chinn, 1994, pp. 320–326; Nieto, 1996). There is, at the very least, a rhetorical commitment to eliminating blatant bias in the curriculum in U.S. public education. Nonetheless, as Anyon (1979) observed in her study of U.S. social studies textbooks, the textbook:

> suggests a great deal about the society that produces and uses it. It reveals which groups have power and demonstrates that the views of these groups are expressed and legitimized in the school curriculum. It can also identify social groups that are not empowered by the economic and social patterns in our society and do not have their views, activities, and priorities represented in the school curriculum ... Omis-

sions, stereotypes, and distortions that remain in "updated" social studies textbook accounts of Native Americans, Blacks, and women reflect the relative powerlessness of these groups. (p. 382)

In the case of foreign language education, although obvious bias has been largely (though by no means completely) eliminated in textbooks and instructional materials in recent years, the underlying ideological and cultural biases for the most part remain unexamined and unaddressed. Although this is no doubt true of the wider curriculum as well, in the case of foreign language education the basics that can be identified are centrally concerned with the actual content and purpose of the formal curriculum, and have the effect of essentially nullifying important elements of the formal curriculum.

An important aspect of the ideological content and functions of the curriculum is visible in the national standards movement. The debate about the content of the national standards in social studies, for instance, has been largely one informed by and grounded in competing ideological perspectives (see Nash, Crabtree, & Dunn, 1997). In the case of foreign language education, the national standards have been far less controversial, in part because the standards themselves are the product of foreign language educators who took their task seriously and produced standards that presupposed a commitment to meaningful language learning on the part of the polity (see National Standards in Foreign Language Education Project, 1996). It is with this assumption, though, that the problem arises, because it is by no means clear that the general public really shares this commitment.

A number of other issues arise as well with respect to subtle bias and internal contradictions in the foreign language curriculum. Most blatant, perhaps, is the label "foreign" itself—a clear identification of the target language of the classroom as "Other" (see National Standards in Foreign Language Education Project, 1996, p. 23; Osborn, 1998a). As such, the target language inevitably becomes something of an object of apathy at best, and of suspicion or even rejection at worst. Recent efforts to change nomenclature, utilizing the term world languages in place of foreign languages, to some extent addresses such concerns, but only at the level of what might be termed *articulated bias*. Regardless of what they are called, in U.S. schools languages other than English are in fact perceived, by both adults and students, as foreign. This perception is in fact only strengthened, we believe, by encouraging the use of what is seen as a politically correct label (i.e., world languages). The risk with such word games, as Apple (1979) noted, is that "historically outmoded, and socially and politically conservative (and often educationally disastrous) practices are not only continued, but are made to sound as if they were actually more enlightened and ethically responsive ways of dealing with children" (p. 144).[6]

In addition, the concept of linguistic legitimacy (that is, what counts and what does not count as a real language) underlies foreign language education in a variety of ways (see Reagan, 1997b). Not only are most human languages excluded from serious consideration as real languages, but even more, the variety of the target language tends to be very selectively chosen. Thus, Spanish classes commonly employ *castellano* as their norm (although certainly less so than in the past), just as French classes use Parisian French as their model. Although there are many compelling reasons for such choices, they nonetheless have important consequences for the foreign language student. First, even where there are local opportunities for students to actually use the target language (Spanish in the Southwest, French in parts of the Northeast, and so forth), the language of the classroom tends to differ dramatically from the local variety, thus again emphasizing the Otherness of the classroom language, and minimizing its actual usefulness for students.

An additional problem in this regard is that posed by the native speaker or heritage language learner of the target language in the foreign language classroom (see Clyne, Fernandez, Chen, & Summo-O'Connell, 1997). It is not uncommon for native speakers of Spanish, for instance, to have difficulties in basic Spanish foreign language classes, largely because of the differences between the normative language employed in the classroom and the language variety of the native speaker (see Ruíz, 1991; Valdés, Lozano, & García-Moya, 1981). Our point here is a simple one: It is not necessarily the native-speaking student who should be seen as the problem, but rather, the attitudes and values related to language held by the school and teachers (including foreign language teachers). As Valdés (1981) noted:

> it is a fact that a surprising number of Spanish-speaking students ... are still being placed in beginning Spanish classes for non-speakers to help them "unlearn" their "bad" habits and begin anew as foreign speakers. It matters not that the student is fluent and has internalized every single grammar rule that the teacher may hope to present. If he says *traiba* for *traía,* many schools will make him "begin from the beginning" ... every day teachers of Spanish casually enroll native Spanish-speaking students in beginning Spanish classes for non-speakers, in which the materials used have been designed exclusively for teaching English-speaking students. The students are expected, in the process, to acquire the standard Spanish dialect as opposed to that normally used in their own speech communities. (p. 7)

Bowers and Flinders (1990) argued that "the language processes of the class can be understood as an ecology of power that advantages certain groups of students over others" (p. 26), and nowhere is this more apparent than in the foreign language classroom. Although all teachers are empowered to some extent by their presumed expertise (just as students are essentially disempowered by their lack of expertise in the subject matter being studied), in the case of the foreign language teacher, not only is content at issue but so too is the ability to communicate in what is in essence the language of the classroom. This difference alone makes the foreign language class different from others, and implies a different and even more significant power differential between foreign language educators and their students. As Craig (1995) noted:

> Traditionally, the [foreign language] teacher's role has been seen as that of an authoritative expert. This view is based on the conception of knowledge as a quantifi-

able intellectual commodity. The teacher, as an expert in a field of inquiry or as an expert speaker of a language, has more of this knowledge than his or her students have. Because this knowledge has a separate existence outside of its knowers, it can be given, or taught, to the learners by the teacher–expert. (p. 41)

The teacher of foreign languages occupies a unique position in the context of public education. She, he, or both often is called on to be the school's unofficial translator–interpreter for foreign documents as well as for dealing with non-English-speaking parents and visitors. Furthermore, because most administrators and supervisors do not possess the language skills to assess a teacher's proficiency, often the evaluation of such teachers is more limited in nature than might be the case in other subject areas. In fact, in our experience foreign language teachers have been known to use code-switching as a strategy to increase the difficulty an administrator may have when observing a lesson. The hope, as we have heard it expressed, is that supervisors will assume that since they hear a foreign language being used, sound and effective instruction must be taking place.

A foreign language teacher's own language proficiency is rarely evaluated, and then usually in a fairly perfunctory manner. This is, interestingly enough, especially true in the case of the less commonly taught languages, where the teacher is likely to be the sole speaker of the target language in the school. Where there are other speakers of the language on staff, as is sometimes the case with bilingual education teachers, it is not uncommon to find foreign language teachers engaged in subtle disputes about relative language competence, especially where other speakers of the language may speak a less prestigious or nonstandard variety of the language. In some school districts, foreign language teachers replace guidance counselors in the context of placement advisor with respect to foreign language classes, and have been known to use this power to guide native speakers (and heritage language learners as well) into independent study courses, thus isolating the student and protecting the teacher from any challenge to linguistic authority in the classroom. This is especially significant, because the native speaker could be validated by the classroom teacher as a knower in the foreign language classroom context. Far from just a language issue, the refusal to recognize the native speaker as a knower may well function as a strategy to make such students invisible, thus preserving and legitimizing the dominant group's way of viewing what is language and who is a language user. Finally, the foreign language teacher controls, to a significant extent, not only the content of the foreign language curriculum, but also serves as the arbitrator of what counts as correct and incorrect use in the target language, as well as preferred lexical and grammatical choices. In addition, the teacher has the opportunity to employ what could be called the official code-switch. The foreign language teacher decides when classroom conversation should be in English and when it must be in the target language, thus effectively controlling classroom discourse (see Gee, 1996; Heath, 1983; Hymes, 1996).

## MAKING THE CASE FOR FOREIGN LANGUAGE EDUCATION

Our comments in this chapter thus far might lead one to assume that we were hostile to the study and teaching of languages other than English in the U.S. context, but in fact nothing could be further from the truth. The fact that there are structural, organizational, and ideological barriers that generally hinder both successful second language learning by English speakers in our society as well as the development of positive attitudes and dispositions toward the learning of other languages merely serves to help to explain why foreign language education has been, and remains, relatively unsuccessful. The challenge before us is to find arguments that are compelling for those outside the field of foreign language education, and then to find ways of ensuring the effective teaching and learning of additional languages in our society.

It is interesting, of course, that of all of the academic subjects normally offered in American public schools, no other discipline is asked to defend its existence in the way that foreign language education is routinely challenged. Imagine, for a moment, applying the arguments against foreign language study to other subjects in the curriculum—be they mathematics, science, reading, geography, history, literature, or whatever. How seriously would we, as a society and as individual educators, take claims like the following:

- I studied algebra, geometry, and calculus in school, and have forgotten all I learned. I don't think that I have ever had any practical use for anything that I had to study in a mathematics class in high school or college, and I can't see any reason to make today's students study such things.
- History may be of interest to a small number of individuals, and they should be allowed to study it, so long as there are enough of them to make it economically defensible. The average person has no need for history or historical knowledge, though.
- It's pretty clear that most Americans know almost nothing about geography. Many can't even name the state capitals! Because we seem to do such a poor job teaching geography, maybe we'd be better off just not offering it at all, except to those students really interested in it.
- What is the point of studying earth science anyway? I've never really needed to know what I learned in those classes in high school. Why would I care if I could identify different kinds of rocks? I'm not a geologist, after all.

Of course, all of these arguments are fundamentally silly. They confuse the utility of a subject for a specific individual or group of individuals with its educational purpose. More than that, they trivialize the disciplines at issue and why we, as a society, believe that children should study these subjects. These claims also beg the question of what exactly is encompassed by the term educated person—a concept on which there is a vast literature in educational philosophy (see, for example, Barrow & Woods, 1988; Hamm, 1989; Hirst, 1974; Peters, 1966, 1967, 1973). When applied to language study, though, such arguments in our society all too often seem to take on a legitimacy that would not apply to any other subject matter. There is, then, a very practical reason for us to offer yet another justification for why foreign languages should be an important and integral component of the curriculum for all students, and it is to the task of outlining such a justification that we now turn.

Earlier in this chapter, we identified three common kinds of arguments that are most commonly used to support foreign language education programs in our society: cognitive, cultural, and pragmatic arguments. We also noted that only the first of the three is really all that credible in factual and empirical terms, and that unfortunately, the cognitive benefits of second language study are most often not politically compelling. So, where does this leave us? It leaves us in need of a more compelling articulation of why students ought to study (and learn) languages other than their own. Fortunately, such a justification is not only possible, but is fully in keeping with the most current educational thought and practice (see Elgin, 2000; Lomas & Osora, 1999).

For us, perhaps the most powerful argument for the need for students to study languages other than their own is that the point of education is to introduce and initiate the individual into our common, human social and cultural heritage, and that this cannot be done adequately without some exposure to the different ways in which human beings, in various times and places, have constructed an amazingly wide variation of languages to meet their needs. If becoming educated is, as many scholars have suggested, the process by which one learns to join in the human conversation, then language skills will inevitably be required if one wishes to join the conversation at anything more than the most trivial level.

On an even deeper level, one can argue that it is in the study of human language—both as an abstract entity and in terms of specific human languages—that one comes closest to what Chomsky called "the human essence." Indeed, one of the more fascinating outcomes of the study of human language over the past few centuries has been the discovery that there is no such thing as a primitive language, that each and every human language (of which there are currently well in excess of 5,000)[7] is a full, complete, and rule-governed entity capable of serving its users and their needs. Furthermore, the recognition that in spite of their many differences, all human languages also share a number of significant common features—that is, what linguists call linguistic universals. It is in these linguistic universals that we may come closest to identifying what it is, exactly, that makes us human.

The study of languages other than one's own cannot only serve to help us understand that we as human beings have in common, but can also assist us in understanding the diversity that underlies not only our languages, but also our ways of constructing and organizing knowledge, and the many different realities in which we all live and interact. Such understanding has profound implications not only epistemologically, but also with respect to developing a critical awareness of language and social relationships. In studying languages other than our own, we are seeking to understand (and, indeed, in at least a weak sense, to become) the Other—we are, in short, attempting to enter into realities that have, to some degree, been constructed by others and in which many of the fundamental assumptions about the nature of knowledge and society may be different from our own. We are, in fact, creating new selves in an important sense. Such creation and recreation forces each of us to reflect more deeply on many of the core questions related to being an educated person, as well as requiring that we become not merely tolerant of differences, but truly understanding of differences (linguistic and otherwise) and their implications. The sort of humility that is learned from studying a language other than one's own is a valuable possession in its own right, though of course language learning is by no means the only arena in which humility can be learned.

The case presented thus far applies only in those instances in which we conceive of the end purpose of education to be the emergence of the educated person. To the extent to which this is not our goal, of course, the argument fails—but then we are faced with what are far more serious problems, at least for those of us committed to the ideals of democracy. In other words, the case for the study of foreign languages rests on the view that all people in a democratic society are entitled to the best and most complete sort of education possible. As the philosopher of education Dewey (1943) so cogently asserted, "What the best and wisest parent wants for his own child, that must the community want for all of its children" (p. 7). The study of human languages must be a part of such education, we would argue, if one is truly concerned with democratic education and education for democracy (see Goodlad, 1994; Gutman, 1987; Soder, 1996). If democracy is removed as part of our conception of education, however, then one is left with little to do but to agree with Adolf Hitler's (1940) assertion that:

> One can, for instance, not see why millions of people, in the course of the years, have to learn two or three foreign languages which thereafter only a fraction of which they can use and which therefore the majority of them forget again completely, for out of a hundred thousand pupils who, for instance, learn French, hardly two thousand will later on be able to use it actually, while ninety-eight thousand, throughout their entire future course of life, will no longer be in a situation where they can make use of what they have learned. During their youth, therefore, they have devoted thousands of hours to a matter which later is of no value or significance to them ... Thus for the sake of two thousand people for whom the knowledge of this language is of use, actually ninety-eight thousand have to be tortured in vain and sacrifice valuable time. (p. 627)

We believe that Hitler was profoundly wrong about the study of foreign languages insofar as life in a democracy is concerned. He was not wrong, though, in recognizing that the widespread study of foreign languages may well not serve the best interests of the state in nondemocratic societies. Control of knowledge of all sorts, and limiting the access of citizens to knowledge, has been and continues to be a central characteristic of modern totalitarian societies of both the right and the left. Knowledge of language and languages is but one piece of the puzzle, though nevertheless a very important piece, in our view.

## QUESTIONS FOR REFLECTION AND DISCUSSION

1. The authors paint a fairly bleak picture of the state of foreign language education in contemporary U.S. society. To what extent to you agree with them? In what ways do you disagree? Why?
2. One of the important underlying aspects of this chapter is the notion of the educated person. It is clear that in many other societies, and at times in our own past, second language skills have been generally considered to be a necessary condition for an individual to count as a educated person. Do you believe that knowledge of a language other than one's own should be required as part of a person's education? Why or why not?
3. Although the authors argue that there is a tie between democratic education and the need for foreign language study, many very repressive societies have in fact been bilingual or even multilingual, whereas many contemporary democratic societies (including the United States) are, or seek to be, monolingual. How would you explain this discrepancy? What lessons can this teach us about foreign language teaching and learning?
4. If it were possible to provide 100% accurate machine translation for all languages, would there still be reasons to study foreign languages? What does this suggest to you with respect to the providing a justification for a place for foreign language in the curriculum?
5. What are the implications of the distinction between basic interpersonal communication skills (BICS) and cognitive academic language proficiency (CALP) for the foreign language curriculum?

## FOCUS ON THE CLASSROOM

1. What are the ways used by students to indicate that foreign language classes are not top priority in their academic lives? What are the implications of these for making classroom practice more effective in the foreign language context?
2. How can foreign language teachers demonstrate the importance of foreign language learning to students, both in and out of the classroom?
3. Do you really believe that all students can learn a foreign language? Why or why not? What are the implications of your beliefs about foreign language learning for your own teaching practice?

4. Given the relatively limited amount of time available to foreign language instruction, do you believe that formal grammatical instruction is important? Would such instruction be more or less significant if we had more time with our students? Why or why not?
5. Why did you originally decide that you wished to be a foreign language educator? What does your answer to this questions tell you about your responses to the other questions in this section?

## NOTES

1. The use of the term Americans to refer to those of us who live in the United States, as well as the use of the adjective American, are obviously problematic. In a very meaningful sense, anyone living in any part of the Americas ought to count as American, and the adjective should refer to things common to all of us. However, standard usage of these terms in the U.S. remains narrow and parochial. One reason for this, we believe, is the lack of appropriate-sounding, non-pedantic alternatives in English. We have, therefore, decided to mix labels as best we can, and trust that readers will understand that when we speak of Americans, our focus is really solely on those people in the U.S.
2. Although there are clear benefits of early second language learning, it is important to note that much of the scholarly literature in the field may have overplayed such benefits, and have underestimated effective second language learning in older students (see, for example, Marinova-Todd, Marshall, & Snow, 2000; Samway & McKeon, 1999, pp. 20–21).
3. The really interesting aspect of this, in our view, is not the fact that most students do not acquire a high degree of competence in the target language, but rather, is the fact that some do. Given the barriers that they face, it is truly remarkable that some individuals do learn second languages in the U.S. school and university context.
4. The exception to this general rule occurs in the context of bilingual education. Content subject matter is taught in languages other than English in such settings, and in dual immersion and two-way bilingual education programs, such instruction is an especially valuable component of the second language learning process.
5. There is a core of truth here, of course. The estimates provided by the Foreign Language Institute for gaining varying degrees of proficiency in different languages makes quite clear the fact that some languages are indeed more difficult than others for native speakers of English to learn. However, in our experience, assumptions made about the relative ease of different languages in the secondary school context are based largely on bias and misinformation.
6. We have chosen to use the term *foreign,* but do so as a way of emphasizing the hidden agenda that goes with the concept of *foreign-ness* in our society. It seems clear to us that when people in the U.S. talk about foreign languages, they mean exactly what

they say—such languages are marks of Otherness. See Osborn (2000, pp. 81–96) for a detailed discussion of this matter. We would also note that in the Canadian context, the preferred terms are *second language* and *second language education*.

7. Estimates of the number of languages in the world today vary dramatically, and in truth, no one really knows how many languages are spoken. Indeed, even determining languages and language varieties and dialects is immensely problematic much of the time. The number 5000 is a relatively moderate estimate (see Nettle, 1999). Skutnabb-Kangas (2000) pointed out, however, that whatever number we select, we should probably double it to encompass all of the different sign languages that are found around the world—a point with which we agree wholeheartedly.

# 2

# From Reflective Practice to Emancipatory Knowledge in Foreign Language Education

> If we want to improve our teaching through reflective inquiry, we must accept that it does not involve some modification of behavior by externally imposed directions or requirements, but that it requires deliberation and analysis of our ideas about teaching as a form of action based on our changed understandings.
>
> —*Bartlett* (1990, p. 203)

There has been a long-standing debate among educators and those interested in education about the nature of teaching. This debate usually takes the form of a dichotomy, with the basic issue being presented as whether teaching is best understood as some sort of artistic endeavor, with the teacher's role seen as roughly comparable to that of the painter or creative writer, or whether teaching is best conceptualized as an application of particular scientific principles in specific settings. At its heart, this dichotomy is concerned with whether teachers are born or made—or, even if some (relatively few) teachers are indeed born, whether others (the vast majority) can be made. This is a very important matter, because most classroom teachers are probably not born teachers. As Van Doren (1959) once insightfully commented,

> Good teachers have always been and will always be, and there are good teachers now. The necessity henceforth is that fewer of them be accidents. The area of accident is reduced when there is a design which includes the education of teachers. Not the training—a contemporary term that suggests lubricating oil and precision parts, not to say reflexes and responses. (pp. 170–171)

The challenge that faces us as educators is determining what kinds of knowledge and skills are essential to competent practice in the classroom. In other words, what we are really concerned with is identifying the knowledge base for successful teaching.[1] The educational psychologist Shulman (1987) identified seven broad categories of knowledge which would, taken together, constitute the major components of the knowledge base for the classroom teacher. On Shulman's account, the teacher needs to have mastered:

- content knowledge;
- general pedagogical knowledge, with special reference to those broad principles and strategies of classroom management and organization that appear to transcend subject matter;
- curriculum knowledge, with particular grasp of the materials and programs that serve as tools of the trade for teachers;
- pedagogical content knowledge, that special amalgam of content and pedagogy that is uniquely the province of teachers, their own special form of professional understanding;
- knowledge of learners and their characteristics;
- knowledge of educational contexts, ranging from the workings of the group or classroom, the governance and financing of school districts, to the character of communities and cultures; and
- knowledge of educational ends, purposes, and values, and their philosophical and historical grounds. (p. 54)

Shulman's conceptualization of the teacher education knowledge base is, by its very nature, quite general and nonspecific. If it is to be useful to us, though, we need to move this knowledge base to the next level of specificity. In other words, how is this knowledge base manifested in the case of the foreign language educator? It is to a discussion of this matter that we now turn.

## THE KNOWLEDGE BASE FOR THE FOREIGN LANGUAGE EDUCATOR

Content knowledge is at the top of Shulman's conceptualization of the teacher education knowledge base, and this is as it should be; clearly one must know a subject in order to teach it effectively. In the context of foreign language education, this means that the foreign language teacher should have achieved a high degree of competence in the target language. This would seem to be axiomatic; it is somewhat puzzling to imagine a language being taught by someone who does not speak it well—and yet in all too many cases, that is in fact the case. In addition to language competence, content knowledge for the foreign language educator includes quite an array of other aspects of language knowledge (see Franklin, Laurence, & Welles, 1999; Guntermann, 1993; Richards, 1998; Wallace, 1991). The language educator should not only speak, understand, read, and write the target language well, but should be familiar with it from both linguistic and sociolinguistic perspectives. A formal understanding of the phonology and morphology of the language is essential for the effective teacher, as is an awareness of the social and cultural contexts in which the target language is used. A knowledge of the historical development of the language is also valuable, as of course, is a broad and deep knowledge of the literature of the language. What this all amounts to is that the language teacher must be thoroughly and deeply familiar with the target language and the speaker community, and must be so at both a pragmatic and theoretical level. Native speakers certainly have some advantages in this regard, but merely being a native speaker of a language in no way prepares one to teach it.

Beyond content knowledge, there is general pedagogical knowledge which is necessary for effective teaching practice regardless of one's area of specialization. Included here, on Shulman's account, "are those broad principles and strategies of classroom management and organization that appear to transcend subject matter" (1987, p. 54). Such principles and strategies are not particularly difficult to identify; they are, in essence, the knowledge and skills that often allow us to differentiate between successful and unsuccessful classroom teachers. An individual may well be a competent user of the target language without being effective (or even in control) of the classroom. Among the principles and strategies that can be considered to be core pedagogical knowledge and skills are instructional planning, lesson presentation skills, questioning skills, interpersonal communication skills, classroom management skills, and knowledge of evaluation approaches and strategies (see, e.g., Cooper, 1990).

The language educator needs not only content and pedagogical knowledge, but also requires specific curriculum knowledge. In other words, it is important for the teacher not only to be competent in the target language, but also to know what aspects of the language are generally taught at different levels. The teacher might well be very versed and knowledgeable about specific linguistic aspects of the target language, but in a classroom context, this specialized knowledge must, to a certain extent, be subjugated to the established and generally accepted curriculum. Thus, in a basic Spanish course, a detailed discussion of the historical evolution of the subjunctive would be both inappropriate and arguably poor pedagogy, regardless of the accuracy of the presentation. Similarly, the vocabulary emphasized at different levels of second language instruction will generally move from most general to increasingly specialized (see Schmitt, 2000).[2] Color terminology, for instance, is arguably an appropriate focus for a beginning language class, as would be terminology to describe family relationships. Terminology used to describe complex sociopolitical issues is probably less so.[3] Finally, an important part of curriculum knowledge on the part of the classroom teacher is an awareness of the ancillary materials generally used by language teachers—realia, music, and so forth.

This brings us to what Shulman (1987) called *pedagogical content knowledge,* which is basically a powerful combination of content, pedagogical, and curricular knowledge. This combination, though, is an instance in which the total is greater than the sum of the parts, because it refers to the specialized articulated and unarticulated knowledge that language educators are able to manifest in classroom practice. This knowledge goes far beyond merely content or pedagogical knowledge; it is, at its base, the understanding not of the target language, but rather of how particular features of the target language are most likely to be acquired by learners.

The effective language educator must also have a detailed and in-depth knowledge of learners, learning and teaching styles, and barriers to learning. Included here would, of course, be the work of Gardner, whose work on multiple intelligences has the potential to revolutionize the teaching of languages and much else (see Gardner, 1991, 1983, 1993; Reid, 1998). Gardner (1993) argued that human intellectual competence is far too complex to be captured by a single conception of intelligence, and instead, proposed a model of at least eight distinct kinds of intelligence: verbal–linguistic, musical, logical–mathematical, spatial–visual, bodily–kinesthetic, interpersonal, intrapersonal, and naturalist. Each of these intelligences can be effectively utilized in foreign language education, and good foreign language teaching will involve all of them in various contexts and settings (see Christison, 1998). It is increasingly important for foreign language educators to be familiar with students with special needs as well, although this is an area in which the education of future foreign language educators clearly is lagging behind the reality of the foreign language classroom.[4]

The language educator must also know about and understand the broader social and cultural context in which she or he is to teach. This includes not only an understanding of the interpersonal interactions among students, but also understanding power relations in the classroom, the school, and the society in general. To function effectively as an advocate of second language learning, the language educator needs to be familiar with issues of educational governance and financing, as well as with the politics and policies in his or her community that impact foreign language learning and teaching.

Finally, the language educator must be able to demonstrate a clear and adequate knowledge of educational ends, purposes, and values, especially with respect to the teaching and learning of foreign languages. In other words, the language educator should be able to clearly and forcefully articulate the rationale for foreign language study, and should be able to explain the ties of foreign language study to other aspects and goals of both liberal and vocational education.

All of this taken together would constitute the knowledge base of the language educator. It is important to understand that this compilation is in fact merely a heuristic device, since each individual foreign language educator must in fact construct his or her own knowledge base. Thus, although an impressive (and even, perhaps, somewhat intimidating) compilation, this conceptualization of the knowledge base for our field is still inadequate. It is inadequate because it relies on an idealized, and somewhat simplistic, conception of what the language educator does, and indeed only hints at what the real tasks of the foreign language educator in the classroom actually are.

## THE REAL-WORLD TASKS OF THE TEACHER

Much of what every classroom teacher actually does during the school day turns out to involve the making of judgments and decisions, often with limited information. Rather than thinking about the role of the teacher in terms of whether teaching is best understood as an art form, a set of technical skills, or some combination of these two extremes, we would suggest that teaching can be more accurately and usefully conceptualized in terms of the role of the teacher as decision-maker. Consider for a moment the many different kinds of judgments and decisions that the typical teacher engages in during his or her normal, daily routine. The teacher makes curricular decisions, methodological decisions, decisions about individual children, their needs and problems, decisions about classroom management and organization, decisions about both personal and professional ethics, and so on—all areas that are, as we have already seen, reflected in the knowledge base for teaching as a profession. The educational philosopher Fitzgibbons (1981) suggested that teachers make decisions of three types: those concerned basically with educational outcomes (that is, with what the goals or results of the educational experience should be), those concerned with the matter of education (that is, with what is, could be, or should be taught), and those concerned with the manner of education (i.e., with how teaching should take place; pp. 13–14).

When a teacher makes decisions, she or he is doing far more than merely taking a course of action or acting in a certain way. The process of decision-making should be a rational one, which means that the teacher (whether consciously or unconsciously) considers and weighs alternatives, and employs criteria to select a given option or course of action. Unfortunately, as Brophy, a well-known educational researcher reported, "most studies of teachers' interactive decision-making portray it as more reactive than reflective, more intuitive than rational, and more routinized than conscious" (quoted in Irwin, 1987, p. 1).[5] Good teaching, however, inevitably requires reflective, rational, and conscious decision-making. As Silberman (1971) argued in his book *Crisis in the Classroom*, "We must find ways of stimulating public school teachers ... to think about what they are doing and why they are doing it" (p. 380). An important element in this process of reflective, rational, and conscious decision-making is that we can reasonably expect a teacher to be able to justify his or her decisions and actions in the classroom. Justification of decisions and actions, as Hamm (1989) explained, is actually a fairly simple and straightforward matter: "To provide a justification for a course of action is to provide good reasons or grounds for that course of action" (p. 163).

To be able to provide such justification, the teacher cannot rely on instinct alone or on prepackaged sets of techniques. Instead, she or he must think about what is taking place, what the options are, and so on, in a critical, analytic way. In other words, the teacher must engage in reflection about his or her practice, just as the physician must reflect about the symptoms and other evidence presented by a patient. The idea of the teacher as reflective practitioner is not a new one; Dewey, the noted American philosopher of education, wrote about the need for reflective thinking throughout his career, and dealt with the role of reflection extensively in both *How We Think* (1910, 1933) and *Logic: The Theory of Inquiry* (1938). For Dewey, logical theory and analysis was a generalization of the reflective process in which we all engage from time to time. Dewey recognized that we can reflect on a whole host of things in the sense of merely thinking about them; however logical, or analytic, reflection can take place only when there is a real problem to be solved. As Dewey (1976) explained:

> The general theory of reflection, as over against its concrete exercise, appears when occasions for reflection are so overwhelming and so mutually conflicting that specific adequate response in thought is blocked. Again, it shows itself when practical affairs are so multifarious, complicated, and remote from control that thinking is held off from successful passage into them. (p. 300)

In other words, true reflective practice can be said to take place only when the individual is faced with a real problem or situation that he or she needs to resolve, and seeks to resolve that problem in a rational manner.

## REFLECTIVE PRACTICE IN FOREIGN LANGUAGE EDUCATION

*Reflective practice* has emerged in recent years in the teacher education literature as an attempt to more fully prepare teachers for their role as classroom decision-makers (see Norlander-Case, Reagan, & Case, 1999; Reagan, Case, & Brubacher, 2000). Reflective practice can be best understood as a cyclical process, moving from reflection-for-practice through reflection-in-practice and on to reflection-on-practice, which then leads on to new reflection-for-practice (Killion & Todnem, 1991; Schön, 1983, 1987).[6] *Reflection-for-practice* refers to the reflective planning and preparation that necessarily precedes the classroom teaching event. Included here are not only the formal lesson and unit planning engaged in by the educator, but also, and arguably more critically, the teacher's analysis of likely pedagogical, learning and management problems that might emerge in a particular class dealing with specific subject matter. All teachers, to some extent, engage in reflection-for-practice, although of course they do so with varying degrees of thoroughness and effectiveness. Reflection-on-practice takes place at the other end of the classroom teaching event; it refers to retrospective reflection on what took place, both positive and negative, during the classroom teaching event. Again, all teachers engage in reflection-on-practice, though again, they do so in very different ways, some of which are far more productive than others. Good reflection-on-practice leads, of course, to new reflection-for-practice, thus completing the cycle of reflective practice.

Distinct in kind from reflection-for-practice and reflection-on-practice is *reflection-in-practice,* which is concerned with the application of what Ponayi (1967) called tacit knowledge in the classroom setting. Reflection-in-practice involves the teacher's ability to utilize unarticulated knowledge about content, pedagogy, and learners in the classroom context. It is this ability to engage in reflection-in-practice that, to a very significant extent, distinguishes the experienced master teacher from the novice. Both may well engage in effective, even exemplary, reflection-for-practice and reflection-on-practice, but only the experiential base of the master teacher allows for reflection-in-practice.

Another way of thinking about the relationships among the different kinds of reflective practice is to note that both reflection-in-practice and reflection-on-practice are essentially reactive in nature, being distinguished primarily by when reflection takes place—with reflection-in-action referring to reflection in the midst of practice, and reflection-on-practice referring to reflection that takes place after an event. Reflection-for-action, on the other hand, as Killion and Todnem (1991) argued, is "the desired outcome of both previous types of reflection. We undertake reflection, not so much to revisit the past or to become aware of the metacognitive process one is experiencing (both noble reasons in themselves), but to guide future action (the more practical purpose)" (p. 15). In other words, reflection-for-practice is in essence proactive in nature.

In summary, it is clear that all three types of reflection will be necessary components of reflective practice on the part of the classroom teacher. It is also important to note here that the relative significance of each of these three components of reflective practice may change over the course of an individual teacher's career; thus, as was noted earlier, for the novice teacher, reflection-for-practice and reflection-on-practice may be the most obvious ways in which his or her practice is distinguished, whereas for the expert or master teacher, reflectivity may be best seen in his or her reflection-in-practice. Furthermore, the process of engaging in reflection-for-practice should be seen not as a linear one, but as an on-going spiral, in which each of the elements of reflective practice are constantly involved in an interactive process of change and development.

In 1977, Van Manen suggested a hierarchical model of levels of reflectivity. According to Van Manen, there are three distinct levels of reflective practice, which can be seen, at least ideally, as paralleling the growth of the individual teacher from novice to expert or master teacher. The first level is concerned with the effective application of skills and technical knowledge in the classroom setting. At this first level, reflection entails only the appropriate selection and use of instructional strategies and the like in the classroom. The second level, according to Van Manen (1977), involves reflection about the assumptions underlying specific classroom practices, as well as about the consequences of particular strategies, curricula, and so forth. In other words, at the second level of reflectivity, teachers would begin to apply educational criteria to teaching practice in order to make individual and independent decisions about pedagogical matters. Finally, the third level of reflectivity (sometimes called *critical reflection*) entails the questioning of moral, ethical, and other types of normative criteria related directly and indirectly to the classroom (see Irwin, 1996). As Irwin (1987) explained:

> This includes concern for justice, equity and the satisfaction of important human purposes within the larger social context. A teacher engaging in this level of reflection, then, would be able to not only make decisions which would be beneficial for the long term development of the students in that classroom but also to contribute to educational policy beyond his/her individual classroom. (p. 5)

Another approach to conceptualizing reflective practice is to view such practice not in an hierarchical manner, but rather, to focus instead on elements that appear to play significant roles in fostering reflection and reflective practice on the part of classroom teachers. Sparks-Langer and Colton (1991), for instance, in a synthesis of the research on teachers' reflective thinking, argued that there are three such elements: the cognitive element, the critical element, and the narrative element. The cognitive element of reflective thinking is concerned with the knowledge that teachers need in order to make good decisions in and about the classroom situation. It is important to note that although all teachers, whether novice or expert, will have similar bodies of knowledge at their disposal, the organization and structuring of this knowledge may differ radically. Research conducted by cognitive psychologists has suggested that the schemata, or organized networks of facts, concepts, generalizations, and experiences, of beginning and experienced teachers are very different in significant ways (see Berliner, 1986; Sparks-Langer & Colton, 1991, pp. 37–38). Because such schemata are constructed by teachers over time as a result of their experiences, it is not surprising that experienced teachers will often be able to make sense of and respond to a given problematic situation in the classroom more quickly and effectively than would novices. Studies that suggest that expert teachers are able to deal with changes in lesson plans and problematic classroom situations far more successfully than are new teachers can be explained, according to Sparks-Langer and Colton (1991), "because (1) many of the routines and the content were available [to the expert teachers] in memory as automatic scripts and (2) their rich schemata allowed the experts to quickly consider cues in the environment and access appropriate strategies" (p. 38). Schemata of the sort discussed here are constructed naturally over time, of course, but their development can be encouraged and supported by reflective practice. In other words, although good teaching practice does indeed depend on a strong experiential base, reflective practice can help us to speed up the development of such an experiential base in new teachers.

The second element of reflective thinking is the *critical element*, which is concerned with "the moral and ethical aspects of social compassion and justice" (Sparks-Langer & Colton, 1991, p. 39). Concerns with issues of social justice and ethics in education are and have been common to educators and educational theorists at least since Plato (see, for example, Chambliss, 1987), and are clearly manifested in such common and important distinctions made by educators as that between educational product goals (i.e., what we want to achieve in the classroom or the school) and process goals (i.e., the restrictions that exist on how our product goals can be achieved; see Teal & Reagan, 1973).

The third element of reflective thinking, the *narrative element*, has to do with teachers' narratives. Teacher accounts of their own experiences in the classroom take many forms, and serve a variety of different functions. A preservice student's journal is an example of one fairly common type of narrative. Other kinds of narrative discourse on the part of teachers include descriptions of critical events in the classroom, various types of logs and journals, conference reports completed jointly by teachers and supervisors or mentors, self-interviewing, and so forth. The key aspect of the narrative element of reflective thinking is that such narratives, whatever their form, serve to contextualize the classroom experience for the teacher and for others, and by so doing, provide us with a much richer understanding of what takes place in the classroom and in the teacher's construction of reality than would otherwise be possible. Narrative accounts are becoming far more common today, especially in the preparation of teachers and in qualitative research on classroom practices (see Connelly & Clandinin, 1990; Goswami & Stillman, 1987; Zeichner & Liston, 1987, 1996), and there can be little doubt that they provide one of the most effective ways in which reflective practice can be encouraged.

A useful way of thinking about both the reflective teacher and the nature of the reflective practice in which he or she will engage has been provided by Irwin (1987), who suggested that:

> A reflective–analytic teacher is one who makes teaching decisions on the basis of a conscious awareness and careful consideration of (1) the assumptions on which the decisions are based and (2) the technical, educational, and ethical consequences of those decisions. These decisions are made before, during and after teaching actions. In order to make these decisions, the reflective–analytic teacher must have an extensive knowledge of the content to be taught, pedagogical and theoretical options, characteristics of individual students, and the situational constraints in the classroom, school and society in which they work. (p. 6)

Notice that this description includes virtually all of the issues that have been discussed thus far. We see that the reflective teacher is first and foremost a decision-maker, who must make his or her decisions consciously and rationally. Furthermore, the reflective teacher must base his or her decisions and judgments on a solid body of content, including technical and content knowledge, which are organized and reinterpreted according to his or her unique experiences. The reflective teacher must also demonstrate both ethical behavior and sensitivity, as well as sociocultural awareness.[7] As Case, Lanier, and Miskel (1986) noted, "The attendant characteristics of professions include conditions of practice that allow professionals to apply this knowledge freely to the practical affairs of their occupation and to use their knowledge, judgment, and skill within the structures of the ethical code of the profession" (p. 36). Finally, it is important to note that reflective practice involves what the teacher does before entering the classroom (e.g., in terms of his or her planning and preparation), in the classroom (functioning as an educator and in all of the other roles expected of the classroom teacher), and retrospectively, after she or he has left the classroom. A good way of visualizing all of this, as suggested earlier, is to think of a spiral, in which we begin with reflection-for-practice, move into reflection-in-practice, and then to reflection-on-practice—which inevitably leads us back to reflection-for-practice in an on-going process.

Such a conceptualization of the reflective teacher makes clear how very much is being expected of the classroom teacher by advocates of reflective practice. Why, one might ask, should a teacher devote so much time and energy to becoming a reflective practitioner? What, in short, are the benefits of reflective practice? There are a number of benefits to be gained from reflective practice, but perhaps among the more compelling is that reflective practice is useful in helping to empower classroom teachers. As Fosnot (1989) noted, "An empowered teacher is a reflective decision maker who finds joy in learning and in investigating the teaching–learning process—one who views learning as construction and teaching as a facilitating process to enhance and enrich development" (p. xi). Most importantly, reflective practice is a tool for individual teachers to improve their own teaching practice, and to become better, more proficient and more thoughtful professionals in their own right (see Wallace, 1991; Zeichner & Liston, 1996).

## THE NATIVE–HERITAGE LANGUAGE TEACHER

Up to this point, we have discussed the foreign language educator who is a native speaker of English. Most foreign language teachers in the United States fall into this category, so it is understandable that this is the primary audience often addressed in the foreign language education literature. However, there are also significant and growing numbers of foreign language educators whose first language is the target language or, indeed, whose native language is a language other than English or the target language (for an interesting contrast, see Braine, 1999). These teachers may themselves be immigrants, or may have grown up in the U.S. as speakers of a heritage language. The challenges faced by such individuals in the foreign language classroom are different in important ways from those faced by native speakers of English. For instance, these teachers must often deal with conflicting language standards, norms, and attitudes, with dated and parochial conceptions of the target culture(s) based on their personal background and experience. In addition, such teachers may face significant challenges with respect to English-medium tests designed for teacher certification. For these native or heritage language teachers, reflective practice provides a powerful means by which their own background knowledge and experiences can be utilized in contextualizing the teaching of the target language. Critical reflection is, in some ways, especially important for this group of teachers, with respect to cultural and linguistic knowledge.

## CRITICAL PEDAGOGY AND PUBLIC SCHOOLING

Until the latter part of the 19th century, it is clear that in the United States the family was the major socializing force in the lives of its members. A wide variety of functions were provided for, to a significant degree, by the family: business (the home was the center of work for most Americans), education (parents were responsible for the education of their children), vocational training (children received job training from their parents), religion (families supplemented the church both in terms of religious instruction and religious practice), correction (families were responsible for disciplining their members), and welfare (care was provided for all members, young and old), and so forth (see Demos, 1970). As American society became increasingly urbanized and industrialized, and as the population of the society became more diverse, state governments gradually began to view education as a means of carrying out a variety of social agendas. The emergence of tax supported, public educational systems, initially in New England and rapidly spreading through the Old Northwest, led to a number of important questions about the role, nature, and purposes of such educational institutions. Among the more significant questions with which Americans were faced were: What is the role of education in a democratic society? What are the purposes of the existing reading and writing schools, the academies, and the grammar schools? Should the schools maintain the status quo and preserve the groups controlling society? Or rather, should the schools be charged with the responsibility of improving the general welfare of all the people? These questions had actually been implicitly addressed earlier in American history by no less a figure than Thomas Jefferson, the first American leader to seek to establish public education as the foundation for the construction of a democratic social order and a means for ameliorating society (see Lee, 1967; Spring, 1994, pp. 37–40; Tozer, Violas, & Senese, 1998, pp. 17–40). More importantly for our purposes here, these same questions are still being debated as we move into the 21st century. As teachers, administrators, parents, and other citizens seek to come to grips with such questions, they need to reflect on their own values, determine individual and group positions, and then develop the kinds of schools and schooling that will not only meet the wants and aspirations of the youth in their classrooms, but also the needs of the society (see Goodlad, 1997).

Freire (1973, 1974) explored the conservative role and functions of the school in a considerable detail. He argued that dominant cultures (for instance, in contemporary American society, the Anglo-American culture) tend to overlook the wants and needs of the dominated cultures that coexist with the dominant culture. Freire suggested that schools, as social institutions involved in the maintenance of the status quo, generally function to impose the values of the dominant culture on dominated cultural groups in the society. Basic literacy skills, such as reading and writing, for instance, can sometimes thus become for dominated groups acts of memorization and repetition, rather than acts of reflection on meaning and critical translation into the child's own culture.

This need not be the case, of course, and when the latter takes place, education becomes transforming, not only to individuals but also for both the dominant and dominated cultures (see McLaren & Leonard, 1993). Although such transformative educational experiences remain relatively uncommon, they have received significant support and attention in American public education, especially among those who consider themselves advocates of critical pedagogy (see, for instance, Giroux, 1991, 1992a, 1992b, 1994, 1997a, 1997b). As McLaren (1989) noted:

> A radical theory of education has emerged in the last fifteen years. Broadly defined as "the new sociology of education" or a "critical theory of education," critical pedagogy examines schools both in their historical context and as part of the existing social and political fabric that characterizes the dominant society. Critical pedagogy poses a variety of counterlogics to the positivistic, ahistorical, and depoliticized analysis employed by both liberal and conservative critics of schooling—an analysis all too readily visible in the training programs in our colleges of education. Fundamentally concerned with the centrality of politics and power in our understanding of how schools work, critical theorists have produced work centering on the political economy of schooling, the state and education, the representation of texts, and the construction of student subjectivity. (p. 159)

In other words, what critical pedagogy is really all about is the recognition that schooling is an intrinsically political activity, and that efforts to present it as objective or neutral are not only misguided but fundamentally misleading and even dangerous. To be sure, schooling can be used to promote democracy and democratic values (see Gutman, 1987), but it also can be (and often is) used to perpetuate an unjust and inequitable status quo. As Giroux explained (1992a), "Central to the development of critical pedagogy is the need to explore how pedagogy functions as a cultural practice to *produce* rather than merely *transmit* knowledge within the asymmetrical relations of power that structure teacher–student relations" (p. 98).

For too long a period of time, the educational problems confronting America and its more than 14,000 school districts have been perceived as fundamentally school problems. Consequently, the attack on those problems has been made primarily by those within the school establishment itself. The many other organizations, groups, and individuals that are also responsible for the problems have been denied access to decision-making and problem resolution (Sarason, 1990). Sarason argued that:

> To a significant degree, the major educational problems stem from the fact that educators not only accepted responsibility for schooling but more fateful, also adopted a stance that essentially said: we know how to solve and manage the problems of schooling in America. Educators did not say: there is much that we do not know, many problems that are intractable to our efforts, and many individuals we are not reaching or helping. (1990, p. 36)

The family of the 21st century will not be solely responsible for the functions of business, education, vocational training, religion, correction, and welfare, but will share those responsibilities with other community agencies. Schools cannot be solely responsible for problems affecting education from the larger society. All community groups who are also affected by those problems should participate in their discussion, analysis, and resolution. This necessitates a systems approach to problem solving by schools and school districts. Only when educational responsibility is shared can education be reformed.

## EMANCIPATORY DEMOCRATIC SCHOOLING AND THE FOREIGN LANGUAGE EDUCATOR

What, then, are the implications of critical pedagogy for the foreign language educator? Foreign language education can certainly be analyzed and critiqued from a critical perspective. As Osborn (2000) argued:

> the traditions that typically frame research and practice in language education have competed with the realities of growing cultural interdependence and a shift in pressure to assimilate in some areas of public life in the United States. As a result, the politics of cultural control have been either deemphasized or overlooked as most in the field have settled for technicist formulas or inquiry into the nature of language learning that springs from positivistic or interpretivistic paradigms. (pp. 123–124)

Such perspectives on our field are invaluable, for they force us to ask fundamental questions about what we are attempting to accomplish, and why. It is all too easy for us to rely on platitudes about the role of foreign language education, just as it is far too easy for us to blame others for the lack of success that foreign language education so often experiences. However, critical pedagogy has implications not only for understanding our failures as a field, but also provides us with some powerful ideas about how foreign language education can function as a positive and constructive force in American education. Critical pedagogy calls for us to re-examine not only the purposes of foreign language instruction, but even more, the hidden (and often not-so-hidden) biases about language, social class, power, and equity that underlie language use. Second language education, in short, from a critical perspective is not only about the teaching and learning of a second or additional linguistic system, but is also about social and cultural knowledge, and perhaps even more, about helping students to develop critical approaches to examining and understanding such knowledge. As Osborn (2000) argued:

> Indeed, most [language educators] recognize that, even under optimum conditions, non-native language learning is difficult. Every day, language teachers throughout the country enter classrooms to attempt what seems to be impossible ... But in the shadow of such pessimistic odds, renewal of our professional vision in the twentieth century occurred with surprising regularity. With such a rich history of effort behind us, the challenges of critical reflection and language education may give one pause, but the greatest traditions of the profession will drive us to rise to the challenge in the twenty-first century ... "[World language education] is unsurpassed in its power to liberate the mind and spirit from the prisons of cultural provincialism, servile ideological conformity, and social class distinctions, thereby freeing the individual person to think for herself or himself." This sentiment ... can begin to be more credible every day. And critical reflection in the language classroom will serve as a powerful means to that end. (p. 124)

It is, then, toward the effective utilization of this means that this volume has been written, and we invite you to join with us in making critical reflection a central part of foreign language teaching and learning.

## QUESTIONS FOR REFLECTION AND DISCUSSION

1. In this chapter, the authors consider the concept of the knowledge base for a foreign language educators in fairly general terms. Can you add specificity to the different elements that they identify as necessary for effective teaching practice? What content have you learned in your (a) language classes, (b) education classes, (c) linguistics classes, and (d) other classes that you believe will prove to be essential in functioning as a classroom teacher?
2. The authors assert that, "Native speakers certainly have some advantages ... but merely being a native speaker of a language in no way prepares one to teach it." Do you agree or disagree with this assessment? Why?
3. Based on your own experiences as a student and as a teacher, do you think that reflection in the classroom setting is really likely to improve teaching

practice? Will it also, in your view, improve student learning? What are the advantages of a foreign language educator focusing on becoming reflective? What are the disadvantages?
4. In the section of this chapter on "Critical Pedagogy and Public Schooling," it is suggested that, "Only when educational responsibility is shared can education be reformed." This makes a certain amount of sense when we are talking about subject matter in which all (or at least most) adults in our society are competent. Does it present special challenges in foreign language education given that most parents, teachers, and administrators do not have functional second language skills? What are the implications of this paradox for shared responsibility with respect to foreign language education?
5. What are the implications of the idea that reflective practice can occur "only when the individual [student] is faced with a real problem that he or she needs to resolve" for the methodology and content of the foreign language classroom?

## FOCUS ON THE CLASSROOM

1. Describe an instance in which you changed your teaching during a lesson. Explain your rationale for the change, and discuss the results.
2. Identify examples of knowledge related to teaching and learning a language that one does not know simply by virtue of being a native speaker of the language. What do you believe are the implications of this special subset of the knowledge base?
3. Describe reflective practice for the foreign language educator in your own words, providing examples of how such practice differs from traditional instructional practice in the context of the foreign language classroom.
4. What are your goals for your students? In other words, what kinds of outcomes would you hope would occur as a result of a student being in your foreign language class? In your answer, be sure to consider not only cognitive–academic goals, but also affective and social goals.
5. Which of the goals identified in your response to Question 4 could be related to critical pedagogy, as well as to foreign language pedagogy?

## NOTES

1. It is interesting to note that the phrase knowledge base has been replaced in recent years in much of the literature (including in National Council for Accreditation of

Teacher Education accreditation materials) with that of conceptual framework. It is clearly both things of course, but the latter phrase, in our view, seems to minimize the importance and significance of content knowledge in a way that the former does not. We have therefore chosen to continue to use the phrase *knowledge base*, although it may seem to be a bit dated to some readers.

2. This observation does not apply, however, in certain specialized kinds of foreign language teaching and learning settings—for instance, in language for specific purposes programs (see Donna, 2000, p. 70).

3. We recognize, of course, that these general claims about appropriateness may not apply in specific settings. Obviously, the issue here is to ensure that the content of the learning experience is appropriate for the particular learners being taught.

4. The issue of whether students with special needs belong in foreign language classes remains a matter of considerable controversy for many foreign language educators. We do not address this matter explicitly here, except to note that it is really moot as far as the reality of the contemporary foreign language classroom is concerned, because such students are increasingly placed in foreign language classes, and this practice seems likely to continue and even, perhaps, to escalate in the immediate future.

5. It is important to note here that this criticism is not so much a criticism of teachers, as it is of the environment in which teachers work. For the quality of teacher decision-making to improve, more is required than simply changing teacher preparation. In addition, the many structural and organizational barriers to reflective practice must also be addressed. Hence, calls for reflective practice properly understood inevitably involve concomitant changes in school organization and culture.

6. Reflective practice in educational contexts is, then, far more than simply thinking about teaching. It involves a deliberate, critical and on-going kind of self-evaluation, and is oriented not just to the understanding of classroom practice, but also toward its improvement.

7. The ethical dimensions of teaching are an incredibly important aspect of teaching as a profession. Goodlad's discussions of the moral dimensions of schooling are central to this point, as are the more focused explorations of teacher ethics and professional codes of ethics in the teacher education literature (see Goodlad, 1994, 1997; Strike, Haller, & Soltis, 1988; Strike & Soltis, 1992).

# 3

# Whose Language Is Real?
# Language Variation
# and Language Legitimacy

> The difference between a language and a dialect is who's got the army and navy.
>
> —*attributed to Max Weinreich*

In everyday speech, people tend to distinguish between languages and dialects as if there were a meaningful distinction between the two. From a linguistic perspective, of course, things are far more complicated than this—and, at the same time, far simpler. The problem, in a nutshell, is that the labels language and dialect are not, in fact, really technical linguistic terms at all. Rather, they express social and political realities. As the aforementioned quote from the linguist Weinreich implies, the distinction between a language and a dialect is merely where a society wishes to draw it, based on social, political, economic, and even military factors. Even the criterion of mutual intelligibility does not work universally to facilitate this distinction: Norwegian, Swedish, and Danish have a high degree of mutual intelligibility, but they are generally viewed, both by their speakers and by others, as distinct languages. At the same time, there are varieties of German that are mutually unintelligible to a significant degree (as there are varieties of English that are mutually unintelligible; see Chambers & Trudgill, 1980, p. 5; also of interest here are Allen & Linn, 1986; Hudson, 1996). Perhaps one of the best examples of this phenomenon in recent years has been the change that has taken place with respect to the language varieties that, until fairly recently, were known collectively as Serbo-Croatian (see Hawkesworth, 1998; Norris, 1993; Partridge, 1972).[1] Following the break-up of the former Yugoslavia and the ethnic tensions that have emerged in the Balkans (see, for example, Glenny, 1996; Lampe, 2000), we are now presented with a number of separate (albeit for the most part mutually intelligible) languages spoken by ethnically distinct groups, among which are Croatian, Serbian, and Bosnian. Even with respect to languages where one might expect greater clarity in this regard, we are often faced with complex and less than satisfying answers. For example, in response to the question, "How many Romance languages are there?" Posner (1996) commented that:

> An answer to this question that has been slightly labeled *sancta simplicitas* is that there is only one: the languages are all alike enough to be deemed dialects of the same language. Another equally disingenuous answer might be "thousands"—of distinctive local varieties—or "millions"—of individual idiolects. (p. 189)

In short, the terms language and dialect are generally used in an ad hoc manner that has little to do with linguistics or with linguistic characteristics. The question, "Is such-and-such a language or a dialect?" is simply not answerable from any body of the linguistic data. The answer, instead, must rely on nonlinguistic and extralinguistic factors, and must be made not by linguists but by the speakers of the language variety at issue and the wider community. From the perspective solely of linguistics, as Alexander (2000) noted, "Each dialect, in fact, is actually a separate language, with its own internally consistent system" (p. 516).

## THE CONCEPT OF LINGUISTIC LEGITIMACY

Language is at the heart of virtually every aspect of education, and indeed, of social life. Language serves as the primary medium through which much learning takes place, and the acquisition of socially and academically appropriate language forms (oral and written) is generally seen as one of the principal goals for the educational experience (see Cleary & Linn, 1993). In addition, it is quite common for individual academic problems to be blamed on, or at least explained by, language differences. Underlying the educational discourse dealing with issues of language are a number of common assumptions about the nature of language, language structure, language difference, and so on, which are shared by both classroom teachers and the general public. Perhaps the most powerful of these assumptions is that concerning what counts as a real language, and, even more important, what does not count as a real language. What is at issue here is what can be called *linguistic legitimacy:* which language varieties are deemed by the society (or some subset of the society) to be legitimate, and which are not.

The concept of linguistic legitimacy is both a timely and important one for educators, and especially for educators involved in the teaching of languages, as it touches on issues of social class, ethnicity, and culture, and is embedded in relations of dominance and power. Linguistic legitimacy as a construct is also important with respect to the implications that it has for the development and implementation of educational policy, as the national controversy about the 1996

# WHOSE LANGUAGE IS REAL?

Oakland, California school district's decision formally to recognize Ebonics (i.e., African American Vernacular English, or AAVE) as the dominant language of many of that district's students, makes clear (see for example, Bennet, 1996; Holmes, 1996; Lakoff, 2000; McWhorter, 1998; Olszewski, 1996; Schorr, 1997; Staples, 1997). Typical of much of the rhetoric surrounding that decision was the columnist Hernandez's assertion that:

> The notion that Black English is a language and that black kids are actually bilingual is ludicrous and patronizing. Ebonics is ungrammatical English. What students who speak Ebonics need to learn is that they are speaking substandard English and that substandard English brands them as uneducated. (p. A-21)

Essentially the same underlying argument, though usually a bit more carefully and moderately articulated, is commonly found in educational settings and among educators. For instance, as is true at many colleges and universities, the California State University (CSU) system has a foreign language requirement. The CSU (1987) catalog described the kinds of languages that can be used to meet this foreign language requirement in the following manner:

> Any natural language other than English used by speakers sharing a common culture is acceptable. Excluded by this definition are artificially created languages such as Esperanto, computer languages, and derivative languages such as American Sign Language or dialects of English. (p. 3)

This is an intriguing passage, as it appears to explicitly distinguish between those systems of communication that count as languages and those which, in some sense, do not. Especially interesting in this passage is the exclusion of Esperanto, American Sign Language (ASL), and dialects of English (which, presumably, would include AAVE). Each of these language varieties is used on a daily basis by significant numbers of people to communicate, and yet none counts as a real language. Underlying this exclusion, of course, is an implicit assumption of the validity of the concept of linguistic legitimacy—that is, that some communications systems are real or legitimate languages and that others are, in some important sense, not.

In this chapter, we challenge this notion of linguistic legitimacy both in general terms and in the specific cases of AAVE, ASL, and Esperanto. Furthermore, we argue that the criteria that appear to be used to distinguish legitimate from illegitimate languages are themselves irrelevant, and that they are often used to disguise personal, political, and ideological biases. In short, we suggest that the very notion of an illegitimate language is simply not defensible, and furthermore, that the distinctions on which notions of linguistic legitimacy rest (including that of the difference between a dialect and a language) are extralinguistic in nature and representative of nonlinguistic, social, and political agendas.

There are a variety of arguments used, implicitly and explicitly, to question (and to reject) the legitimacy of various language varieties. The objections are often language-specific, which is to say that the objections to one language variety will be different from those applied to another. There are also, however, underlying commonalities in different challenges to linguistic legitimacy. In the following section of the chapter, we present and respond to the language-specific objections to the legitimacy of AAVE, ASL, and Esperanto, and then discuss, in somewhat broader terms, the general themes that hold these objections (and other language-specific objections to linguistic legitimacy) together conceptually.

## THE DEBATE ABOUT AFRICAN AMERICAN VERNACULAR ENGLISH

There are few debates about language that are capable of producing the kind of heat and passion produced by discussions of AAVE, especially with respect to educational issues. In 1979, the *Martin Luther King Junior Elementary School Children v. Ann Arbor School District* decision led to a vociferous debate about the nature and status of AAVE not unlike that which recently took place with respect to the decision of the Board of Education in Oakland, California, to recognize Ebonics as the primary language of a significant proportion of students in the school district (see Chambers, 1983; Lakoff, 2000, pp. 227–251; McWhorter, 1998; Smitherman, 1981, 1998; Whiteman, 1980; Wolfram, 1998). In both instances, it is clear that strong emotions on both sides of the debate have all too often effectively drowned out more moderate, defensible voices.

Many well-meaning individuals, educators and noneducators alike, have raised grave reservations and concerns about both *King v. Arbor* and the Oakland policy with respect to AAVE. The concerns that have been articulated most commonly include doubts about the nature and origins of AAVE, its recognition in educational settings, and perhaps most important, its effects on student learning and achievement. Also raised have been fears about the implications of identifying speakers of AAVE as non-English speakers, as well as concerns about the social and economic language needs of speakers of AAVE. A fairly typical critical response to the Oakland decision is that of Maxwell (1997), an African American columnist:

> Oakland, like many other districts nationwide, is failing in part because grown-ups there lack the courage to call Ebonics what it is: a bastardization that has few redeeming elements ... Ebonics is acceptable in rap, poetry and fiction. But it has precious few redeeming qualities in the real world and, therefore, must be avoided in public. (p. B-2)

Although this response, like that offered by Hernandez (1996), is clearly polemical in nature, the underlying concerns it reflects are very real and legitimate, and are certainly shared by many people, regardless of race. These are concerns that do need to be addressed and which can, we believe, be addressed in a very compelling manner. At this point, although a complete treatment of the social phenomenon of AAVE is obviously not possible here, it may be useful to present a basic overview of what is actually known about the nature and origins of AAVE, as well as a brief discussion of possible educationally sound responses to the presence of large numbers of speakers of AAVE in the schools.

An appropriate place to begin our discussion is with the label for AAVE, which is actually highly problematic. Other expressions and terms that have been, and continue to be, used in the literature to refer to AAVE include the very dated *nonstandard Negro English* (NNE), *Black English Vernacular* (BEV), *Black English,* and *Ebonics,* among others. Each of these labels has its own problems and limitations, as does AAVE.[2] All of these labels share the common problem that they imply that we are talking about a single language variety, that this variety is simply a variant of English, and that it is spoken by Blacks. Each of these assumptions is actually misleading at best. First, there is no single language variety that constitutes AAVE. In fact, there are a series of related language varieties (distinguished by both geographic variables and those of age, gender, social class, and so forth; see McWhorter, 1998; Mufwene, Rickford, Bailey, & Baugh, 1998; Wolfram & Fasold, 1974, pp. 73–98). Second, the relationship of AAVE to mainstream American English[3] is an area subject to considerable debate, as indeed is the extent to which AAVE can be said to constitute a language distinct from English. In fact, one of the problems with the label Black English is that it seems to create a false dichotomy between White English and Black English, which is simply not reflective of linguistic reality (see Labov, 1972a, p. xiii). Finally, although the vast majority of speakers of AAVE are African American, not all African Americans use AAVE, nor are all native users of AAVE Black (see Mufwene et al., 1998; Schneider, 1989, pp. 4–5; Stewart, 1975, pp. 237–239). This having been said, the collection of language varieties that generally fall under the label AAVE do coexist with other varieties of American English, and are notably similar to one another and significantly different from other varieties of American English (see Labov, 1972a, pp. 36–37; McWhorter, 1998). Given the lack of consensus about the best label for this collection of language varieties, as well as the problems with each of the alternatives, then, we have chosen to employ what we take to be the least offensive and most accurate term—*African American Vernacular English,* or *AAVE* (see Lanehart, 1998). What is most important to note in this regard is that the debates about what to call AAVE are themselves reflections of the very nonlinguistic and extralinguistic issues that color all aspects of the debates about AAVE. As Trabasso and Harrison (1976) noted with respect to the definition of what is Black English:

> It is a political question since language has served as an instrument of political and cultural control whenever two cultures meet. It is a social question since certain forms of speech are admired, prestigeful, codified and promulgated while others are accorded low esteem, stigmatized, ridiculed and avoided. It is an economic question

since many feel that "speaking proper" or some variety of Standard English is required for success in middle-class America. (p. 2)

The contemporary social and educational debates about AAVE rest on two fundamental and distinct arguments (see Schneider, 1989, pp 2–3). The first of these two arguments focuses on the nature of AAVE in general terms, and especially with respect to prescriptivist judgments about what constitutes proper English, and how such judgments are related to the use of AAVE. The second argument concerns the relationship between AAVE and other varieties of American English, and is often presented in the terms of whether AAVE is really a distinctive language in its own right or whether it is simply a variety of American English. Each of these arguments is important both from a linguistic and an educational standpoint, and each merits our attention here.

That the nature of AAVE as a language should be at issue in contemporary discussions is, although perhaps somewhat understandable socially and educationally, nevertheless profoundly puzzling from a linguistic perspective. As Schneider (1989) noted, "For more than twenty years, the dialect spoken by Black Americans has been among the most salient topics of linguistic research in the United States" (p. 1), and there is a huge body of very competent linguistic research dealing with various aspects of AAVE (see Baugh, 1983; Burling, 1973; DeStefano, 1973; Dillard, 1972, 1975; Kochman, 1972, 1981; Labov. 1972a, 1972b, 1978; McWhorter, 1998; Mufwene, 1993; Mufwene et al., 1998; Smitherman, 1977). Indeed, it could be quite credibly argued that in sociolinguistics the study of AAVE has provided a central framework for much contemporary research. In other words, from the perspective of linguistics, the status of AAVE has long since been answered: AAVE is a series of related language varieties, spoken primarily by African Americans, which are rule-governed and which differ in significant ways from other varieties of American English (see, for example, Baugh, 1983; McWhorter, 1998; Mufwene et al., 1998; Whatley, 1981).

Among the most obvious differences found in varieties of AAVE are phonological and syntactic rules that differ from those of mainstream American English. For instance, with respect to its phonological system, AAVE-speakers tend to lack the nonprevocalic /r/ (as in *car ca'* and *from f'om*). In addition, the two *th* sounds common in mainstream American English (/ θ / and / ð /) are absent in AAVE, being systematically replaced with /t/ and /d/ respectively in initial positions (thus, *thin tin* and *this dis*), and with /f/ and /v/ in medial and final positions (*mother mov'uh* and *both bof*). The simplification of final consonantal clusters (such as /sk/, /st/, /nd/, and so on), which is found in spoken mainstream American English in cases such as *wes' coast* for *west coast*, is in AAVE used even more regularly (as in *wes' end* where mainstream American English would require *west end*). Finally, the phonology of AAVE is characterized by the nasalization of vowels before nasal consonants and the loss of the consonant, the vocalization and loss of the nonprevocalic /l/, and a number of other features (see Luelsdorff, 1975; Trudgill, 1995, pp. 51–53). The important thing to note here is that all of these phonological characteristics of AAVE are rule-governed, and are in all meaningful respects comparable to the phonological rules found in any human language. For speakers of AAVE, none of these phonological features can be considered to be errors or mistakes (see Mufwene et al., 1998; Perry & Delpit, 1998; Wolfram, 1979).

With respect to syntax, AAVE tends to differ most markedly from other varieties of American English in its verbal system. Some of the differences identified in the AAVE verbal system are relatively minor, and can be explained by normal processes of language change. This is the case, for instance, with the absence of the third-person singular present tense marker /-s/ in AAVE verbs (as in *she like* and *he go*). Explaining the absence of the copula (that is, the verb *to be*) in the present tense in AAVE is a somewhat more complex matter. This feature of AAVE may be due to the hypothesized creole origins of the language, but could also be explained by a phonological process that takes the contraction tendency in mainstream American English to a further level by adding a deletion rule (thus, *he is > he's > he*). Most significant in the AAVE verbal system is a feature that is called the invariant *be*, which is used by AAVE-speakers to identify the habitual aspect of a finite verb (see Labov, 1993). Thus, the meaning of the AAVE sentence, *She be around* is best conveyed by the mainstream American English *She is usually around*, whereas the AAVE *she around* would be best conveyed in mainstream American English as, *She's around right now*. The implications of this distinction in the classroom context are made clear in the following conversation between a teacher and an AAVE-speaking student reported by Heath (1983):

> A teacher asked one day: "Where is Susan? Isn't she here today?" Lem answered "She ain't ride de bus." The teacher responded: "She *doesn't* ride the bus, Lem." Lem answered: "She *do* be ridin' de bus." The teacher frowned at Lem and turned away. (p. 277)

This is a wonderful example of how a teacher's ignorance of a student's language variety can impede effective communication and lead to misunderstandings in the classroom. Lem did, in fact, respond appropriately to the teacher's question: He indicated that Susan had not ridden the bus on the day in question. The teacher, focusing on what she took to be an error in mainstream American English, attempted to correct Lem by rephrasing his answer. Lem not only understood the teacher's correction, but he recognized that she had not understood his point, and replied by using a form of the habitual aspect to emphasize that indeed Susan did normally ride the bus, but that she hadn't done so on this particular day. The teacher at this point merely abandons the conversation, no doubt convinced that Lem has communication problems. She is, of course, partially correct: Someone in the conversation has missed the point although we would argue that it wasn't Lem. As Warren and McCloskey (1993) cogently noted,

> It appears that most Black English-speaking children understand more Standard English pronunciation and grammar than they use ... What aspects of Standard English they do not understand may be relatively superficial, at least from a linguistic standpoint (although perhaps not from a social one). The greater problem may be that their Standard English-speaking peers and teachers do not understand Black English. (p. 222)

The key issue to be kept in mind with respect to the syntactic features of AAVE, in any event, is that these features are consistent and rule-governed; in short, they function precisely as do syntactic rules in other languages.

A much-discussed aspect of AAVE has to do with how this collection of language varieties developed—that is, with what the origins of the features previously discussed might be. Most linguists today would accept what is called the *decreolist view*, which maintains that the differences between mainstream American English and the varieties of AAVE can be best explained with respect to the creole origins of AAVE (Mufwene et al., 1998; Trudgill, 1995, p. 50; see also Todd, 1990). As Traugott (1976) has commented,

> Viewed from the perspective of English-related pidgins and creoles, there seems to be no question that aspects of VBE [Vernacular Black English] can best be explained in the light of centuries of linguistic change, and development from a pidgin to a creole, through various stages of decreolization, to a point where VBE, though largely assimilated into the various English vernaculars, still has features which clearly distinguishes it from them. To claim that VBE derives from a creole, therefore, is to focus on its social and linguistic history, and on the relative autonomy of the Black community in America. (p. 93)

It should be noted here that recent research has suggested that in many urban areas of the United States, the process of decreolization has not only stopped, it may actually have been reversed. In other words, as the urban Black population has been increasingly marginalized socially and economically, the language varieties that they speak may have begun to diverge from the surrounding mainstream varieties of American English (see Bailey & Maynor, 1987, 1989; Butters, 1989). Among the linguistic features that may be developing in some contemporary AAVE varieties, for instance, is the use of the future resultative *be done* that has been documented by the sociolinguist Baugh, as in the sentence, *"I'll be done killed that motherfucker if he tries to lay a hand on my kid again"* (quoted in Trudgill, 1995, p. 61).

What of the classroom context of AAVE? The debate about AAVE is fundamentally an educational one, concerned with the most appropriate manner of meeting the needs of a particular group of students. Arguably the most significant lesson to be learned with respect to the needs of AAVE-speakers is that language difference does not in any way constitute language deficit. Although this has become something of a politically correct cliché in recent times, it is nonetheless worth emphasizing because although teachers and others may rhetorically accept the distinction between differences and deficits, all too often the distinction is not reflected in actual belief and practice. Speakers of AAVE continue to be disproportionately misdiagnosed and mislabeled with respect to both cognitive and speech–language problems, and this alone would constitute a compelling justification for additional teacher preparation with respect to language differences, and specifically those differences commonly found in the language of AAVE-speakers (see Perry & Delpit, 1998; Wolfram, 1979).

Embedded in much contemporary educational discourse about AAVE are, in fact, strongly held views of linguistic inferiority. A powerful example of this tendency is found in a book by Orr (1987), entitled *Twice as less: Black English and the performance of Black students in mathematics and science*. The thesis offered by Orr, an experienced classroom teacher, was that "For students whose first language is BEV [Black English Vernacular] ... language can be a barrier to success in mathematics and science" (1987, p. 9). Orr's argument is that certain linguistic features of AAVE (such as prepositions in the expression of selected quantitative relationships, as–than modes of expressing comparisons, etc.) can result in erroneous understanding of certain key mathematical relationships.

The position argued by Orr in *Twice as less* is one that is firmly grounded in a view known as linguistic relativity. This view, which has its origins in the late 18th and early 19th century work of the German scholar von Humboldt, was given its clearest and most popular articulation in the work of Sapir and Whorf—after whom it is commonly named as the Sapir-Whorf Hypothesis. In essence, the Sapir-Whorf Hypothesis is concerned with describing the relationship between the language that we speak and our thoughts and thought processes.[4] As Whorf himself argued, "we dissect nature along lines laid down by our native languages ... by the linguistic systems in our minds" (quoted in Crystal, 1991, p. 306). A more recent articulation of this view is provided by Lee (1996):

> Although all observers may be confronted by the same physical evidence in the form of experiential data and although they may be capable of "externally similar acts of observation," a person's "picture of the universe" or "view of the world" differs as a function of the particular language or languages that the person knows. (p. 87)

In its most extreme forms, such as that found in Orr's work, this view of the relationship between thought and language is in fact deterministic in nature. Although there may well be elements of truth in a weak version of the Sapir-Whorf Hypothesis (see Elgin, 2000, pp. 49–71; Lee, 1996), there is widespread agreement among linguistics that the sort of strongly deterministic relationship between thought and language posited by Orr is simply not credible.

The fundamental problem with Orr's book, is not so much that her views reflect a fairly extreme version of linguistic relativity, but rather, that she is simply wrong about her facts. Not only is the linguistic base with regard to what we actually know about the structure of AAVE dated and inaccurate, but, as Baugh cogently argued, "despite claims to the contrary, Orr's book merely serves to perpetuate racist myths about the relationship between language and thought" (1988, p. 403).

Basically, then, what the case of AAVE would seem to emphasize is that there is a fundamental distinction between what might be called language-as-system (i.e., language as a linguistic phenomenon) and language-as-social marker (the sociological role of language). Further, in every society there is a hierarchy of linguistic variations, generally reflective of social class. It is this distinction that helps us to understand why, in contemporary American society, AAVE and mainstream American English can have the same linguistic status, while having markedly different sociolinguistic status. The many jokes that were circulated in our society, both orally and especially on the Internet, about the Oakland policy in fact provide vivid evidence of just this difference—the humor was clearly grounded in both racist beliefs and flawed understandings of the nature of human language in general and AAVE in particular (for extended and powerful discussions of this point, see Rickford & Rickford, 2000; Scott, 1998).

## RECOGNIZING AMERICAN SIGN LANGUAGE

Challenges to the legitimacy of ASL have increased in recent years as efforts have been made to include it as a foreign language option in many secondary schools, colleges, and universities (see Belka, 2000; Jacobs, 1996; Wallinger, 2000; Wilcox & Wilcox, 1997). Among the more commonly raised objections to ASL have been those that are concerned with the nature of ASL (i.e., with its status linguistically and psycholinguistically), the degree to which ASL can be considered to be foreign, the degree to which advocates of ASL are using the concepts of language and culture metaphorically rather than literally, and last, whether a nonwritten language is an appropriate choice for students, given the commonly articulated purposes of foreign language instruction in educational settings.

Many objections to the teaching of ASL as a foreign language, as well as to its use in the education of deaf children, are based on the idea that ASL is in some manner linguistically and psycholinguistically inferior to spoken language. Characteristic of this view is Myklebust's assertion that, "Sign language cannot be considered comparable to a verbal symbol system" (quoted in Lane, 1992, p. 45), and the Dutch scholar van Uden's claim that, "The informative power of the natural sign language of the deaf is extremely weak" (van Uden, 1986, p. 89). However common and popular such views may be, though, they are nonetheless clearly and demonstrably false in both spirit and detail. As Chomsky (1988) once commented in an interview, "If deaf people have developed sign language, then there are no intellectual defects at all. Many people who are not deaf think that deaf people have deficits because we just don't understand their language" (p. 196).

Indeed, since the 1960 publication of Stokoe's (1960/1993) landmark study, *Sign Language Structures*, there has been a veritable explosion of historical, linguistic, psycholinguistic, and sociolinguistic research dealing with ASL (see Fischer &

Siple, 1990; Lillo-Martin, 1991; Lucas, 1989, 1995, 1996; Lucas & Valli, 1992; Metzger, 2000; Siple & Fischer, 1991; Valli & Lucas, 1995), as well as with other natural sign languages (see Edmondson & Karlsson, 1990; Emmorey & Reilly, 1995; Kyle & Woll, 1985; Lucas, 1990; Prillwitz & Vollhaber, 1990a, 1990b; Rée, 1999). The result is that we now know far more about the nature and workings of natural sign languages than we did in 1970, and the now well-established research base was summarized by Hoffmeister (1990) as follows:

> ASL is a language that has been misunderstood, misused, and misrepresented over the past 100 years. It is structured very differently from English. The structure of ASL is based on visual–manual properties, in contrast to the auditory–spoken properties of English. ASL is able to convey the same meanings, information, and complexities as English. The mode of expression is different, but only at the delivery level. The underlying principles of ASL ... are based on the same basic principles found in all languages. ASL is able to identify and codify agents, actions, objects, locations, subjects, verbs, aspects, tense, and modality, just as English does. ASL is therefore capable of stating all the information expressed in English and of doing this within the same conceptual frame. ASL is able to communicate the meaning of a concept, through a single sign or through a combination of signs, that may be conveyed by a word or phrase (combination of words) in English. (p. 81)

In fact, as a result of this growing body of research concerned with the linguistics of natural sign languages, a 1985 UNESCO report went so far as to assert as an operating principle that, "We must recognize the legitimacy of the sign language as a linguistic system and it should be accorded the same status as other languages" (quoted in Lane, 1992, p. 46).

Perhaps among the more intriguing objections to viewing ASL as a foreign language in American educational settings that have been raised in recent years is that offered by Mancing, head of the foreign language department at Purdue University. Professor Mancing argued that:

> In no way do I impugn the integrity of ASL as a legitimate academic subject or as a well-developed, intellectual, emotional, subtle, sophisticated language ... It is all of that, but since it is [*American*] Sign Language it is not foreign by definition. (Quoted in "Sign language," 1992)

The issue raised by Mancing is essentially one of definition. The obvious, ordinary language sense of "foreign" in the phrase term "foreign language" is that the language is foreign to the learner. To employ Mancing's definition would require that we also exclude native American languages, such as Navajo, and even perhaps Spanish, which is at least as indigenous to North America as English, and is certainly widely spoken as a native language in the United States. In short, although the argument that ASL is not foreign may initially appear to be compelling, this is in fact far from the case. The extent to which a particular language is foreign, in short, has to do with the extent to which it is new or different to the learner. The danger in the argument presented by Mancing is that by granting the legitimacy of ASL as a language, but denying its foreignness, one is presented with what falsely appears to be a balanced position—yet another way in which a particular language or linguistic system can be effectively delegitimized.

Traditional defenses for the study of foreign languages as a part of a liberal education often rely on the close connection between language and culture. It is commonly argued that only through the study of a people's language can their culture be properly understood, and that such study can provide an essential international or global component in an individual's education. Critics of the acceptance of ASL as a foreign language have suggested that it does not meet this aspect of foreign language education on two counts. First, because the terms language and culture, when applied to ASL and the culture of the Deaf community, are used metaphorically rather than literally, and second, because it is an indigenous rather than international language. As Kerth, chairman of the German and Slavic Languages Department at SUNY, Stony Brook, attempted to explain:

> I think these people who talk about deaf culture and foreignness are using it in a metaphorical way, not literally, and when you get into the realm of metaphor the meaning gets obscured. Most would read a foreign language as one not spoken by Americans. (Quoted in "Sign language," 1992).

With regard to this claim that discussions of the deaf culture are metaphorical rather than literal, all one can say is that this is a serious distortion of what writers on (and members of) that culture have actually said, written, and meant. There are a number of works devoted to the history, sociology, and anthropology of the American deaf community, written by both deaf and hearing scholars (see, e.g., Bragg, 2001; Cohen, 1994; Fischer & Lane, 1993; Lane, Hoffmeister, & Bahan, 1996; Padden & Humphries, 1988; Reagan, 1990a, 1992, 2000b; Schein, 1989; van Cleve, 1993; Wilcox, 1989). These writings do not suggest that the concept of cultural deafness is to be understood metaphorically; indeed, the overwhelming sense of these works is that the term is used in an absolutely literal sense (for a comparable British perspective, see Gregory, 1992; Gregory & Hartley, 1991). Indeed, one of us has written extensively on this topic, and has very much intended his description of both the language and the culture of the deaf community to be taken not only seriously, but quite literally.[5] In short, the preponderance of the evidence clearly supports the view that the deaf community constitutes a cultural community in precisely the same way as would any other cultural community.

Kerth's second claim is closely related to the idea that ASL is not foreign. However, here the suggestion is that because ASL is used almost exclusively in North America, it cannot provide students with an international or global perspective. This is true in the case of ASL, of course, to the same extent that it is a valid criticism of the study of the indigenous languages and cultures of North America, as noted earlier. The study of the Hopi, for instance, is also not international in the narrow sense that is being applied to ASL and the deaf community. However, one could certainly argue that the point of such an international requirement in a student's education is to expose the student to cultures and languages different from his or her own, and that there is no logical reason for this exposure necessarily to entail study of a culture and language of a different country.

One of the more common arguments, at least at the tertiary level, against accepting ASL as a foreign language has been that it is not a written language, and hence does not have a literature to which students can be exposed. This objection actually has two separate components; first, the claim that ASL is not a written language, and second, that it does not possess a literature. Although it is technically not quite true that ASL is not a written language—there actually are several notational systems that can be used for reducing it to written form—it is true that it is not a commonly written language. Indeed, the written language of the American deaf community is in fact English. Having granted, then, this first objection, what of the second—that is, the claim that there is therefore a lack of a literature in ASL?

Because ASL is not normally written down, it obviously does not have a written literature in the way that French, German, Russian, and English, among others, do. Of course, the same might be said of the vast majority of the languages currently spoken around the world. What ASL does have is a literary tradition comparable to the oral traditions found in spoken languages (see Reagan, 1995a). Frishberg, for instance, has identified three major indigenous literary genres in ASL: oratory, folklore, and performance art. Frishberg (1988) compellingly argued that:

> ASL has been excluded from fulfilling foreign or second language requirements in some institutions because of claims that it has no … tradition of literature … [However,] a literary aesthetic can be defined prior to a written literary tradition, as in the case of Greek and Balkan epic poetry. We know that other languages which are socially stigmatized nonetheless adapt literature through translation and develop their own literary institutions. Non-Western cultures without writing traditions convey their traditions of history and philosophy within community-defined forms of expression. And, finally, the presence or absence of writing (systematized orthography) has little relationship to the existence of a traditional verbal art form. (pp. 165–166)

Furthermore, it can be argued that the advent of the movie camera, and more recently, the VCR, have made possible the compilation and transmission of the literary traditions and even the canon of ASL in a way simply not possible before this century. Nor is it the case that such a literature is merely possible in theory; the extensive body of ASL literature exists as a fact (see, e.g., Bahan, 1992; Jacobowitz, 1992; Low, 1992; Rutherford, 1993; Wilcox, 2000). In short, ASL does have a well-developed literature, albeit one not easily reducible to a written form, which is now both accessible and worthy of serious study (see Peters, 2000).

## ESPERANTO AND OTHER PROBLEMS

The third case that we wish to examine here is that of Esperanto, by far the most successful of the many artificially created international auxiliary languages (see Nuessel, 2000a; Richardson, 1988). The title for this section of the chapter comes from a colleague of ours, who recalled using a textbook about American education many years ago that concluded with a chapter entitled, "Women, Minorities and Other Problems." The idea that women and minorities constitute educational problems is of course powerfully offensive, but the fact that the author of that textbook apparently did not even recognize this tells us a great deal about the values, attitudes, and beliefs common at the time the book was written. Similarly, the fact that Esperanto (and, as we have seen, AAVE, ASL, and many other language varieties) can be and often is seen as a problem for educators and others to resolve is offensive in precisely the same way. No language is, or should not ever be viewed, as a problem—the language itself, whatever it is, is a uniquely interesting human creation. The challenges that are associated with language and language diversity are social, economic, political, and cultural issues rather than linguistic issues, and need to be understood and addressed on this basis. With this important caveat in mind, we turn now to our discussion of the case of Esperanto.

Challenges to the legitimacy of Esperanto have been raised on a number of grounds. Among the more common objections are the claim that Esperanto is an artificially constructed language, and thus not a natural human language; that Esperanto is a failed (although perhaps interesting) historical experiment that is now simply historical trivia; that individuals waste their time studying Esperanto when they could be learning another (presumably more useful) language; that Esperanto as a linguistic system is limited by its lack of a cultural community and literary tradition; and finally, that Esperanto is, despite the idealism of its creator and supporters, really not terribly usable—and that, in any event, the matter has largely been made moot by the international dominance of English.

These criticisms of Esperanto have been repeatedly and compellingly refuted by a number of writers (see, e.g., Auld, 1988; Edwards & MacPherson, 1987; Forster, 1987; Janton, 1993; Richardson, 1988). Esperanto is, as its critics have argued, an artificial language insofar as it was deliberately created—although why, exactly, this should count against its legitimacy as a language is far from self-evident. Indeed, supporters of Esperanto often cite the logic and regularity of Esperanto as one of the language's principal strengths (see Janton, 1993; Moore, 1980; Richardson, 1988), and it is likely that this regularity—made possible by the initial artificial construction of the language—is one of the reasons for Esperanto's relative ease of acquisition (see Maxwell, 1988). It is especially intriguing that relative ease of acquisition should count against linguistic legitimacy, given the emphasis in the pedagogical literature on the need to facilitate the language learning process for second language users, not to mention the plethora of advertisements in travel and airline magazines promising fluency in French, Spanish, German, and even Japanese with little effort and in remarkably short periods of time. However, having raised the issue of Esperanto's artificial origins, it is also important to note that Esperanto is by no means frozen in time—the language has been subject to the same processes of change found in other human languages, although change in Esperanto has to some extent been limited by the general acceptance by users of the language of Zamenhof's *Fundamento de Esperanto* (1905/1963) as a foundation for the language.

The claim that Esperanto is a failed historical experiment is also an interesting one, as it is not clear what criteria are being used to judge success and failure.[6] Certainly Esperanto has not become the common second language worldwide that its supporters would like, but alternately, it is spoken by a small but significant number of individuals around the world, despite serious oppression in a variety of settings and apathy in a number of others (see Jordan, 1987; Large, 1985, pp. 100–105; Lins, 1990; Nuessel, 2000a). One could, it would seem, argue just as compellingly that, given its 20th century history, Esperanto has been surprisingly successful and prosperous (see Janton, 1993, pp. 129–133; Tonkin, 1997).

Claims related to the usability of Esperanto, as well as to the de facto dominance of English around the world, are equally suspect. Esperanto is in fact demonstrably usable, as any number of Esperantists who have traveled to various parts of the world can attest (for discussions of educational and classroom uses of Esperanto, see Glossop, 1988; Goodman, 1978; Quick, 1989; Tonkin, 1988). Additionally, even if Esperanto were not particularly usable in communicative interactions, it has clear-cut pedagogical and propaedeutic advantages that facilitate, sometimes dramatically, the learning of other languages (see Fantini & Reagan, 1992; Frank, 1987; Leon-Smith, 1987; Markarian, 1964; Sherwood, 1982, 1983; Symoens, 1989; Szerdahelyi, 1966; Williams, 1965). As for the dominance of English, although it is true that English is widely spoken, it is also true that it is widely spoken badly, and in any event, the vast majority of the world's people speak no English whatsoever. Furthermore, when English speakers converse in English with non-native users of the language, there is inevitably a problem of equity and, indeed, of cultural and linguistic domination involved (see Pennycook, 1994, 1998, 2000; Phillipson, 1992). The same, of course, is also true of every other language of wider communication, and, for that matter, at least potentially true of every other ethnic language.

Finally, the claims of its critics notwithstanding, Esperanto does not exist in a culture-free context; there is in reality a vibrant, creative, and productive international Esperanto community, defined largely by common language use, which shares a substantial and growing literature (see Gregor, 1976; Janton, 1993, pp. 91–128; Richmond, 1993; Tonkin, 1977). Indeed, as Tonkin (1987) argued:

> Literature in Esperanto has continued to be an important part of the linguistic culture, as others have followed Zamenhof's lead in translating major literary works and in writing original works of their own ... For example, the 900-page anthology of Esperanto poetry *Esperanto antologio*, published in 1984, contains selections from no less than 163 poets, many of them authors of one or more volumes of poetry. There is also a steady stream of novels and short stories appearing in Esperanto,

along with occasional plays. Many of the major classics of Western literature, and numbers of non-Western masterpieces, have been published in Esperanto translation. (pp. 268–269)

In a remarkably fair, if somewhat depressing, account of the current status of Esperanto, Cohen (2000) commented:

Will Esperanto go the way of the eight-track? Though it may claim superiority to global English, Esperanto probably can't compete with it ... Esperanto will remain viable only if an unrealistically broad consensus of individuals continuously opt for compromise. So long as all roads lead to Wall Street, English will prevail ... Esperanto may be with us for some time. But even if it doesn t last—even if this is good-bye—Esperanto deserves respect for its century-long struggle to find an equitable common ground amid the confusion of languages. And if language extinction continues to accelerate, perhaps someday soon we'll want to take a new look at an old attempt at an entirely different model of globalization. (p. 62)

Although hardly a ringing endorsement of Esperanto, this passage nonetheless does identify some of the key issues surrounding the status and future of Esperanto as a common international language. In short, whatever its prospects for the future may appear to be, it is also clear that the rejection of Esperanto as a legitimate language would appear to be based on some very debatable, and generally problematic, factual claims.

## TOWARD A CRITIQUE OF LINGUISTIC LEGITIMACY

The challenges to the legitimacy of AAVE, ASL, and Esperanto would appear to be quite different, and this is hardly surprising, because they are in many significant ways very different linguistic systems with very different histories, user communities, and so on. And yet, there are some remarkably similar common themes. In all three instances, concerns about the legitimacy of the language inevitably involves related concerns about culture, and specifically, about the perceived lack of a cultural community tied to the language. The language communities that choose to use each of the languages under consideration are, in essence, themselves delegitimated as well—the African-American cultural community is simply not discussed at all in the context of AAVE, whereas in the case of ASL, the deaf community is seen by outsiders as unsophisticated and parochial, and speakers of Esperanto are routinely seen as fringe idealists (see Forster, 1982). Ling, for instance, a well-known and respected scholar, went so far in attempting to delegitimize the feelings and concerns of the deaf community as to argue that, "Members of the adult deaf community are not, by virtue of their deafness, experts on the education of hearing-impaired children and to argue otherwise is comparable to claiming expertise in pulmonary medicine simply because one breathes" (quoted in Neisser, 1983, p. 113). Indeed, as this quote suggests, in all three of the cases discussed here, the very existence of a concomitant cultural community is often denied by those challenging the legitimacy of the language. Furthermore, questions are raised about the linguistic structures of all three languages—AAVE is dismissed as simply broken English, ASL is rejected as a derivative of English or as syntax-free or syntactically limited, and with respect to Esperanto, it is commonly asserted that the artificial creation of the language constitutes grounds for rejecting its status as a real language. Finally, it is interesting to note that challenges to the linguistic legitimacy of AAVE, ASL, and Esperanto are very commonly offered by those who are not themselves competent in the respective language. This fact is, on its own, quite intriguing, because under normal circumstances we would not consider individuals who do not speak a language to be credible judges about the value and structural components of the language.

We see, then, that the challenges to the legitimacy of all three of these language varieties have been based on a variety of assumptions that, on careful examination, prove to be both empirically and conceptually problematic. In all three cases, it can be argued that the resistance to the language under consideration is misguided, misleading, and inappropriate. However, the debate is not simply a matter of misunderstanding. Rather, it reflects more general issues of language and cultural rights in society, and the way in which such rights are often overlooked or ignored. What is actually at issue in this debate is the question of how the Other in society is perceived and treated, and the extent to which the dominant group in society is willing seriously to countenance pluralism. By challenging the legitimacy of particular languages (whether AAVE, ASL, Esperanto, or another language), we in essence denigrate and even reject the speaker communities of these languages, their cultures, and their worlds. The rejection of the linguistic legitimacy of a language—any language used by any linguistic community—in short, amounts to little more than an example of the tyranny of the majority. Such a rejection merely reinforces the long tradition and history of linguistic imperialism in our society. The harm, though, is done not only to those whose languages we reject, but to all of us, as we are made poorer by an unnecessary narrowing of our cultural and linguistic universe. As Archbishop Tutu (1983) once noted about oppression in apartheid-era South Africa, "at present nobody is really free; nobody will be really free until Blacks are free. Freedom is indivisible" (p. 45). The same is true, we argue, with respect to language, language rights, and linguistic oppression. So long as we reject the legitimacy of others' languages, we inevitably set overly parochial limits on our own culture, language, and world.

It is important to note that calling for the recognition of the legitimacy of all human languages and language varieties, and rejecting the false categorization of some language varieties as nonlegitimate, as has been done here, does not in and of itself constitute any particular prescription for educational practice. Accepting a child's language as legitimate does not necessarily require that the child be taught through the medium of that language variety, nor does such acceptance automatically preclude instruction in or the learning of another language. The specifics of how speakers of AAVE, for instance, are to be schooled are in no way limited by the recognition of their language as real and legitimate.

This having been said, there are nonetheless clear social and educational implications that do in fact follow from the rejection the concept of linguistic legitimacy. Perhaps most important in this respect is that the discourse related to the education of children from different language backgrounds must reflect the recognition of their languages and linguistic experiences as real, valuable, and appropriate, and should seek to build on the individual child's background, to as great an extent as possible, in seeking to meet his or her needs. Our discourse, as Foucault compellingly argued, does indeed affect our perceptions and understandings as well as embodying "meaning and social relationships [and] constitut[ing] both subjectivity and power relations" (Ball, 1990, p. 2). Thus, our discourse about language and language diversity, in both social and educational settings, must itself be carefully reconsidered and subjected to critical reflection.

It is not, however, only with our discourse that we must be concerned. Also clearly at issue is teacher knowledge, especially as such knowledge relates to language broadly conceived. Although teachers today are without doubt asked to function in classrooms in which language diversity is a daily fact of life, their preparation to deal with language diversity is all too often at best minimal. If classroom teachers are to be expected to function, in essence, as applied linguists in their classrooms (as does, in fact, appear to be the case), then it becomes both urgent and essential that they receive appropriate preparation and training to enable them to meet such challenges (see Reagan, 1997a). At stake, too, are the kinds of research problems that are explored, and finding ways to ensure that indefensible linguistic prejudices are not closing off potentially valuable areas of research.

In short, what is required is a change of both attitudes and practices with respect to our thinking about and responding to linguistic diversity in society and in the classroom. These changes, based on a better understanding of the nature of language, do not, as noted earlier, lead to any specific prescriptions for practice. What they do accomplish, though, is to ensure that the linguistic needs of all children will be considered alongside their social, cultural, and educational needs. Whether we call what they speak a language, a dialect, or a language variety is really irrelevant. What does matter is how we address their needs, and that is what we should be discussing and debating.

## LINGUISTIC LEGITIMACY AND THE FOREIGN LANGUAGE EDUCATOR

For the foreign language educator, the implications of our discussion thus far in this chapter are profound. Language educators are very much at the forefront of the education that students receive with respect to the nature of language and language variation. Foreign language educators need to be aware of the issues surrounding the concept of linguistic legitimacy, as do all teachers, but they also need to understand the specific implications of these issues for the foreign language classroom.

Students in the foreign language classroom need to be exposed not only to the mainstream variety of the target language, but also need to learn about other variations of the target language. It is by no means inappropriate for us to focus primarily on Parisian French in the French classroom, but it is very much a mistake to exclude from our teaching the different varieties of French spoken around the world (see, for instance, Hale, 1999; Natsis, 1999; Valdman, 2000). Furthermore, in at least some instances local varieties of the target language may actually be incorporated into the formal school curriculum. This would, for instance, make sense in Spanish classes located in areas where there are large numbers of native speakers of the language who speak a non-mainstream variety of Spanish. It makes little sense, we would suggest, to teach a variety of the target language that has few local uses, when another variety might prove quite useful. Again, this is not to say that students should not learn the mainstream variety of the target language (or, in a case like Spanish, one of the mainstream varieties). However, if our students' second language interactions are most likely to take place with Spanish speakers for whom *troca* rather than *camión* is the recognized term for truck, then surely both Spanish forms should be learned. What we are advocating here is fairly simple: Foreign language education should be informed by an understanding and sensitivity to the sociolinguistic aspects of the target language (for the case of French, see Ball, 1997; Lodge, Armstrong, Ellis, & Shelton, 1997; Walter, 1988; for the case of Spanish, see Klee, 1998; Mar-Molinero, 1997, 2000; for the case of German, see Johnson, 1998; Stevenson, 1997).

Beyond such sociolinguistic understanding, though, the foreign language classroom is also an ideal place to help students to begin to develop what can be called critical language awareness. In other words, the study of language needs to include not only the communicative and cultural aspects of language, but also the often implicit political and ideological issues related to language. Students need to understand the ways in which language is used to convey and protect social status, as well as how it can be used to oppress and denigrate both individuals and groups. The foreign language classroom can either reinforce negative language attitudes and prejudices, or can be used to empower students to better understand the social roles of language in society (see Lippi-Green, 1997). The choice is very much ours to make in our classrooms and in our interactions with our students.

---

## QUESTIONS FOR REFLECTION AND DISCUSSION

1. Identify some of the major varieties of the language that you teach (or plan to teach). Which varieties are the socially preferred varieties? Which varieties are socially stigmatized? How do these language attitudes reflect historical and contemporary power relations in society?
2. To what extent do you believe that your own background and education have adequately prepared you to address issues of language diversity in

the target language? What are the implications of your answer for (a) the foreign language curriculum in general, (b) the preparation of foreign language teachers, and (c) the need for professional development for foreign language educators?

3. What, in your view, are the most important implications of the concept of linguistic legitimacy for the teaching of foreign languages in the U.S. context? In your answer, be sure to include both curricular and methodological implications.

4. Are you convinced by the authors' arguments about AAVE? About ASL? About Esperanto? Do you think that these language varieties ought to be taught as foreign languages? Why or why not? If you respond differently to the cases of AAVE, ASL, and Esperanto, try to articulate what the differences among these three cases are for you.

5. In recent years, some avid fans of the various *Star Trek* television series have begun to study the Klingon language, an alien language created for the series. There is now a dictionary and grammar of Klingon (see Okrand, 1992), as well as a Klingon Language Institute, a postal course for learning Klingon, numerous translation projects (including the Klingon Shakespeare Restoration Project, the Klingon Bible Translation Project, the Extended Corpus Project, the Klingon Writing Project, the Klingon Educational Virtual Environment, and so on), and multiple Web sites. Do you believe that the authors' arguments about linguistic legitimacy ought to apply to the case of Klingon? Why or why not? Should students be able to meet a foreign language requirement by studying Klingon?

## FOCUS ON THE CLASSROOM

1. How do you think your students would define the concept of real language? What are the implications of this for foreign language education?

2. Compare and contrast the status of AAVE as a variety of American English with some of the nonmainstream varieties of the language(s) you teach. What do you believe your students need to learn about these nonmainstream varieties, and why?

3. How can a foreign language educator explain the concept of language variety to students? Why is this a concept that students of foreign languages need to understand?

4. In the context of the foreign language classroom, the correction of student errors plays an important role. Under what circumstances can we say that a sentence created by a student is wrong? Under what conditions is such a judgment on the part of the teacher inappropriate? Why?

5. Are there native speakers of the target language you teach locally available to you? Do any of these native speakers use different varieties of the target language? What are the implications of this for classroom instruction?

## NOTES

1. The deliberate construction of a single Serbo-Croatian language took place following a 1954 agreement at Novi Sad. Although the two varieties of the language are obviously quite close, they are distinguished not only by their orthography (Serbs use the Cyrillic alphabet, whereas Croatians use the Latin alphabet), but also by lexical differences. Even during the period in which the languages were officially unified, there were tensions (primarily on the part of Croatian intellectuals) related to the apparent dominance of Serbian forms. As Lampe (2000) noted:

   > Could a common Serbo-Croatian orthography and dictionary fairly be called Croato-Serbian as well? Croatian reservations turned into public protests when the first two volumes of the dictionary were published [in 1967]. Serbian variants of these two, overlapping, grammatically identical languages were consistently chosen over the Croatian variants. (p. 305)

   In the years following the break-up of the former Yugoslavia, efforts to emphasize the distinctive nature of each variety of the language have intensified, and there are now separate dictionaries, and so on, for Croatian, Serbian, and Bosnian (see, Kroll & Zahirovič ..., 1998, Šušnjar, 2000; Uzicanin, 1996; Vitas, 1998), not to mention the emergence of Macedonian in the Republic of Macedonia (see Kramer, 1999a, 1999b). Typical of the rhetoric found in such works is the following description of the Bosnian language:

   > The Bosnian language is spoken by 4.5 million people: Muslims, Serbs, and Croats living together for centuries in Bosnia and Herzegovina ... The Bosnian language is a symbiosis of the Serb and Croat languages, which are Slavic tongues, with strong Turkish and German influences. Bosnian is written in two alphabets: Cyrillic and Roman. (Uzicanin, 1996, p. 7)

   This, then, is a very clear example of Weinreich's point about the difference between a language and a dialect.

2. One of the more serious concerns about many of the labels used to refer to AAVE is that the use of Black in this context is not simply misleading, but is in fact fundamentally racist, as there is no equivalent concept of White English. For a more in-depth discussion of this point, see Lanehart (1999).

3. We have chosen to use the term mainstream rather than standard to refer to the socially dominant and preferred variety of a language, primarily because we are concerned that the term standard may be taken to imply a level of linguistic superiority that does not, in fact, exist. In fact, the use of the term standard to refer to a single

variety (albeit the socially dominant variety) is itself a manifestation of what Cameron labeled the "ideology of standardization" (1995, pp. 38–39); see also Lippi-Green (1997, pp. 53–62).

4. Perhaps the most common illustration of the Sapir-Whorf Hypothesis has been the example of the number of words in Eskimo languages for snow. Although there are credible examples that one could offer in support of the Sapir-Whorf Hypothesis, this particular example—widespread though it certainly is—is in fact nothing more than a fiction (see Pullum, 1991, pp. 159–171).

5. See, for instance, Reagan (1988, 1989, 1990a, 1990b, 1992, 1997b, 2000b, in press-b).

6. This is not, however, to suggest that the history of efforts to create artificial languages is not worth study; indeed, we believe that just the opposite is the case. Such efforts, regardless of how effective they have been, have much to teach us about the nature of human language and about language attitudes. Especially interesting in this regard is Eco's masterful work, *The Search for the Perfect Language* (1995); also worth noting are Guérard (1922), Knowlson (1975), Large (1985), and Yaguello (1991).

# 4

# Constructivist Epistemology and Foreign Language Teaching and Learning

> Constructivism is not a theory about teaching. It's a theory about knowledge and learning.
>
> —*Catherine Fosnot* (1993, p. vii)

One of the more puzzling and complex concepts that foreign language educators must deal with is the question of what it actually means to know or to learn a second language (see, for example, Cooper, 1975; Wardhaugh, 1993, pp. 208–249). Although people who speak a single language often believe that such knowledge is easily determined and demonstrated, individuals who have second language skills inevitably know better than this. The notion of knowing a language is in fact highly problematic, as is the notion of learning a language.[1] This is an especially important point for foreign language educators to understand, because underlying all pedagogical practice, ultimately, are questions of epistemology. The way in which we think about knowledge and what it means to know are directly and necessarily linked to all aspects of how we teach. In foreign language education, this can be seen clearly, for example, in the well-documented and close relationship between behaviorist epistemology and learning theory and the audiolingual method (see Chastain, 1976, pp. 109–129; Littlewood, 1984, pp. 17–21).

In recent years, a number of academic disciplines, not the least of which are mathematics and science, have undergone significant changes in the epistemology that underlies their pedagogical practice, moving increasingly toward constructivist approaches to epistemology and learning theory (see Cooper, 1993; Davis, Maher, & Noddings, 1990; Fensham, Gunstone, & White, 1994; Kamii, Manning, & Manning, 1991; Mintzes, Wandersee, & Novak, 1997; Nelson, 1996;

Spivey, 1997; Steffe, Cobb, & von Glasersfeld, 1988; Tobin, 1993; Wood, Cobb, & Yackel, 1995). This change in learning theory has, in essence, involved a change in the metaphors that we use to conceptualize knowledge, teaching, learning, and knowing (see Tarsitani, 1996).

Although to some extent arguably implicit in many contemporary discussions about communicative language teaching, and often fairly clearly embodied in actual foreign language teaching practice, constructivist approaches to epistemology and learning theory have only recently, and relatively rarely, been explicitly examined in terms of their implications for foreign language teaching and learning (see Blyth, 1997; Craig, 1995; Kaufman & Grennon Brooks, 1996; Kumaravadivelu, 1994; Nyikos & Hashimoto, 1997; Stevick, 1996; Williams & Burden, 1997). In this chapter, we consider the potential contributions of constructivism to foreign language teaching and learning by providing a broad overview of the core assumptions and concepts of constructivism, and then by exploring the ways in which constructivism can inform and promote effective pedagogical practice, as well as a better understanding of such practice, in the foreign language context. Next, we turn to a short introduction to the use of metaphors and metaphorical language as windows into our own understanding and practice.

## METAPHORS IN EDUCATIONAL DISCOURSE

It is reasonable to wonder why the metaphors[2] that we select to describe such concepts as teaching, learning, and knowing really matter. After all, by their very nature, metaphors are intended to be nonliteral (see Lakoff & Johnson, 1980). And yet, the metaphors that we select and use do matter, because they reflect underlying beliefs and attitudes and, even more, because the metaphors themselves take on significant pedagogical power. There is a wealth of metaphorical language in the discourse of classroom teachers that relates directly and indirectly to pedagogy and pedagogical issues. As Miller and Fredericks (1988) argued, the use of metaphors is a worthwhile topic for our attention because, "Metaphorical expressions are so pervasive in ordinary and academic life ... they must reflect a 'fundamental core' of shared meaning. By using these expressions, people must assign meaning. Metaphors are not simply random events but are ways of "structuring" and extending experience" (pp. 263–264).

Metaphors and metaphorical language, in short, function at least in part to structure the individual's construction of reality, as well as to mediate his or her experiences with underlying, and often implicit, assumptions, values, and beliefs. As Lakoff and Johnson (1980) suggested, "Metaphors may create realities for us, especially social realities. A metaphor may thus be a guide for future action. Such actions will, of course, fit the metaphor. This will, in turn, reinforce the power of the metaphor to make experience coherent. In this sense metaphors can be self-fulfilling prophecies" (p. 156).

If it is indeed the case that metaphors not only play a role in the way in which individuals construct their realities, but also serve as guides for practice, then it would seem to be evident that the study of the kinds of metaphors and metaphorical language employed by teachers and other educators about teaching and learning ought to be of considerable concern to anyone interested in understanding and improving educational practice (see Nattinger, 1993). Siegelman (1990), for instance, believed that metaphors have the potential to generate new ideas and meanings between listener and speaker. Thus, if the goal is to help people better communicate their personal realities, metaphors can provide an infrastructure for supporting shared cultures (see Nuessel, 2000b).

An interesting and significant feature of much educational discourse is the use of language in nonliteral but nonetheless meaningful ways. The use of metaphors (including the use of similes and other sorts of metaphorical language use) is perhaps the best example of nonliteral language use. Metaphors are widely used in education and in other kinds of public discourse, and often play key roles in discussion and debates. Green (1971) suggested that, "Indeed, it may be that metaphors are necessary if we are to think about important matters at all. No major philosopher in the history of the subject has escaped their use and no major field of knowledge in the modern world can do without them" (p. 56).

Metaphors, at root, are basically unstated analogies, involving the implicit comparison of two different kinds of things, one of which is intended by the speaker to be taken literally, the other figuratively. Examples of common educational metaphors would include the claims that "education is growth," "critical thinking is a tool," and "teachers mold and shape children." Taken literally, each of these claims is clearly not only false, but absurd (see Scheffler, 1960, pp. 49–59; see also Scheffler, 1979). However, it is nevertheless true that we do in fact understand each of these statements quite clearly in the non-literal way in which each is intended. Metaphors, in short, are used because they have value to us. As Green (1971) noted, "The main virtue of the metaphor is that it calls our attention to certain similarities between two things. It carries the mind over from one thing to another by calling attention to resemblances. In other words, a metaphor is a way of establishing 'thought-full' relations between things" (p. 57).

The analysis of metaphors in educational discourse often provides us with important insights, and the use of metaphors can help us to develop clearer understandings and appreciations of complex issues and concepts. Consider the kinds of metaphors that are often used by teachers. In a fascinating study of classroom teacher discourse, Miller and Fredericks (1988) found that five broad families of metaphors were commonly used:

- teaching as a conduit
- teaching as a biological process
- teaching as a process of building

- teaching as war
- teaching as the manifestation of emotional responses

The metaphor used to describe the classroom in fact tells us a great deal about the teacher. The frequent use of war or military metaphors ("in the trenches," and so forth), for instance, suggests that the teacher perceives the classroom as something of a battleground. Insofar as this is the case, we would expect (and indeed would be likely to find) that concerns of classroom management and control are at the top of such a teacher's worries. This, in turn, will be reflected in the approach to students taken by the teacher.

With this brief background in mind, we turn now to a discussion of one of the more powerful contemporary metaphors for teaching and learning—constructivism, both as a learning theory and as an epistemology.

## CONSTRUCTING CONSTRUCTIVISM

Although *constructivism* has gained considerable attention in the educational literature in recent years, there is no clear definition or consensus of what is meant by the term (see Duffy & Jonassen, 1992; Forman & Pufall, 1988; Fosnot, 1996a; Kafai & Resnick, 1996; Merrill, 1992; Nicaise & Barnes, 1996; Schwandt, 1994; Steffe & Gale, 1995). As Richardson noted, "One cannot think of constructivist teaching ... as a monolithic, agreed-upon concept ... There are fundamental theoretical differences in the various constructivist approaches" (1997b, p. 3). Indeed, there is even debate about whether constructivism is best understood as an epistemology, an educational philosophy, a pedagogical approach, a theory of teaching, or a theory of learning (see Kaufman & Grennon Brooks, 1996, p. 234). Arguably the best articulation of the nature of constructivism in the educational literature is that of Fosnot (1996b), who compellingly suggested that:

> Constructivism is a theory about learning, not a description of teaching. No 'cookbook teaching style' or pat set of instructional techniques can be abstracted from the theory and proposed as a constructivist approach to teaching. Some general principles of learning derived from constructivism may be helpful to keep in mind, however, as we rethink and reform our educational practices (p. 29).

Such a view of constructivism essentially confirms its status as an epistemology—a theory of knowledge and learning, rather than a theory of teaching (see von Glasersfeld, 1993, pp. 23–24). As an epistemology, constructivism, in essence, entails the rejection of traditional transmission-oriented views of learning, as well as behaviorist models of learning. Instead, emphasis is placed on the individual learner's construction of his or her knowledge. Beyond this, though, constructivism assumes not only that learning is constructed, but also that the learning process is a personal and individual one, that learning is an active process, that learning is collaborative in nature, and that all learning is situated (see Merrill, 1992, p. 102). In other words, what constructivism offers is a radically different view of the nature of the learning process—a view that is grounded in a rejection of what von Glasersfeld called the "domination of a mindless behaviorism" (1995a, p. 4). This view includes, as Fosnot (1996b) noted, a number of general principles of learning, including:

- Learning is not the result of development; learning is development. It requires invention and self-organization on the part of the learner.
- Disequilibrium facilitates learning. Errors need to be perceived as a result of learners' conceptions and therefore not minimized or avoided ... Contradictions, in particular, need to be illuminated, explored, and discussed.
- Reflective abstraction is the driving force of learning. As meaning-makers, humans seek to organize and generalize across experiences in a representational form.
- Dialogue within a community engenders further thinking. The classroom needs to be seen as a "community of discourse engaged in activity, reflection, and conversation" ...
- Learning proceeds toward the development of structures. As learners struggle to make meaning, progressive structural shifts in perspective are constructed—in a sense, big ideas ... These "big ideas" are learner-constructed, central organizing principles that can be generalized across experiences and that often require the undoing or reorganizing of earlier conceptions. This process continues throughout development. (pp. 29–30)

It is important to stress here that constructivist epistemology is more than simply an alternative to other approaches to epistemology; rather, it entails a rejection of some of the core assumptions that have been shared by western epistemology for some two and a half millennia (see Gergen, 1982, 1995). As von Glasersfeld argued, "the crucial fact [in understanding constructivism is] that the constructivist theory of knowing breaks with the epistemological tradition in philosophy" (1995a, p. 6), which is why it has been labeled not merely postmodernist, but postepistemological by some writers (see Noddings, 1990).

Up to this point, we have discussed constructivism as a single entity, although keeping in mind Richardson's warning that it is in fact far from monolithic. In reality, it has become fairly commonplace in discussions of constructivism to distinguish between what are often taken to be two fundamentally distinct, competing types of constructivism (see Cobb, 1994, 1996; Magadla, 1996). The first type of constructivism, radical constructivism, is fundamentally an epistemological construct that has been most clearly and forcefully advocated in the work of von Glasersfeld (1984, 1989, 1993, 1995a, 1995b, 1996). Radical constructivism has its philosophical roots in Piaget's genetic epistemology (Piaget, 1976, 1979, 1986,

1993, 1996; Sinclair, Berthoud, Gerard, & Veneziano, 1985), and is essentially a cognitive view of learning in which "students actively construct their ways of knowing as they strive to be effective by restoring coherence to the worlds of their personal experience" (Cobb, 1996, p. 34). Radical constructivism is premised on the belief that an individual's knowledge can never be a true representation of reality (in an observer–independent sense), but is rather a construction of the world that she or he experiences. In other words, knowledge is not something that is passively received by the learner; it is, quite the contrary, the result of active mental work on the part of the learner. Thus, from a radical constructivist perspective, knowledge is not something that can merely be conveyed from teacher to student, and any pedagogical approach that presumes otherwise must be rejected.

The alternative to radical constructivism is social constructivism, which has as its primary theoretical foundation the work of Vygotsky (1978, 1986; see also Frawley, 1997; Lantolf, 2000; Moll, 1990). Social constructivism, although accepting the notion that the individual does indeed construct his or her own knowledge, argues that the process of knowledge construction inevitably takes place in a sociocultural context, and that therefore knowledge is in fact socially constructed. As Driver, Asoko, Leach, Mortimer, and Scott (1994) argued with respect to science education, "it is important ... to appreciate that scientific knowledge is both symbolic in nature and also socially negotiated ... The objects of science are not phenomena of nature but constructs that are advanced by the scientific community to interpret nature" (p. 5).

The tension between radical and social constructivism, between the personal and the social construction of knowledge, is to a significant extent more apparent than real, and in any event, is certainly amenable to resolution on a practical level, criticisms to the contrary notwithstanding (see, e.g., Cobern, 1993; Confrey, 1995). As Cobb asserted, "the sociocultural and cognitive constructivist perspectives each constitute the background for the other" (1996, p. 48), and von Glasersfeld recognized that "we must generate an explanation of how 'others' and the 'society' in which we find ourselves living can be conceptually constructed on the basis of our subjective experiences" (1995a, p. 12).

Perhaps the most reasonable way to articulate the common, shared elements of radical and social constructivism is to talk about learning as socially mitigated but personally constructed, a formulation that at the very least moves us away from a strong bifurcation of radical and social constructivism and allows us to move on to a discussion of the implications of constructivist epistemology in general for teaching practice.

## CONSTRUCTIVIST TEACHING

Although it is obviously important to keep in mind that constructivism is not, and could not be, a pedagogical theory or approach per se, it is also true that certain characteristics of the constructivist-based classroom can be identified. For example, Grennon Brooks and Brooks (1993) and Kaufman and Grennon Brooks (1996, p. 235) identified eight characteristics that have been observed in constructivist classrooms:

1. Use raw data and primary sources, along with manipulative, interactive, and physical materials.
2. When framing tasks, use cognitive terminology, such as classify, analyze, predict, create, and so on.
3. Allow student thinking to drive lessons. Shift instructional strategies or alter content based on student responses.
4. Inquire about students' understandings of concepts before sharing your own understandings of those concepts.
5. Ask open-ended questions of students and encourage students to ask questions of others.
6. Seek elaboration of students' initial responses.
7. Engage students in experiences that might engender contradictions to students' initial hypotheses and then encourage a discussion.
8. Provide time for students to construct relationships and create metaphors.

What these characteristics, taken together, are all about really focuses on what could be called *guided discovery,* or more accurately, *structured induction* in and as the learning process. These characteristics function as descriptive and normative attributes in that they have not only been observed in practice, but in that they have also been used for evaluation purposes. It is important to note here, incidentally, that "Many of these attributes are not unique to constructivist teaching but are representative of good teaching in general" (Kaufman & Grennon Brooks, 1996, p. 235)—a point that would seem to confirm von Glasersfeld's claim that "Constructivism does not claim to have made earth-shaking inventions in the area of education; it merely claims to provide a solid conceptual basis for some of the things that, until now, inspired teachers had to do without theoretical foundation" (1995a, p. 15). Furthermore, although it is the case that "constructivist principles of learning do not automatically engender principles of teaching ... [since] learners construct meaning on their own terms no matter what teachers do," (Winitzky & Kauchak, 1997, p. 62), it is also true that:

> Constructivist theorists would maintain ... that learning is better or more effective when teachers use constructivist teaching methods, like culturing and keying bacteria as opposed to lecturing about bacteria. Constructivist teaching typically involves more student-centered, active learning experiences, more student–student and student–teacher interaction, and more work with concrete materials and in solving realistic problems ... Nevertheless, students still create their own meanings based on the interaction of their prior knowledge with instruction, and the meanings they make may not be the ones the teacher had in mind, no matter how constructivist the instruc-

tion ... Teachers create constructivist learning experiences for students based necessarily on what they, the teachers, find salient. But what is salient to the teacher is not necessarily so to the learner. (Winitzky & Kauchak, 1997, pp. 62–63)

With this significant caveat in mind, we are ready to turn next to an examination of the implications of constructivist epistemology for the specific case of foreign language education.

## CONSTRUCTIVISM IN FOREIGN LANGUAGE PEDAGOGY

Constructivism has a wide range of implications for language educators in terms of its significance for research and its relevance for pedagogical practice. With respect to the former, studies of the social nature of language learning and acquisition are increasingly grounded in constructivist epistemological positions. Writing about developments in bilingual education, for instance, Faltis (1997) noted that "a shift toward the constructivist, social nature of learning and language acquisition is also increasingly evident in new research efforts" (p. 194). Similarly, the veritable explosion in discourse studies is ultimately, albeit often implicitly, linked to constructivist approaches to understanding, whether one is concerned with academic discourse (see Achard, 1993; Bourdieu, Passeron, & de Saint Martin, 1994; Fairclough, 1995; Reagan, in press-a), classroom discourse (see Bartolomé, 1998; Craig, 1995; Measures, Quell, & Wells, 1997; van Lier, 1996; Woods, 1996), or scientific discourse (see Boulter, 1997; Gunnarsson, Linell, & Nordberg, 1997). Indeed, Gunnarsson (1999) went so far as to suggest that:

> The complexity of the construction of knowledge has been focused on by scholars dealing with scientific discourse. Proceeding from ideas within the social constructivist tradition, they have developed a methodology for the purpose of understanding how science is created through discourse ... the social construction of scientific facts [has been described] as an antagonistic struggle among scientists, leading to a deliberate diminishing of the results of others and a leveling up—to a generalized level—of one's own results. Scientific facts are regarded as mere works; rhetoric determines what become scientific facts. (p. 111)

The implications of such a view of the nature and role of scientific discourse for the classroom are significant:

> It is the growing recognition of the significance of the social construction of conceptual understanding in science that has coincided with the development of a suitable methodology for investigating social situations involving talk. Science is now often seen within science education research as intimately constructed, through discourse, within communities of knowers. The following themes in research and discourse in science teaching and learning arise from the synthesis of con-

# CONSTRUCTIVIST EPISTEMOLOGY 63

structivism and sociolinguistic methodology and can be seen in the major work in progress:

- The *complexity* of classroom discourse which has complex interactions with the ways teachers teach, the resources they use and with the particular phenomenon of science being studied;
- *Communities* in science and science classrooms having characteristic discourse patterns;
- *Collaboration* in classroom settings allowing the authentic practice of science and the development of appropriate discourse;
- *Critiques* of science, its methodology, its boundaries, its status, and its language as a cultural construct. (Boulter, 1997, p. 242)

Such research foci emphasize, not surprisingly, the social construction of language and discourse, but there is room as well for concern with the personal or individual construction of language. One powerful way in which we can conceptualize the personal construction of language has to do with the linguistic notion of idiolects: "The unique characteristics of the language of an individual speaker are referred to as the speaker's *idiolect*. English may then be said to consist of 400,000,000 idiolects, or the number equal to the number of speakers of English" (Fromkin & Rodman, 1993, p. 276). In other words, a transfer or transmission-based view of language learning is simply incompatible with the final outcome of such learning, as each individual speaker (whether native or non-native) in fact constructs his or her own understanding of the target language, which will in turn be modified and can be evaluated by comparison with other speakers of the language. This is not, of course, to minimize in any way the key role played by interaction in the process of language learning; as Nelson (1996) cogently observed:

> Competence in constructing and using culturally defined categories of entities (objects, events, properties, etc.) has been shown to involve a number of different linguistic components, including superordinate labels and the vocabulary of inclusive hierarchies. These verbal components can account for aspects of conceptual development previously held to be perceptually based (e.g., grouping along lines of shape similarity) or logically based (e.g., set relations). The verbal contributions to the development of cultural categories are integrated with experientially derived categories ... The coordination and integration processes involved in the assembling of cultural taxonomies ... exemplify the more general problem encountered during the preschool years of reconfiguring individual experientially based representations established independently of linguistic input to accommodate knowledge systems displayed in language. This reconfiguration cannot be accomplished through individual constructive processes alone, but requires implicit and explicit collaboration with knowledge bearers ... (p. 332)

Although Nelson's focus was on language acquisition in early childhood, the same general claim would apply, we believe, to foreign language learning with respect to the complementary and interactive roles of the individual and the social construction of language. This is an important aspect of a constructivist approach to understanding foreign language learning, because it emphasizes not only the individual construction of meaning, but also, the potential for the misconstruction of meaning and therefore the need for collaboration and interaction with the knowledge bearer—that is, generally speaking, the teacher. This brings us to the implications of constructivist epistemology for foreign language pedagogy.

In the context of the foreign language classroom, the application of constructivist epistemology would necessarily undergird virtually all classroom practice. As Williams and Burden (1997) explained:

> The literature on language teaching provides comprehensive accounts of different language teaching methodologies and is rich with ideas and techniques for teaching a language. However, what has become increasingly clear to us is the fundamental importance to teachers of an understanding of what is involved in the process of learning to inform and underpin our teaching of the language. Teachers' own conceptions of what is meant by learning, and what affects learning will influence everything that they do in the classroom. At the same time, in order to make informed decisions in their day-to-day teaching, teachers need to be consciously aware of what their beliefs about learning and teaching are. (pp. 1–2)

This is true not only of foreign language teaching, but of all teaching. To be sure, foreign language pedagogy does indeed have many common features with other sorts of teaching—but it is also distinct in some key ways. Successful foreign language learning entails far more for the learner than merely learning content and skills. Gardner (1985) suggested that, "Languages are unlike any other subject taught in a classroom in that they involve the acquisition of skills and behaviour patterns which are characteristic of another community" (1985, p. 146), whereas Crookall and Oxford argued that, "Learning a second language is ultimately learning to be another social person" (1988, p. 136). It is this need for the learner to reconstruct one's personal identity that is at the heart of foreign language learning, and it is in this process of reconstruction, rather than merely in terms of learning vocabulary and grammatical forms, that constructivist epistemology may be most useful. It is also a constructivist perspective that allows us to recognize, as Anward (1997) argued, that certain kinds of foreign language pedagogy are in fact internally contradictory: "Put bluntly, we could say that in the context of language drills students are often taught language resources that cannot be used in that very context" (p. 129).

A point that needs to be stressed here is that constructivist epistemology, although certainly having clear implications for classroom practice, is concerned first and foremost with helping us to understand the learning process itself, rather than with dictating pedagogical practice. As Fosnot (1993) emphasized in the quote with which this chapter began, "Constructivism in not a theory about teaching" (1993, p. vii). Furthermore, as will be clear in the following discussion of

# CONSTRUCTIVIST EPISTEMOLOGY 65

constructivist pedagogy in the foreign language context provided, much of the common pedagogical practice of foreign language teachers (especially those utilizing communicative approaches in foreign language teaching) is fully compatible with constructivist learning theory. In other words, the power of constructivist epistemology for foreign language education may well be more in its explanatory, legitimating, and justificatory power than in terms of any specific implications that it may have for classroom practice.

An example of a constructivist approach to foreign language teaching is provided by a teacher in an introductory Spanish class whose lesson focuses on the use of the verb *gustar* to express personal likes and dislikes. The class begins with the teacher presenting the following short passage in Spanish, in which *gustar* is used in a number of different ways:

> A mi me gusta bailar, pero a Ana no le gusta bailar. A mi hermana le gustan las flores, pero a mi padre no le gustan las flores. A mis hermanos les gustan la música americana. A mi me gustan todos los tipos de música. Juan y Diana les gusta hablar frances. A Kelly y a mi nos gusta hablar español. ¿Qué te gusta a ti?

The teacher then employs pictures, realia, and dramatic techniques to facilitate students understanding of the meaning of the passage, even though the students have not yet learned the specifics of the use of *gustar*. Next, the teacher elicits both individual and class involvement using the basic forms of *Me gusta* + singular subject (as in *me gusta el vino*). After several instances in which the correct forms of this type have been produced, the teacher introduces a plural subject (*me gustan las flores*), and asks a student, *¿Te gustan las flores?* Utilizing various elicitation techniques, the teacher then moves around the classroom, alternating the use of the first and second person forms and the singular and plural forms and introducing negative forms (*No me gustan las flores*). Students are encouraged to converse in dyads, in a round-robin fashion, asking questions and giving answers. The teacher provides corrective input only as needed, generally using stress to indicate a student error and encourage student self-correction. During this activity, the teacher would also introduce the *Me gusta* + infinitive form (*Me gusta bailar*), and would then encourage students to use constructions of this type to indicate activities that they enjoy. At this point, the teacher might also introduce the third person form (*Le gusta el chocolate*) and have students discuss the likes and dislikes of other students in the class, based on the information obtained earlier in the class. By the end of the class, the students will have begun to master the use of the verb *gustar*; additional practice and further development of the use of *gustar* will be needed, of course, but students should already be in a position to offer a reasonably accurate description of how *gustar* is used—and should be able to do so without ever having explicitly encountered a formal explanation of the grammatical rules involved. Similar approaches can be used to teach virtually any linguistic structure, semantic relationship, or lexical item in the target language, as well as helping students to develop their own personal competence in (and hence construction of) the target language broadly conceived. In fact, a fairly compelling case could be offered for the claim that the greater the difference between a particular structure or vocabulary item in the learner's mother tongue and the target language, the more appropriate and effective a constructivist approach to language learning may prove to be. This point is similar to, and certainly compatible with, that made recently by Widdowson (1998):

> We now know much more than our predecessors about what makes language real for its users, and we know what learners have to do if they are to aspire to be foreign language users themselves. My main point is that this heightened understanding about language, communication, community, and social identity has also to be applied to the contexts of the classroom and the realities and identities of language learners. To do this is really only to recognize, as our predecessors have done, that what we are teaching is not language as experienced by its users but a *foreign* language which, as a subject, has to be designed for learners. (p. 332)

Thus, in a similar vein, telling students about the difference between the verbs *ser* and *estar* in Spanish might well be less useful than simply having them employ the verbs and gradually come to know, in part as a result of teacher correction, when each is appropriate (although in fact, it is important to note, constructivist pedagogy would not actually rule out explicit grammatical instruction if it was useful in helping students to construct their own understandings of the features of the target language).

And what of the case of a student who has misconstructed[3] some aspect or feature of a second foreign language? In an interesting discussion of the role of technology in foreign language education, Phillips (1998) reported on a powerful example of the role of technology in facilitating what is, in essence, a reconstruction of student understanding based on native speaker feedback:

> What technology, when used well, has wrought is the following e-mail exchange between a seventh grader in Sleepy Hollow, New York and a peer in Padre las Casas, Chile ... When a U.S. youngster, named Chema, sent a message of introduction to a Chilean keypal, some of the adjectives used in the message ended in *o* and some ended in *a* in spite of the student's record of more accurate responses on the worksheets, audio tapes, and computerized drills that came with the classroom text package. Chema received a response that said, *Me alegré mucho de recibir tu mensaje, pero aclárame amigo o amiga. ¿Cuál es tu sexo?* 'I'm really glad to receive your message, but make it clear whether you are a [male] friend or [female] friend. Are you male or female?' Maybe, like so many language learners in the past, Chema will never travel to a country where Spanish is spoken, but today's student will communicate real messages with users of the target language. That single instance caused learning to occur for Chema, her teacher reported that she never again made an agreement error when talking about herself. (p. 27)

In all of the instances that have been discussed here, although explicit and directive teaching is certainly possible, and often both appropriate and valuable, the alternative of teacher modeling and individual student construction of the linguistic

# CONSTRUCTIVIST EPISTEMOLOGY

target has much to commend it as well. In addition, it is important to note that constructivist learning theory would require that we attend seriously to the context in which language learning takes place—recognizing, for instance, that the methods and activities that facilitate language learning in one context might differ significantly from those in another. Williams and Burden (1997) provided a summary of what they consider to be the ten basic propositions involved in applying constructivist learning theory to foreign language education, and these 10 propositions include:

1. There is a difference between learning and education.
2. Learners learn what is meaningful to them.
3. Learners learn in ways that are meaningful to them.
4. Learners learn better if they feel in control of what they are learning.
5. Learning is closely linked to how people feel about themselves.
6. Learning takes place in a social context through interaction with other people.
7. What teachers do in the classroom will reflect their own beliefs and attitudes.
8. There is a significant role of the teacher as mediator in the language classroom.
9. Learning tasks represent an interface between teachers and learners.
10. Learning is influenced by the situation in which it occurs (pp. 204–208).

Constructivist epistemology has, then, clear implications for classroom practice, the curricula, student evaluation, and indeed virtually all aspects of the teaching–learning process (see Henning, 1995; Zietsman, 1996), including teacher professional development (see Keiny, 1994). Although not explicitly discussed here, constructivist epistemology also has the potential to impact in significant ways the preparation of foreign language educators (see Condon, Clyde, Kyle, & Hovda, 1993; Rainer & Guyton, 1994; Richardson, 1997a), and the challenge of preparing such educators to engage in reflective and analytic classroom practice (see Parker, 1997; Reagan et al., 2000; Richards & Lockhart, 1994; Zeichner & Liston, 1996). The ultimate purpose of taking constructivist epistemology seriously in foreign language education is helping teachers to learn to empower students to acquire language more effectively. As von Glasersfeld (1989) argued:

> Good teachers ... have practiced much of what is suggested here, without the benefit of an explicit theory of knowing. Their approach was intuitive and successful, and this exposition will not present anything to change their ways. But by supplying a theoretical foundation that seems compatible with what has worked in the past, constructivism may provide the thousands of less intuitive educators an accessible way to improve their methods of instruction. (p. 138)

## QUESTIONS FOR REFLECTION AND DISCUSSION

1. In this chapter, the authors argue for the importance of metaphors as important windows into the attitudes, beliefs, and views of the teacher. What metaphors would you use to describe your role as a foreign language educator? What do these metaphors indicate about your underlying beliefs and attitudes? How might these metaphors be reflected in your own classroom practice?
2. What, in your view, is the difference between knowing German and knowing about German? What are our goals in the foreign language classroom with respect to these two kinds of knowing? How are these goals reflected in our methodology and assessment?
3. In this chapter, Crookall and Oxford are quoted as suggesting that, "Learning a second language is ultimately learning to be another social person." Based on your own experiences as a second language learner, do you agree or disagree with this position? What are the implications for Crookall and Oxford's view for foreign language teaching and learning?
4. What do you see as the fundamental distinction between the student's construction of knowledge in the foreign language classroom and the student's misconstruction of knowledge? What are the implications of this distinction for foreign language teaching and learning?
5. What does it mean to you to learn a second language? What are the implications of your view for teaching in a foreign language classroom setting?

## FOCUS ON THE CLASSROOM

1. When and why are student errors or mistakes beneficial in the context of the foreign language classroom? What are the implications of your answers for teaching methods in foreign language education?
2. What can you as the foreign language teacher do to encourage oral language practice as students engage in the construction of their own knowledge of the target language? What barriers discourage oral language practice and how can you minimize these?
3. What can you as the foreign language teacher do to encourage written language practice as students engage in the construction of their own knowledge of the target language? What barriers discourage written language practice, and how can you minimize these?
4. Can grammatical knowledge be learned as a constructivist activity, and if so, how can this be done?

5. What do you believe are the effects of national, state, and local standards in foreign language education on classroom practice? How do such standards complement or contradict constructivist conceptions of learning in the foreign language context?

## NOTES

1. Indeed, some authors and researchers have insisted on using only the term acquisition when referring to second languages (see, e.g., the work of Krashen and Terrell, 1983). The same is true with respect to terms like bilingual, which refers not to any particular degree or level of competence, but instead is used to describe an incredibly wide range of varying degrees of competence in two languages. Thus, in some contexts, bilingual may be used to refer to an individual with only very limited second language skill, and in others, only native competence in two languages would constitute bilingualism. For an extended and clear discussion of this topic, see Elgin (2000).
2. It is important to emphasize that our concern here, and the focus in the literature on metaphors in discourse, is on metaphorical language rather than simply on metaphors. Thus, included in this discussion are not only pure metaphors, but also similes and other forms of metaphorical language. For an extended discussion and explanation of this matter, see Lakoff and Johnson (1980); also of interest are Ortony (1980), Smith (1981), and Taylor (1984).
3. The idea that students can misconstruct knowledge is also an important one. The concept of knowledge construction does not in any way entail that all constructions of knowledge are equally valid, nor that some are not demonstrably false.

# 5

# Critical Curriculum Development in the Foreign Language Classroom

> I believe that ... the only true education comes through the stimulation of the child's powers by the demands of the social situations in which he finds himself. Through these demands he is stimulated to act as a member of a unity, to emerge from his original narrowness of action and feeling, and to conceive of himself from the standpoint of the welfare of the group to which he belongs.
>
> —*John Dewey* (1897/2000, pp. 92–93)

We now turn our focus directly onto the foreign language curriculum—and in particular, to the concept of curriculum development. Typical approaches to both developing curricula and to understanding curricula often focus on an essentially hierarchical view of the curriculum development process, in which one begins with broadly philosophical issues and then moves through the articulation of specific goals and aims, and culminates in the identification and description of units, lessons, and activities that are intended to accomplish particular objectives. Although such an hierarchical perspective on curriculum has its benefits heuristically, and although it does indeed emphasize the importance of the connections and overlappings inherent in the curricular process, it also presents a serious challenge to understanding the development, implementation, and evaluation of democratic, and especially critical, approaches to curriculum. Indeed, one could fairly easily argue that such a top-down model of curriculum is in fact anathema, or at the very least is antithetical, to the core principles that a more democratic and critical approach to curriculum requires, both in general and in foreign language education in particular. Martel (2000) articulated this point quite succinctly when noting that:

# CRITICAL CURRICULUM DEVELOPMENT

> there is a sense today that ideas, institutions, and political structures resting on the vertical [hierarchical] axis represent a deficit model of human organisation. Largely products and constructs of the Western world and of its political culture, like the Nation-State, products exported with Western Europe's historical world-wide displacement of its internal competitions and wars, they are not adapted to meet the budding axial shift [to collaborative/horizontal frames]. They are not structures based on peace and sharing. On the contrary, they are based on competition and even warfare. (p. 154)

This point can, of course, be applied to the issue of curricula and curriculum development in the broader sense, as the process or construct of curriculum development as now practiced in U.S. foreign language education is, quite obviously and deliberately, a construct and product of the Western world and its intellectual tradition. The same can be said of the products of such a process, including most notably the recent popularity of national standards in various disciplinary areas. As the curriculum theorist Apple (1996) argued,

> While the proponents of a national curriculum may see it as a means to create social cohesion and to give all of us the capacity to improve our schools by measuring them against "objective" criteria, the effects will be the opposite. The criteria may seem objective; but the results will not be, given existing differences in resources and in class and race segregation. Rather than leading to cultural and social cohesion, differences between "we" and the "others" will be socially produced even more strongly, and the attendant social antagonisms and cultural and economic destruction will worsen. (pp. 32–33)

How, then, can critical language educators proceed in the classroom? Certainly the curriculum writ large, as well as our objectives, classroom activities, and so on, cannot and should not be randomly and arbitrarily designed and implemented. There is, in short, clearly a need for a instructional plan that seeks to further the aims of what might be termed *emancipatory praxis*. Arguing for a holistic model that incorporates and celebrates the social and cultural contexts of the schooling process, Kincheloe, Slattery, and Steinberg (2000) pointed out that some view curriculum as:

> A process of understanding the self in relation to the world, not simply the concrete information students must memorize or master. Contemporary scholars analogize instruction to a personal journey, with the teacher as travel guide, advisor, author, wise mentor or philosopher more concerned with the growth, maturity, and empowerment of each student that with the information each student regurgitates on standardized tests. In this conception, evaluation becomes an authentic expression of each student's unique understanding and application of learning. (p. 300)

Reflecting the process Osborn (2000) described as macrocontextualization, critical curriculum development in the foreign language classroom must proceed from the context of the world, the self in relation to the world, and the role of language and language education in the shaping of both independent of and dependent on the others. We advocate the understanding of collectivities, but no longer in the sense of a them to be studied, but as a contextually defined construct. This theoretical starting point makes its way into, and is manifested in, practice in three ways:

- the critical language curriculum is built around problem posing;
- the critical language curriculum is holistically constructed, overarching disciplinary bounds as defined in the academic world; and
- the critical language curriculum requires evaluation not as a measure of linguistic skill, but as an expression of language awareness.

We now turn to a detailed discussion of each of these aspects of critical curriculum development in the context of contemporary foreign language education in the United States.

## PROBLEM POSING

Asking the right questions is among the most important and powerful activities that students can learn. A fundamental component of asking the right questions, of course, is in being able to pose the right questions. As the noted critical pedagogue Freire (1972/2000) noted:

> Problem-posing education does not and cannot serve the interests of the oppressor. No oppressive order could permit the oppressed to begin to question: Why? While only a revolutionary society can carry out this education in systematic terms, the revolutionary leaders need not take full power before they can employ the method. In the revolutionary process, the leaders cannot utilize the banking method as an interim measure, justified on grounds of expediency, with the intention of later behaving in a genuinely revolutionary fashion. They must be revolutionary—that is to say dialogical—from the outset. (p. 198)

Key points of problem posing in education are illuminated in this passage. Problem posing will not serve the interests of the oppressor, because it constantly strives to answer the question, Why? Second, problem posing in foreign language education can be incrementally implemented. There is no need for current curricula to be rewritten from a problem-posing perspective. Foreign language educators can implement critical curriculum pieces incrementally, beginning at any time. The dialogical or change-oriented focus of the classroom activities becomes a critical pedagogy immediately accessible to practitioners. Problem posing originates as a form of praxis the first day one uses it. Wink (2000) provided a powerful explanation of how problem posing can impact the classroom:

# CRITICAL CURRICULUM DEVELOPMENT 73

> Problem posing brings interactive participation and critical inquiry into the existing curriculum and expands it to reflect the curriculum of the students' lives. The learning is not just grounded in the prepared syllabus, the established, prescribed curriculum. Problem posing opens the door to ask questions and seek answers, not only of the visible curriculum, but also of the hidden curriculum. Problem posing is very interested in the hidden curriculum, which is why many are uncomfortable with it. Problem posing causes people to ask questions many do not want to hear. (p. 61)

Problem posing in the foreign language classroom involves constructing units around questions, issues, concerns, and puzzles related to language. Such units can and should have specific communicative outcomes in mind, and should be tied to the formal curriculum in appropriate ways. They should also, however, help students to begin to examine language, language use, and language attitudes (both their own and others') more critically. For instance, even in an introductory level class, one might explore advertisements, both in the U.S. media and in the foreign media. Among the issues that might be raised in such a unit are:

- How are different languages utilized in such advertisements?
- How are speakers of particular languages represented?
- What are the social, cultural, economic, political, ideological (and so on), messages that are conveyed in such advertisements?
- How are these messages consistent with or inconsistent with stereotypes found in different societies?
- What level of fluency would be required to understand foreign language texts in various advertisements?

It is essential to note that such questions will inevitably involve the incorporation of the skills of reading, writing, listening, and speaking in contextualized and communicative activities as students begin to explore the component parts of how these portrayals are made and what they mean. It is also, of course, significant to note that these same questions are the sort of questions that teachers themselves need to be asking about the entire curriculum that they teach.

In the U.S. context, for example, one might consider analyzing the series of television commercials for Taco Bell that feature the chihuahua with a Spanish accent (and often, a military uniform). In contrast, one could point out the Seville STS automobile ad, in which a picture of the globe includes the Mercedes symbol superimposed in the northeastern United States with the caption, "Stuttgart, wir haben ein Problem." In more general terms, advertisements for private schools that assert that "In our school, 'I can't' is a foreign language" also convey important, and indeed not-so-subtle, messages to the reader. Finally, there are cartoons, such as the *Rocky and Bullwinkle* classics, in which the antagonists speak with foreign (and, in this case, what one takes to be Russian-sounding) accents.[1]

Such media trivializations of non-English languages, and the messages that they convey, can then be contrasted with the use of English (and other foreign languages) in the media of other societies, where English in particular is most often used to indicate far more positive values and attributes.[2] The exploration and examination of such advertisements will not, of course, prepare students to visit foreign countries and purchase squash from a street vendor, but they may very well prepare them to live beside speakers of non-English languages, and increase their understanding of both the open and hidden messages about language and language usage that surround us all. In our view, we would argue that the latter is actually a more educationally appropriate use of the time than much of what currently takes place in classrooms.

## HOLISM AND THE CRITICAL CURRICULUM: THE ROLE OF INTERDISCIPLINARY UNITS

> While it unquestionably has high rhetorical appeal, curriculum integration presents daunting challenges to those who would like to see it more widely embraced as an alternative or counterpart to subject-based curriculum ... With its promise of unifying knowledge and modes of understanding, interdisciplinary education represents the pinnacle of curriculum development.
> —*David Ackerman (1989, p. 37)*

We now turn our focus directly onto the concept of curricular integration with other subject areas. Connecting with other disciplines has, at least until recently, not been a particularly strong point of foreign language curriculum and instruction, often because planners in the other core areas have failed to recognize the potential contributions our field can provide, and also because we have tended to focus on what can be done within the foreign language classroom with respect to disciplinary connections rather than looking for ways in which connections might be made between foreign language classes and other classes. As the latest state frameworks and national standards attest, however, interdisciplinary links have the potential to help students to create a powerful nexus among the issues that they study (see National Standards in Foreign Language Education Project, 1996). In fact, as foreign language education takes its much-coveted place among the core subjects offered in the schools, encouraging students to make these associations will prove invaluable for a number of reasons, some cognitive (such connections more accurately represent the reality of the nature of knowledge) and others pragmatic (connections to other subjects and disciplines help students to see the relevance of foreign language study).

Since 1991, a growing number of educators working within and among the core content areas have advocated the development and implementation of interdisciplinary curricula as an important aspect of educational reform and renewal (see

Lonning, DeFranco, & Weinland, 1998; National Council of Teachers of Mathematics, 1991). An important aspect of the literature concerned with the interdisciplinary curriculum has been its emphasis on the hurdles faced by educators in integrating course content across disciplinary lines, which constitute a challenge of considerable scope and difficulty (Davison, Miller, & Methany, 1995; Lonning & DeFranco, 1997). Within the field of foreign language education, researchers and educators have looked for ways to effectively move beyond the traditional barriers of the classroom in terms of both pedagogy and instructional content (Biron, 1998; Gehlker, Gozzi, & Zeller, 1999; Osborn, 1998a, 1998b; Overfield, 1997). These efforts reflect the values and articulated goals of the *Standards for Foreign Language Learning*:

> The conscious effort to connect the foreign language curriculum with other parts of students' academic lives opens doors to information and experiences which enrich the entire school and life experience. Those connections flow from other areas to the foreign language classroom and also originate in the foreign language classroom to add unique experiences and insights to the rest of the curriculum. (National Standards in Foreign Language Education Project, 1996, p. 49)

Contemporary educational thought in general tends to be decidedly supportive of interdiscplinary approaches to teaching and learning (see Shrum & Glisan, 2000), and we would certainly agree that the linking of foreign language with content in language courses (and, indeed, across the whole curriculum) is certainly a worthwhile goal. However, desire alone is insufficient to direct and guide efforts of this type to successful fruition. A model for the initial planning stages of interdisciplinary curriculum development in and for foreign language courses is crucial.

Jacobs (1989) noted that, "in contrast to a discipline-field based view of knowledge, interdisciplinarity does not stress delineations but linkages" (1989, p. 8). Ackerman (1989) moved the interdisciplinary agenda forward by proffering intellectual and practical criteria to be considered as a "framework for teachers and curriculum developers deliberating over whether to adopt a curriculum integration approach for some portion of their instructional program" (p. 25). Perhaps most significant elements of Ackerman's framework are the concepts of validity for, validity within, and validity beyond the discipline (see also Lonning et al., 1998, p. 315). Briefly summarized, these criteria require that an interdisciplinary theme or organizing center be important to relevant fields of study—that is, that they not be a contrived connection. Furthermore, the criteria must facilitate the learning of other concepts within the individual disciplines, and must give the student a "metaconceptual bonus" (Ackerman, 1989, p. 29; see also pp. 27–30). Within these criteria, however, one finds both the genesis of new ways of thinking about such units and about the limitations of current models for the foreign language classroom.

As Lonning et al. pointed out, the "selection of appropriate themes seems to be the key to providing instruction that is potentially more meaningful when taught in an interdisciplinary fashion than when the concepts are taught separately" (1998, p. 312). The model they proposed for the integration of math and science includes moving from standards and state frameworks, through a revision and evaluation process in selecting an applicable theme, to a refinement of activities that balance mathematics and science content. In an analogous fashion, units in the foreign language classroom can become interdisciplinary as they move from the usual textbook chapter topics to overarching and extendable curricular themes, especially insofar as such themes overlap and are tied to curricular content in other subject areas.

Yet, even as the newest standards challenge both the traditional grammatical and even solely communicative approaches to foreign language education, curriculum planners may well find it perplexing to attempt to design an appropriate interdisciplinary theme for the foreign language class. A good place to see this problem is with the notion of teaching culture. Simply put, the challenge is to determine which themes or topics can be included under the broad banner of traditional culture, and how far and to what extent it is appropriate to deviate from time-honored categories when they seem too rigid, given new directions in the field. Understandably, Shanahan's (1998) contention that there are minimally five major approaches to the conception of culture with relevance for the foreign language classroom pointed to a lack of clarity about culture as the point of departure for non- or extra-linguistic course content in the foreign language classroom. Shanahan included capital "C" culture and lowercase "c" culture, cultural studies that included political aspects, cross-cultural communicative facets, and an ecumenical cultural approach that focused on the affective rather than the oppositional approaches of the primarily cognitive notions of culture.

The uncertainty about defining culture arises with good reason, since for both language educators and others alike, the concept of culture is both a fuzzy and complex one. Lessow-Hurley (1996) for instance, perceptively pointed out that, "Culture is something we all have but often find difficult to perceive. Culture, like language, is dynamic, changing to meet the needs of the people it serves. All cultures have coherent, shared systems of action and belief that allow people to function and survive" (p. 95). Goodman on the other hand, relied on more traditional definitions of culture in asserting that culture is the "learned, socially-transmitted heritage of artifacts, knowledge, beliefs, values and normative expectations that provides the members of a particular society with the tools for coping with recurrent problems" (p. 338). Although the definitions offered by many are not mutually exclusive, such a catch-all category is difficult to use in planning interdisciplinary units with other core curricula, even given the theoretical power and applicability of Ackerman's criteria (1989) and Lonning et al. (1998) model for other disciplines.

In practice, of course, it is quite difficult, if not impossible, to meaningfully separate the linguistic content of the foreign language course from its concomitant cultural components. As Kramsch (1993) explained:

> One often reads in teachers' guidelines that language teaching consists of teaching the four skills [reading, writing, listening, and speaking] "plus culture." This dichot-

omy of language and culture is an entrenched feature of language teaching around the world. It is part of the linguistic heritage of the profession. Whether it is called (Fr.) *civilisation*, (G.) *Landeskunde*, or (Eng.) *culture*, culture is often seen as mere information conveyed by the language, not as a feature of language itself; cultural awareness becomes an educational objective in itself, separate from language. If however, language is seen as social practice, culture becomes the very core of language teaching. Cultural awareness must then be viewed both as enabling language proficiency and as being the outcome of reflection on language proficiency. (p. 8)

As Osborn (in press) stressed, cultural items included in the foreign language curriculum will be more similar to the home culture, the target culture, or both, and as a result critical interdisciplinary units will need to utilize themes and activities that include both connective validity and comparative integrity. Connective validity and comparative integrity imply that themes for interdisciplinary units possess features that simultaneously resonate as authentic with both members of the represented culture and experts in the field of study, thus achieving a balance among elements of disciplinary epistemology (see Reagan, 1999) and multicultural perspectives.

Connective validity requires that any interdisciplinary unit include the following aspects:

- A thoughtful integration of communicative aspects in the skills of reading, writing, listening, and speaking;
- A contextualization or subjectification of the domestic (or "home culture") perspective; and
- Primary attention paid to the related global or local realities of pluralism, including any role played by language diversity. (Gerwin & Osborn, in press; Osborn, in press)

An interdisciplinary unit focusing on defining who we are, defining who they are, for example, might involve activities in the foreign language classroom, the social studies or history classroom, the English or language arts classroom, and the drama classroom. The integrated, interdisciplinary unit we suggest should focus on cultural identity themes that can be investigated through sources in the foreign language classroom. Documents, videos, audio recordings, and other media are examples of such sources, including the ones described earlier in this chapter in relation to problem posing. The language teacher, utilizing the examples of commercials, cartoons, and advertisement or other target language realia as communicative catalysts, then includes activities related to reading, writing, listening, or speaking in any combination. Although all of the activities need not specifically relate to the connections in each of the other classes, the point of connection should involve the acquisition of information in the target language as demonstrative of how we identify ourselves and portray dissimilar others. A unit should also include a concerted attempt to subjectify the home perspective. Giroux (1997a) referred to a culture of positivism that in the case of the language classroom can lead students to understand, in error, that knowledge, including knowing one's identity is apolitical or beyond the influence of culture. The critical foreign language curriculum is built in cooperation with the other contributing disciplines to enable student understanding of the home perspective as one created from within a specific time and place framework (i.e., that it is not suprahistorical), and to hear other voices that seek to challenge the dominant perspective with an often dissenting view. In this way, students grow to understand through the contextualization of the perspective that the identity being constructed in any narrative—literary, historical, linguistic, dramatic, or otherwise—represents a dominant ideology, not an unbiased fact.

Connective validity also suggests that a theme attends to the realities of global pluralism. If a theme does not relate to cultural diversity in some international or transnational way, then a connection to the language classroom is likely contrived. The theme of defining who we are, defining who they are, however, most certainly attends to the realities of diversity both at home and abroad.

In a related vein, Wong (1993) attempted to raise warnings about the potential misuse of comparative approaches to literature:

> A key instructional means of eliciting insight being comparison and contrast, at every turn we need to decide what to compare a marginalized literature to, and to what end. If this is done from a fallacious assumption of one's impartiality, however well-intentioned, the purpose of broadening the curriculum, namely, to honor the articulation of previously suppressed subjectivities, will be seriously undermined. (p. 112)

A growing body of evidence suggests that cultural information as presented in classrooms is often culturally reductionist or misrepresentative (Brosh, 1993, 1997; Osborn, 1999, 2000; Reagan & Osborn, 1998; Wieczorek, 1994). Osborn (in press) contended that cross-cultural comparisons should be screened in an attempt to avoid defining cultural issues as cleanly dichotomous, including characteristics as follows:

- An *emic* voice in representing the cultural information;
- An absence of bifurcatious categorization; and
- An explicit articulation of multiple perspectives within the "home" culture.

The emic perspective is central to a unit theme or activity that possesses comparative integrity. If the classroom activities, discussions, or presentations attempt to act as paternalistic agent for representing a target cultural perspective, the derived depictions will unavoidably be both self-serving and reductionist. The avoidance of bifurcation, in relation to the unit we are proposing, implies that the teacher attempts to disclaim the use of us and them categories. Although seldom so blatant, discussions of the American versus foreign perspective present the same problem in a language classroom. Such categories, obviously, trivialize the complexity of diversity as expressed in society and significantly call into question the ethical and educational value of any interdisciplinary unit. As well, by calling student attention to the multiple perspectives of who we are and who they are within both the home and target cultures, language teachers provide a dialectical understanding of cultural mediation for the students, and thus engage in the dialogical process advocated so compellingly by Freire (1973, 1974, 2000). Put simply, no issues related to identity are unidimensional, nor are they uncontested.[3] Tensions and resistance exist in all cultural identity issues, and illuminating such facets for students is vitally important to the integrity of critical foreign language instruction.

## CRITICAL ASSESSMENT AND EVALUATION

Authentic assessment should be the cornerstone of evaluation in the critical foreign language curriculum. Focusing on a student's expression of her or his emancipatory knowledge, the assessment seeks to understand the new ways in which student construct, deconstruct, and reconstruct the world as related to language diversity. Students can be presented with textual material in any accessible language, target or home, and asked to explore the world and the word contained and represented within. Receptive and productive language skills can be tested, to be sure, but the point of the assessment is not to measure proficiency in using arbitrary language code. Returning to the example we have used throughout the chapter, that of constructing collective identities, we now propose how evaluation in such a unit (interdisciplinary or stand alone) might be carried out. Assume that the students have lower intermediate language skills, as might be seen in a second year high school course. Students might be asked to look at a map of the *Mundo Hispanico* and describe why, in the case of the United States, only portions of the map are highlighted (such as Florida, Texas, California, New York City, and Chicago). Students may utilize grammar that involves the subjunctive if they answer an essay question such as "If a speaker of Spanish in Hartford, Connecticut (notably absent from the map) saw this map, how might he or she feel about his or her membership in the Spanish-speaking world?" Written accuracy could be evaluated if the teacher desires, or more holistic approaches could be employed. Students might listen to a speech in a German class related to the Turkish *Gastarbeiter* in Germany. Questions related to how their group identity is constructed by the speaker may test comprehension in this critical, problem-posed example.

## IMPLICATIONS FOR FOREIGN LANGUAGE PEDAGOGY

Moving toward a critical pedagogy in the foreign language classroom requires fundamental changes not only to curriculum development, but also to the way we conceptualize what curriculum is. Themes of family, health, and weather or other vocabulary and grammatically driven syllabi will give way to units built around the context in which language education takes place. This process of macro-contextualiztion in the foreign language classroom becomes a genesis for curricula, instruction, and evaluation that are sensitive to the issues of diversity, and optimistic in their regard for social justice.

Curriculum planners desiring to move toward interdisciplinary, thematic units can strengthen educational experiences for students by helping them break down some artificial disciplinary barriers imposed by educational practice. At the same time, however, reaching across disciplines can be approached from a carefully planned and thoughtful attempt to balance the exigencies of academic rigor and sensitivity to realities of cultural pluralism. The politics of school knowledge will continue to influence curricular decisions, and an awareness of the issues raised in developing cross-cultural understanding will empower developers to move forward in a most effective and ethical manner.

Teacher educators and teachers can begin to develop a critical awareness of instructional issues as well. How we present material related to cultural comparisons and academic connections is as important as what we choose to present in terms of achieving the goals of equipping students to live in an increasing diverse society. Language classes as part of the core curriculum will indeed be faced with challenges as we broaden our own horizons in addition to those of our students. Interdisciplinary thematic units can serve as a powerful tool for connections and comparisons as we fulfill the agenda set by the newest and most ambitious standards.

It is unquestionably ironic that second (foreign) language education has seemed to come late to the realm of interdisciplinary unit development, since the foreign language field, unlike any other, is by its very nature concerned with bridging disciplines. The category culture, in common use, has included strong components of studies of history, political science, food science, literature, economics, media studies, and so forth. Although collaborations with other disciplinary specialists within the academic setting may seem restricted because the fluency required to discuss complex topics in the second language often eludes students, in reality the newest standards and mandates provide multiple opportunities for connections and comparisons in the second language classroom. The integration of second language education into the core will be enhanced as practitioners in the field become skilled in the development of integrated, interdisciplinary units including the language classroom in the core.

## QUESTIONS FOR REFLECTION AND DISCUSSION

1. This chapter begins with a quote from the well-known American philosopher of education, John Dewey. What in your view are the implications of Dewey's comments for the development of critical curricula in foreign language education? In other subject areas?

# CRITICAL CURRICULUM DEVELOPMENT 81

2. The authors assert that, "Certainly the curriculum writ large, as well as our objectives, classroom activities, and so on, cannot and should not be randomly and arbitrarily designed and implemented." Do you agree with this claim? Why or why not? What does the claim tell you about the assumptions the authors are making about the nature of the foreign language curriculum?
3. Explain in your own words what problem posing entails, and how this concept relates to teaching a foreign language. Can you give examples of student-based problem posing in the foreign language classroom?
4. Can you suggest a series of interdisciplinary themes that might tie the foreign language curriculum to other subjects? What are the barriers to the successful implementation of such interdisciplinary themes? How can these barriers be addressed effectively?
5. How would you distinguish between a foreign language curriculum and a critical foreign language curriculum? How would the differences between the two be manifested in actual classroom practice?

## FOCUS ON THE CLASSROOM

1. What kinds of topics are covered in foreign language classes that might also be important in mathematics classes? To what extent might these topics provide a foundation for interdisciplinary instruction?
2. What kinds of topics are covered in foreign language classes that might also be important in different science classes? To what extent might these topics provide a foundation for interdisciplinary instruction?
3. What kinds of topics are covered in foreign language classes that might also be important in social studies classes? To what extent might these topics provide a foundation for interdisciplinary instruction?
4. What kinds of topics are covered in foreign language classes that might also be important in English or language arts classes? To what extent might these topics provide a foundation for interdisciplinary instruction?
5. What kinds of topics are covered in foreign language classes that might also be important in other classes? To what extent might these topics provide a foundation for interdisciplinary instruction?

## NOTES

1. Such advertisements abound, in both printed and video forms, and it is quite easy for the teacher to begin to collect examples of advertisements that make use, in some way, of foreign languages. We have also found, however, that this is a very

useful activity for students in foreign language classes, at all levels, to be asked to engage in. Indeed, it is often an eye-opening experience for students to begin to critically assess advertisements, and understand the hidden and covert messages that such advertisements often convey.
2. For an excellent discussion of the issues raised here, see Lippi-Green's book, *English With an Accent: Language, Ideology and Discrimination in the United States* (1997).
3. The complex issue of the relationship between language and identity is explored in Dicker (1996, pp. 1–33).

# 6

# Foreign Language Teaching as Social Activism

Se vogliamo che tutto rimanga come è, bisogna che tutto cambi.

—*Giuseppe di Lampedusa* (quoted in Augarde, 1991, p. 129)

Although advances have abounded in recent years with respect to our understanding of the way in which schools, and particularly curricula, contribute to and reproduce existing inequalities in the United States, some scholars have argued that the field of sociology of school knowledge has nevertheless been marginalized within the social sciences (see Ladwig, 1996). At least some of this marginalization may result from a lack of understanding of how such advances are applied (or not applied) in practice. As Dewey observed, when scholars connect the broader social view of education and educational reform to general cases, "it will lose its isolated character; it will cease to be an affair which proceeds only from the over-ingenious minds of pedagogues dealing with particular pupils" (1900/1902/1943, p. 8). One of the issues often overlooked in all of this, however, is that we tend to entertain an overly constrained view of the teaching profession. Although admittedly we are far from completely understanding everything involved in teaching, there has been a very real growth in our understanding of the cognitive dimensions of the craft, notably through reflective practice. In this regard, as we noted earlier, Reagan et al. (2000) identified three levels of reflective practice:

> At this first level, reflection entails only the appropriate selection and use of instructional strategies and the like in the classroom. The second level involves reflection about the assumptions underlying specific classroom practices, as well as about the consequences of particular strategies, curricula, and so on ... Finally, the third level of reflectivity (sometimes called critical reflection) entails the questioning of moral,

ethical, and other types of normative criteria related directly and indirectly to the classroom. (p. 22)

Critical reflection, as discussed in chapter 2, thus becomes prerequisite to the critical pedagogy that we are advocating here. Teachers who cannot reflect critically possess little hope of providing their students meaningful opportunities to reflect on the issues of language diversity and critical language awareness. In short, criticisms that critical pedagogy is not applicable to the real world of the classroom teacher, go far beyond a simple lack of understanding about critical pedagogy. Those who doubt the practicality of using critical pedagogy in teaching are also extremely likely to have an overly constrained understanding of the profession of teaching. Simply put, teaching is much more than the conveyance of material to be memorized and regurgitated. It is, as well, an art and science of engaging students intellectually and emotionally in their understanding of the world. Superficial conceptualizations of teaching (and, indeed, of learning) in fact place at risk many of the promising trends in contemporary educational practice in the United States:

> For we are beginning to recognize again that teaching is a fundamentally moral enterprise. How we treat children who are different, how we deal with antisocial behavior, and how we decide what is to be taught are all essentially moral decisions. As moral agents, teachers must have enough control of their teaching to ensure that they cannot be forced to act against the interests of their students. (Irwin, 1996, p. 114)

Most experienced teachers will relate that in fact they cannot be forced to act against what they consider to be the best interests of themselves, the community, or the students, as their own priorities would dictate. Teachers typically refer to the adage that "when that classroom door closes," and proclaim their own veto power over any mandate, curricular, legal, administrative, or otherwise.[1] Only challenges of moral or professional impropriety wield power to dissuade a teacher from exercising her or his own form of academic freedom. We contend that this power, when practiced, represents curricular nullification, and an awareness of its principles and practices can become part and parcel of any teacher education program desiring to move teachers from those who simply understand what is transpiring in relation to the sociological nature of schooling, to those who have the power to change it. As Wink (1997) argued in regard to transformative models of lesson design:

> The fundamental belief that drives these classroom behaviors is that we must act; we must relate our teaching and learning to real life; we must connect our teaching and learning with our communities; we always try to learn and teach so that we grow and so that students' lives are improved, or for self and social transformation ... This new approach to teaching and learning challenges teachers to have complex pedagogical skills. (p. 118)

Language teaching is a political act. There is no escaping the veracity of this maxim, even if we shroud curriculum in the illusion of neutrality or attempt to convince teachers that they are engineers of instruction following the architecture of such curricula. Teaching by its very nature is a form of social activism. Curricular nullification can be a tool of empowerment with immense socially transformative potential.

## FOREIGNNESS AS IMPRIMATUR

There is a real sense in which foreignness, as a conceptualiztion of the Others represented within and beyond foreign language curricula and instruction, serves as the official sanction under which we, as foreign language educators, operate. Language study, as it currently exists in our educational systems, functions to identify that which is foreign, by constructing the ideologically charged concept within the common sense realm of our students and colleagues. Let us examine in detail the concept of foreignness, then, as it applies in this regard. The concept of foreignness, as explored by Osborn (1998a, 1999), should be viewed as having four component parts, the external, the internal, the dynamic, and the value identification. These component parts, taken together, constitute foreignness in the context of U.S. secondary language curricula—which is to say, that this conceptualization of foreignness is that which is presented and taught to over four million students annually, primarily by native speakers of English. Foreign language learning, then, is presumed to have some educational value due to one or more of the following:

- national economic concerns;
- national defense concerns;
- leisure activities, especially travel outside the country;
- promoting multicultural awareness or acceptance;
- an ascribed ability to validate speakers of the language within this society; and/or
- a recognized relationship to historical, traditional, and mainstream Western education or contemporary U.S. educational practice or society.

Beyond this, though, foreignness is not a singular entity, but rather refers to a continuum ranging from more foreign to more familiar. To the degree that the speakers of any given language pose (or are perceived to pose) a threat to the economic, political, or ideological security of mainstream U.S. society, the extent to which the language is seen as foreign is increased. We have seen this phenomenon in action in both the cases of German, during both the First and Second World Wars (see Benseler, Lohnes, & Nollendorfs, 1988), and more recently with respect to Russian during the Cold War (see Kagan & Rifkin, 2000; Lubensky & Jarvis, 1984; Magner,

1984). Along the same lines, when a particular language has no historical or recognized relationship to Western education and culture, the language again falls toward the more foreign end of the foreignness continuum. There is, of course, an interesting exception to this phenomenon, and that is where particular learners or groups of learners may identify with the target language even though it is perceived by the dominant culture as very foreign—as has been the case with Swahili to some extent, and with Arabic to a considerable extent (see Rouchdy, 1992). Incorporated into the concept of foreignness are a number of separate components, among which are the beliefs that the target language community is:

- outside the traditional mainstream;
- not American;
- typically geographically isolated (especially within the U.S. context); and
- in need of validation from the mainstream population.

It is also important to note that the concept foreignness differs in terms of the form and content of the curriculum, with the former being related to educational value and the latter related to the use of non-English language in the United States. These form and content conceptualizations are evident in both foreign language textbooks and formal curricula. The sanction of ascribing foreignness to non-English languages in the U.S. setting comes with a paradoxical price—namely, the marginalization of our endeavor to teach the target language. In other words, to this point foreign language educators have been so successful in convincing our constituency that non-English languages are more or less foreign in the U.S., we have had to consistently reaffirm the rationale for our existence in the educational realm. We have, in short, to some extent taught ourselves out of a job!

Although in general terms creating independent learners is a positive educational outcome, in foreign language education we have often not created independent learners, but rather, independent ideologues. The proponents of this oppressive ideology are the college-bound populace and members of the dominant culture who have passed through our doors, taking a language, but learning nothing at all. Indeed, they have learned, and have learned a considerable amount, albeit perhaps not learning focused on communicative competence. Perhaps it is time that we, as foreign language educators, begin to more clearly recognize exactly what it is that our students have learned.

Language study is important in the U.S. context—perhaps now more than ever as the diversity in our country no longer is annihilated in the crucible of assimilation, but is instead embraced as a national strength. Championing language diversity in the language classroom becomes the mandate for social activism in the critical pedagogy of the foreign language classroom. To that end, we must begin to dismantle the frameworks of foreignness currently in place in curriculum, instruction, and evaluation. Curricular nullification can serve as one starting point to that end, and it is to a discussion of the nature and process of curricular nullification that we now turn our attention.

## CURRICULAR NULLIFICATION, REVISITED

We have spoken and written of curricular nullification at some length (see Osborn, 1998a, 2000; Reagan, in press-a; Reagan & Osborn, 1998). In essence, *curricular nullification* is an effective pedagogical strategy for instructional planning and delivery that acts in a dialectical fashion to challenge curricular mandates that are opposed to or incompatible with the ends of social justice. Teachers exercise curricular nullification every day when the classroom door closes and they begin to conduct classes in the way that they believe to be most appropriate, often regardless of explicit mandates and curricular guidelines. Teachers effectively proclaim and use their own veto power over any mandate, curricular, legal, administrative, or otherwise, which they believe to be in conflict with their professional and ethical responsibilities. It is this veto power over curricular mandates, both explicit and implicit, which is the focus of the concept of curricular nullification.

We have discussed curricular nullification as consisting of a variety of distinct oppositions, which may be useful to review briefly at this point. Specifically, curricular nullification can take place in terms of the following oppositions:

- subtractive versus additive curricular nullification
- ethical versus unethical curricular nullification
- dissonantal versus harmonious curricular nullification
- intentional versus consequential curricular nullification.

*Subtractive curricular nullification* is the act of failing to engage in behaviors that are curricularly and institutionally mandated, including the omission of required topics from the course or syllabus. A teacher of Spanish who refuses to teach the *ustedes* form as a formal plural, reasoning that it encourages an attitude of elitism and reinforces social class hierarchies, is demonstrating an example of subtractive curricular nullification. It is important to contrast subtractive curricular nullification with appropriate curricular modification. When teachers change course content for students having special needs, for example, they may reduce course content in the hope of meeting curricular mandates or goals. Subtractive curricular nullification, in contrast, is an active effort to contradict, oppose, and nullify objectives by virtue of the omission. Note well that some cases of subtractive curricular nullification could be unethical, and more extreme ones might actually constitute professional malpractice. For instance, a teacher of sex education who fails to provide students with information regarding sexually transmitted diseases is a powerful example of subtractive curricular nullification that is indeed malpractice.

*Additive curricular nullification* is the act of engaging in behaviors beyond those mandated in the curriculum, again with the intent of contradicting, opposing, or nullifying objectives. Imagine, for instance, the case of a middle school biology teacher, who, when finishing a unit on evolution, closes with the comments, "And if you wish to believe that you come from monkeys like the book says, that's OK with me, but I know that *I* was created in God's image." This teacher has engaged in additive curricular nullification—the lesson on evolutionary theory was taught, but the addition of the comment was contradictory to curricular mandates, and was arguably the more powerful component of the teaching that had taken place. In a foreign language setting, if the hidden curriculum of the course includes a goal of keeping the target language, its speakers, and their associated cultures foreign, then a teacher who empowers her or his students to interact with those speaking the language in their own community in sociologically relevant discourse, is providing an excellent example of additive curricular nullification. We caution again, however, that additive curricular nullification in extreme cases could be unethical or represent professional malpractice, as might be the case of a secondary teacher who encourages underage students to visit a bar to explore cultural differences in attitudes toward alcohol consumption.

Curricular nullification can be either ethical or unethical. *Ethical behavior* here refers to professionally recognized, appropriate, and sanctioned behavior (see Strike & Soltis, 1992). Certainly we recognize that, to an extent, what is taken to constitute ethical versus unethical behavior may vary historically and by location.[2] This fact notwithstanding, though, such a qualification of curricular nullification is relevant for the world of the activist practitioner who obviously could be terminated for unethical behavior (see also Reagan et al., 2000, pp. 57–75). As Strike and Soltis (1992) pointed out,

> a kind of rational ethical thinking that goes beyond personal beliefs and values is essential both to professional ethics and to the moral education of all members of society. Ethics is a public as well as a personal matter. If we are correct, then it would seem to follow that teachers have a special obligation to help their students see and share the potential objectivity and rationality of ethical thinking so that we can all lead morally responsible lives together. (p. 5)

*Dissonantal curricular nullification* is essentially what takes place when there is either an explicit, or even more an implicit, conflict between the curriculum and the teacher's own value and belief system. We appreciate the concept of cognitive dissonance, as employed by Wicklund and Brehm (1976), since it is helpful in understanding the distinction highlighted here:

> Any bit of knowledge that a person has about himself or the environment is a "cognition," or "cognitive element" ... The relationship between two cognitive elements is *consonant* if one implies the other in some psychological sense. Psychological implication can arise from cultural mores, pressure to be logical, behavioral commitment, past experience, and so on ... If having cognition $A$ implies having cognition $B$, a dissonant relationship exists when the person has cognitions $A$ and the obverse or opposite of $B$. (1976, p. 2)

Given any cognitive element or value, curricular nullification may be psychologically implied by that element or may be its obverse or opposite. As to the example at hand, if one teaches for the goals of social justice and discovers that a curriculum supports hegemony, an act of curricular nullification may be harmonious or dissonantal. Indeed, for some teachers, all acts of curricular nullification may be dissonantal. For others, any act of nullification may be harmonious. This distinction is one of an internal check in much the same way ethical–unethical represents an external check, and we would contend that these two elements should be employed in conjunction with each other when evaluating the advisability of an act or acts of curricular nullification.

It is also the case that, phenomenologically, acts of curricular nullification can be either intentional or consequential. Obviously, only the intentional acts are those to be considered in constructing the critical foreign language pedagogy. The intentional, harmonious, and ethical forms that can be utilized as socially transformative pedagogy and thus, social activism, helps teachers recognize the potential of their pedagogical repertoire.

## TOWARD PRACTICING PRAXIS

As language teachers employ critical reflection, curricular nullification, and other forms of activism in their practice, the foreign language classroom moves from serving as a definer of deviance (i.e., as we have seen, foreignness) to an educational agency for social change. In other words, we begin to develop a praxis based on what Giroux (1997a) called critical multiculturalism:

> In opposition to a quaint liberalism, a critical multiculturalism means more than simply acknowledging differences in stereotypes; more fundamentally it means understanding, engaging, and transforming the diverse histories, cultural narratives, representations, and institutions that produce racism and other forms of discrimination ... An insurgent multiculturalism takes as its starting point the question of what it means for educators and cultural workers to treat schools and other public institutions in which teachers, students, and others engage in daily acts of cultural translation and negotiation ... Within this perspective, pedagogy is removed from its exclusive emphasis on management and is defined as a form of political leadership and ethical address. (pp. 237–239)

At the core of such critical multiculturalism is the concept of discourse itself. As McLaren and Giroux (1997) asserted in *Revolutionary Multiculturalism*:

> The excess of language alerts us to the ways in which discourse is inextricably tied not just to the proliferation of meanings, but also to the production of individual

and social identities over time within conditions of inequality. As a political issue, language operates as a site of struggle among different groups who for various reasons police its borders, meanings, and orderings. Pedagogically, language provides the self-definitions upon which people act, negotiate various subject positions, and undertake a process of naming and renaming the relations between themselves, others, and the world. Educational theory is one of the discursive faces of literacy, pedagogy, and cultural politics. It is within theory and its concern with the prohibitions, exclusions, and policing of language along with its classification, ordering, and dissemination of discourse that knowledge becomes manifest, identities are formed and unformed, collective agents arise, and critical practice is offered the conditions in which to emerge. At the current moment of dominant educational practices, language is being mobilized within a populist authoritarian ideology that ties it to a tidy relation among national identity; culture, and literacy. As the cultural mask of hegemony, language is being mobilized to police the borders of an ideologically discursive divide that separates dominant from subordinate groups, whites from Blacks, and schools from the imperatives of democratic public life. (p. 16)

We advocate in this regard that language classrooms themselves become sites of challenging hegemonic ideologies, of liberating students from oppressive cognitive, intellectual, and sociological constructs that have thus far been created or reinforced in our context. We seek to deter the psychological violence inflicted on oppressed segments of our society for which we, ourselves, can be held partially responsible. As Scott (1972) explained:

Another reaction that commonly occurs when a deviant label is applied is that within the community a feeling arises that "something ought to be done about him." Perhaps the most important fact about this reaction in our society is that almost all of the steps that are taken are directed solely at the deviant. Punishment, rehabilitation, therapy, coercion, and other common mechanisms of social control are things that are done to him, implying that the causes of deviance reside within the person to whom the label has been attached, and that the solutions to the problems that he presents can be achieved by doing something to him. This is a curious fact, particularly when we examine it against the background of social science research on deviance that so clearly points to the crucial role played by ordinary people in determining who is labeled a deviant and how a deviant behaves. This research suggests that none of the corrective measures that are taken can possibly succeed in the intended way unless they are directed at those who confer deviant labels as well as those to whom they are applied. (p. 15)

The critical pedagogy of foreign language education begins to apply those corrective measures to both oppressor and oppressed. The label of foreign language does indeed need to go, but not in a shell game of political correctness, but as the outcome of a fundamental reordering of the conditions, the guiding principles and practices, and the social outcomes of foreign language education.

## TOWARD A CRITICAL ACTIVISM

Critical theories of education, although enlightening, often stop short of providing practical advice to the classroom teacher. The reason for this omission is likely multifaceted. In the first place, scholars often have not taught in the preuniversity level for many years, if ever, and the practical considerations elude them—they have, in short, little or nothing to say. Second, critical advances do not always lend themselves well to practical advice, since the generalized assumptions one must make about a teacher's range of curricular and instructional options are unrealistic. And finally, the myriad of variables that enter into teaching, in fact, make any formulaic assertions about a critical foreign language pedagogy either oversimplified, naive, or impossible. Nevertheless, there is a broad range of emancipatory avenues of educational reform available to practitioners, and such avenues must be the consideration that will become the litmus test of any critical pedagogy's ability to move from the margins to the mainstream in educational settings and dialogue.

In a nutshell, five theoretical underpinnings will be advanced by any critical activist pedagogy in the foreign language classroom. First, teachers should recognize how current practice supports what might be called miscommunicative competence. Then, students must be assisted in their development of multiple literacies, including Freire's (2000) concepts of both reading the word and world. Third, students and teachers will need to develop language awareness that is critically sociopolitical in character. Fourth, students should become cross-culturally communicative, not simply communicatively competent. Finally, teachers will need to recognize and act upon their own status as cultural and intellectual workers.

## QUESTIONS FOR REFLECTION AND DISCUSSION

1. The authors discuss benefits of foreign language study related national economic concerns or leisure activities, especially travel outside the country. What reasons would you give your students for studying a foreign language? What benefits could students enjoy from the ability to communicate with native speakers of non-English languages in the United States?
2. How is in need of validation from the mainstream population achieved in language study? How does foreignness as a concept serve to validate the foreign language teaching profession?
3. Give an example of curricular nullification in the foreign language classroom that is additive, ethical, and dissonantal. Give an example of curricular nullification in the foreign language classroom that is subtractive and unethical.

4. How do teachers engage in curricular nullification when they are observed by superiors?
5. The authors suggest that in many ways, we may in fact prepare students to have miscommunicative competence. What kind of potential changes to U.S. society would be observed if all college-educated people were really able to be cross-culturally communicative? How would these benefits relate to the goals of contemporary foreign language education?

## FOCUS ON THE CLASSROOM

1. Carefully examine a foreign language textbook. Identify two activities in the textbook that you would not use with students. Explain why you would not use these activities, and what one might to do make them more appropriate.
2. If you were asked to sum up your love of the target language in five words, what would these words be?
3. If you were asked to sum up the content of the foreign language textbook examined in question 1 above in five words, what would these words be?
4. To what extent are your responses to the two previous questions the same? To what extent are they different? What are the implications of this for the teaching of foreign languages?
5. Design an activity that highlights one aspect of life for native speakers of the target language in the United States. How might you use this activity in the foreign language classroom?

## NOTES

1. It is interesting to note that just as there is a teacher veto in the classroom, so too is there a student veto. In essence, the idea here is that in the context of the public school classroom, each student does in fact possess the ultimate veto with respect to learning. Although the teacher can do many things to encourage, facilitate, and motivate learning, it is nevertheless true that at some point and at some level, the student must be willing to learn (or, at the very least, not willing to not learn).
2. This does not mean, however, that we believe that all ethical matters and norms are relative and of equal worth (see Reagan et al., 2000, pp. 65–75).

# 7

# Language Rights as Human Rights: Social and Educational Implications

La tyrannie est toujours mieux organisée que la liberté.

—*Charles Péguy* (quoted in Augarde, 1991, p. 169)

The reality of multilingualism is exceedingly complex: Multilingualism can be an individual or a social phenomenon, can be differentially spread across different spheres of language use, can be viewed quite different normatively, and can reflect ideological, political, economic, cultural, and ethnic identity in a host of different ways (see Edwards, 1994). Further, in the educational context, multilingualism can be constructed either in terms of the means of education (e.g., media of instruction, focus of curricula, and so on), or with regard to educational outcomes. It is this complexity, in part, that makes multilingualism such an incredibly controversial aspect of educational policy and practice (see Cenoz & Genesee, 1998; Corson, 1999; Kaplan & Baldauf, 1997; Wagner, 1989). One aspect of multilingualism that is especially important for language educators to understand is that of language rights.

As we enter a new millennium, the world in which we live is very different than it was a mere century ago. Since 1901, the changes are probably nowhere more visible, recognized, and utilized than in the scientific and technological spheres. So too, have our social, cultural, and political realities changed, although not always in such obvious ways. One area in which we can clearly see significant evolution in social thought is with respect to the discourse on human rights (e.g., Spring, 2000). As the British philosopher Almond (1993) noted:

> The Second World War involved violations of human rights on an unprecedented scale but its ending saw the dawn of a new era for rights. Following their heyday in

the seventeenth century ... rights played a crucial role in the revolutions of the late eighteenth century. In the nineteenth and early twentieth centuries, however, appeal to rights was eclipsed by movements such as utilitarianism and Marxism which could not, or would not, accommodate them ... The contemporary period has seen a further shift in their fortunes and today they provide an accepted international currency for moral and political debate. In many parts of the world, irrespective of cultural or religious traditions, when issues or torture or terrorism, poverty or power are debated, the argument is very often conducted in terms of rights and their violation. (p. 259)

Indeed, the latter half of the 20th century has witnessed a veritable explosion of interest in and concern with human rights. To some extent of course, such interest and concern have been self-serving. As with young children who master the concept of unfairness when it applies to them far more quickly than when it applies to others, we tend to be more aware of violations of our own rights than of our violations of others' rights. Discourse about human rights, and on the violation of human rights, in the international realm also serves multiple purposes, and is often used as a convenient weapon to distract or to delegitimize a political opponent.

The use and misuse of rights discourse to achieve other kinds of ends sometimes, quite understandably, leads to a tendency to simply ignore or dismiss the issue altogether as merely another sort of meaningless political rhetoric. Rights do matter, though, as does discourse about rights. Discussions and debates about rights impact legislation, social policy, and ultimately, the quality of life of both groups and individuals. As Phillipson, Rannut, and Skutnabb-Kangas (1995) argued:

The history of human rights shows that the concept of human rights is not static. It is constantly evolving in response to changed perceptions of how humans have their fundamental freedoms restricted, and the challenge to the international community to counteract injustice. (p. 16)

The 20th century, then, has witnessed not only challenges to and abrogations of human rights, but also growing awareness and articulation of such rights. One area in which such awareness has been relatively late to develop, despite on-going and often egregious violations of group and individual rights, is that of language. As recently as the mid-1980s, Gomes de Matos wrote that, "Although ours has been said to be 'the age of rights' ... there has not yet been a thorough, well-documented, carefully thought out discussion of the crucial problem of the human being's linguistic rights" (1985, pp. 1–2). Given the centrality of language to self-identification and to our sense of who we are, and where we fit in the broader world, it is interesting that a concern with language rights has taken so long to emerge. And yet, such concern has emerged in recent decades, and the scholarly and political literature dealing with issues of language rights has increased dramatically both quantitatively and qualitatively (see, e.g., Annamalai, 1986; Benson, Grundy, Itakura, & Skutnabb-Kangas, in press; Herriman & Burnaby, 1996; Olivier, 1993; Phillipson, 2000; Skutnabb-Kangas, 2000a,

2000b; Skutnabb-Kangas & Phillipson, 1995). Although it is clear that we have a long way to go in terms of raising consciousness about language rights, and although such rights are far from universally recognized (let alone observed), the fact that the issue itself has been put on the table for discussion and debate is itself a promising development.

In this chapter, we present an overview of the concept of language rights as a component of more general human rights as it has emerged in recent years, especially in such international agreements as the *Universal Declaration of Human Rights* and the *U.N. Declaration on the Rights of Persons Belonging to National or Ethnic, Religious and Linguistic Minorities*. The implications of the concept of language rights for education are explored, and selected cases of the violations of children's language rights in various educational settings are presented. Finally, we discuss the implications of language rights for the foreign language educator.

## CONCEPTUALIZING LANGUAGE RIGHTS

The fundamental challenge presented by debates about language and language policy, as we see in the next chapter, is essentially one of achieving balance between the competing goods of social unity and access on the one hand, and respect for and toleration of diversity on the other. Basically, the question that policy-makers are trying to address in such debates is the extent to which pluralism, as a necessary condition for a democratic social order, applies to the issue of language. At the heart of this discussion, of course, is the issue of language rights. In other words, to what extent, and in what ways, are language rights human rights? Also relevant here is the related question of whether rights (in this case, language rights) apply only to the individual, or whether there are rights that are group rights (i.e., rights that apply to a community rather than solely to the members of that community by virtue of some common, shared feature of the individuals in the community; see Coulombe, 1993; Tollefson, 1991, pp. 167–200, 1995). This is actually a far more complex matter than it might at first seem, since language rights are "preeminently *social,* in that they are only comprehensible in relation to a group of other human beings with whom the language is shared and from which personal and cultural identity is achieved" (MacMillan, 1982, p. 420). In other words, debates about language rights are unique in that, as McRae argued, "societies characterized by linguistic pluralism differ from those characterized by racial, religious, class or ideological divisions in one essential respect, which stems from the pervasive nature of language as a general vehicle of communication" (1978, p. 331). This having been said, the concept of group rights is itself somewhat problematic, potentially leading to an apartheid-style mandate of ethnic obligation (see Degenaar, 1987, for a compelling discussion of the concept of group rights), even as the alternative of linguistic imperialism looms large (see Pennycook, 1994, 1998; Phillipson, 1992). The challenge, in short, is a very real one, with very real and significant outcomes for people's lives.

In working toward a conception of language rights, a good place to begin the discussion is with *The U.N. Declaration on the Rights of Persons Belonging to National or Ethnic, Religious and Linguistic Minorities* (18 December, 1992), in which the international community attempted to articulate the nature of the human and civil rights that ought to be accorded members of minority groups (see Skutnabb-Kangas, 1994). This *Declaration* was a follow-up to the *Universal Declaration of Human Rights*, necessitated by the widespread violation of the second article of the *Universal Declaration of Human Rights*, which prohibits discrimination against individuals based on language. Specifically, three articles of the *Declaration* are relevant for our purposes here. First, Article 2.1 prohibits what might be termed active discrimination against members of minority groups:

> Persons belonging to national or ethnic, religious and linguistic minorities (hereinafter referred to as persons belonging to minorities) have the right to enjoy their own culture, to profess and practice their own religion, *and to use their own language, in private and in public, freely and without interference or any form of discrimination.* (Article 2.1, our emphasis)

This, in a sense, is the negative force of the *Declaration*, in that it focuses on simply prohibiting actions and policies that unfairly target minority groups. The *Declaration* goes far beyond this negative constraint, however, and in Articles 4.2 and 4.3 specifies what can be called positive language rights:

> States shall take measures to create favorable conditions to enable persons belonging to minorities to express their characteristics and to develop their culture, language, religion, traditions and customs, except where specific practices are in violation of national and contrary to international standards. (Article 4.2)

> States should take appropriate measures so that, whenever possible, persons belonging to minorities have adequate opportunities to learn their mother tongue or to have instruction in their mother tongue. (Article 4.3)

These explicit statements of both negative and positive aspects of language rights differ in significant ways, of course, from the constitutional provisions governing the issue of language rights in the United States, and indeed, of those in many countries. They are even further, in many instances, from actual government policies and practices, especially (although by no means exclusively) with respect to the rights of indigenous peoples. In fact, a central feature of the draft *Declaration of Indigenous Peoples Human Rights*, which was developed by the Working Group on Indigenous Populations of the United Nations Sub-Commission on Prevention of Discrimination and Protection of Minorities in the 1990s (see Spring, 2000, pp. 35–37), was focused on the issue of language rights in education:

> Indigenous children have the right to all levels and forms of education of the State. All indigenous peoples also have this right and the right to establish and control their

educational systems and institutions providing education in their own languages, in a manner appropriate to their cultural methods of teaching and learning. (Article 15)

With this background in mind with respect to the nature and focus of language rights as human rights, we can move to an examination and discussion of specific violations of children's language rights in a variety of contexts.

## VIOLATIONS OF LANGUAGE RIGHTS

In the preface to her powerful and compelling book *Linguistic genocide in education—or worldwide diversity and human rights?*, Skutnabb-Kangas (2000) emphasized both the ties between linguistic diversity and language rights and the relatively weak treatment of language rights in contemporary global society:

> Linguistic human rights are a necessary (but not sufficient) prerequisite for the maintenance of linguistic diversity. Violations of linguistic human rights, especially in education, lead to a reduction of linguistic and cultural diversity on our planet ... language in education systematically gets a poorer treatment than other basic human characteristics. Very few international or regional human rights instruments grant binding educational linguistic human rights, despite pious phrases. The present binding linguistic human rights in education clauses are completely insufficient for protecting and maintaining linguistic diversity on our globe ... (p. xii)

Not only are language rights in the educational context insufficiently protected—they are in fact routinely ignored and violated around the world (see Crystal, 2000; Grenoble & Whaley, 1998; Nettle & Romaine, 2000). Although even a reasonably thorough overview of such violations is made impossible by their ubiquity, it is possible to identify and examine briefly a few cases for heuristic purposes, and it is to this task that we now turn.

### *The Nonexistence of Kurdish*

One of the most interesting examples of the denial of linguistic rights is provided by the current status of Kurdish, especially in the eastern parts of Turkey. Kurdish is an Indo-European language spoken in Turkey, Iraq, Iran, and Syria by some 25 to 30 million people. The division of the Kurds among a variety of other nations, without any recognized homeland of their own, has meant that they have been subjected to considerable oppression, not the least of which has been linguistic oppression. As Matras (1990) noted:

> The majority of Kurds in Iran, Syria and Turkey are considered illiterate in their native tongue. In these countries official policy has prevented the autonomous development of a literary variety by denying Kurds education in their own language as well

as the right to distribute printed material in Kurdish. Linguistic and literary projects have thus been restricted to clandestine activities of oppositional movements. (p. 1)

In what Skutnabb-Kangas (2000a) termed a "close to surrealistic" passage (p. 515), Turkish Law No. 2820 on Political Parties asserts:

> It is forbidden to claim that there exist minorities in Turkey. It is forbidden to protect or develop non-Turkish cultures and languages. (Section 81 22 April, 1983)

The two seemingly contradictory parts of this legislation—first, that there are no minorities in Turkey, and second, that the promotion of the languages and cultures of such groups is forbidden—although presenting something of a logical challenge for anyone familiar with the concept of the disjunctive syllogism nevertheless mirrors official Turkish government policy for most of the 20th century. Indeed, legislation in Turkey explicitly identifies the mother tongue of all Turkish citizens as Turkish (arguably a unique definition of mother tongue), mandates that only Turkish may be used as the medium of instruction in educational institutions, forbids the use of the Kurdish language in public, and bans all publications in Kurdish (Skutnabb-Kangas, 2000a, pp. 514–523; Skutnabb-Kangas & Bucak, 1995, p. 353). Perhaps the most puzzling aspect of the official Turkish position on Kurdish historically has been the unwillingness to even recognize the existence of Kurdish as a distinct language, even in the face of virtually universal agreement about its existence by linguists (see Campbell, 1995; Payne, 1990). As Okumus poignantly noted:

> If Kurds in Turkey attempt to use only some of the most fundamental minority rights, to speak and maintain their own language, identify as a Kurd, and enjoy and maintain Kurdish culture through books, films, cassettes, etc., or through a Kurdish cultural organisation, they can be sentenced to at least 50 years of imprisonment. (Quoted in Skutnabb-Kangas & Bucak, 1995, p. 348)

### *The Case of Post-Soviet Estonia*

The collapse of the Soviet Union has resulted in significant changes in both language policy and language practice in many parts of the former Union of Socialist Soviet Republics (see e.g., Schlyter, 1998; Taagepera, 1993). In the three Baltic republics (Estonia, Latvia, and Lithuania), the changes have been complicated by the complex historical developments of the second half of the 20th century (Clachar, 1998; Lauristin & Vihalemm, 1997). As Ozolins (1994) explained:

> The Baltic states are attempting to redefine their languages from a minority status that they had *de facto* acquired (despite the blandishments of official Soviet policy regarding the status of languages of the republics) to a full national status as the language of state and administration, and of most social discourse. Yet this is occurring

in a peculiar context where the national languages are not the most wide-spread language in their respective states: while all Baltic nationals are fluent in Russian, only some of the non-Baltic recent migrants are fluent in the local languages. (p. 161)

This situation is nowhere clearer than in Estonia, where 81% of the population speak Estonian, but 93% speak Russian. The paradox that exists in Estonia and the other Baltic nations is one whose origins lie in the migration of large numbers of Russian speakers in the years following the 1940 occupation of the three Baltic republics by the Soviet Union. Under normal circumstances, the language rights of immigrants are, by international convention if not in common practice, protected. However, if the immigration is the result of foreign occupation, then the international conventions do not apply in the same way. This, then, is the dilemma of the Baltic states. As a result of past extensive military presence coupled with the non-integration of the Russian-speaking diaspora in the Baltic republics, the breakup of the Soviet Union left large numbers of Russian speakers in these nations (roughly 30% of the total population in Estonia) in what is essentially a stateless status (see Rannut, 1995).

The issue of citizenship for non-speakers of Estonian has proven to be an intensely controversial one. As Taagepera (1993) explained, "the main issue in Estonia was language ... More specifically, the Estonian demand was for bilingualism on the part of the Russians, not a prohibition of Russian ... Yet some colonists demanded the right to remain monolingually Russian, oblivious to the fact that this imposed bilingualism solely on Estonians—as had been the case during the Soviet occupation" (pp. 222–223). Whereas it is certainly possible that some sort of official bilingualism will emerge in the future, such a development would appear to be most unlikely in the immediate future:

Fifty years hence the language issue might fade, and Russian might even become a second official language, as Swedish is in Finland. In the foreseeable future, however, Estonian has to remain the only official language, because the Russian colonization was such a very recent experience ... Most important, many colonists in Estonia were as yet not ready for Finnish-type bilingualism, which implies that public servants and most members of the minority group know both languages. The issue of a second official language could be seriously discussed only when the former colonists would have become as bilingual as Estonians had been forced to be under Soviet occupation. (Taagepera, 1993, p. 225)

The current status of Russian speakers in Estonia (and elsewhere in the Baltics) is thus an uncomfortable one at best (see Bezberezhyeva, 1998). Perhaps the most visible point of tension is, not surprisingly, that of education, where the government is moving toward the elimination of Russian-language schools as a way of ensuring linguistic assimilation into the national language. The rights of Russian speakers are clearly at stake, but given the historical and demographic context of the situation, so too are the rights of Estonian speakers in their own land (see Vihalemm & Lauristin, 1997).

It is interesting to note that more than a dozen separate human rights missions have been sent to Estonia since independence, often with a concern for language rights, and that none of these missions "have found any gross or systematic violation of human rights" (Rannut, 1995, p. 208). It is cases such as this that make clear how very complex issues of language rights can actually be.

## The Case of the United States

What of the United States? The proponents of the U.S. English Movement and their allies are correct in noting that there is no official language in the United States, and that our language policies have emerged in a somewhat chaotic and inconsistent fashion. More to the point, though, language policies and language practices at all levels of U.S. society have historically involved extensive violation of individual language rights, and in fact continue to do so. There is, to put it mildly, absolutely no reason whatever to believe that the sorts of changes advocated by the supporters of the U.S. English Movement are likely to change this situation. If anything, the rhetoric of such groups suggests just the opposite (see Baron, 1990; Corson, 2001; Crawford, 1992a, 1992b, 2000; González & Melis, 2001a, 2001b; Macedo, 2000). The right of the child to an education in his or her native language is violated on a daily basis throughout the United States, of course, but even beyond this, the denigration and exclusion of languages in both school and society constitutes an on-going assault on meaningful language rights (see Reagan, 1997a, 1997b). The history of U.S. language policy has been accurately summarized as follows:

> Except for very brief periods during which private language rights have been tolerated and certain limited public rights have been permitted, the history of language policy in the United States has generally been one of the imposition of English for an ever wider range of purposes and the restriction of the rights of other languages. (Hernández-Chávez, 1995, p. 141)

Indeed, if we look at the history not only of immigrant languages, but even more, the history of indigenous languages in North America, what we find is not merely a history of neglect, but in fact what is arguably a history of deliberate cultural and linguistic genocide (see Boseker, 1994; Hernández-Chávez, 1995)—a history shared, unfortunately, with the treatment of indigenous peoples and their languages both in Canada (Fettes, 1992, 1994, 1998) and in Latin America (see Aikman, 1999; Hamel, 1995a, 1995b; Hornberger, 1999; King, 2000; Marr, 1999).

## The Case of the Deaf

In chapter 3, we explored the issue of the "linguistic legitimacy" of American Sign Language; that earlier discussion of that topic laid the necessary foundation for a further examination of the issue of language rights and the deaf. The medical and sociocultural perspectives of deafness not only lead to different understandings of deafness and the deaf, and to different social and educational policies for the deaf (see Baynton, 1996; Johnson, Liddell, & Erting, 1989; Safford & Safford, 1996, pp. 90–121; Walworth, Moores, & O'Rourke, 1992), but also lead to very different approaches to the issue of language rights in the deaf community.[1] For those accepting the medical model of deafness, discussions of language rights are basically irrelevant. The deaf do not constitute a minority group in the sense intended in the passages, but rather, are seen as disadvantaged members of a particular spoken language community. Thus, the medical perspective leads to what is essentially a compensatory view of language rights, which will focus on ensuring access through what is assumed to be a common language. This means that interpreting services and similar support will be provided to the deaf, because this is a way of compensating for a deficit. Although certainly well meaning, such an approach is of course profoundly paternalistic, and is clearly grounded in a understanding of deafness as a disability. The alternative conceptualization of language rights and the deaf, which has been forcefully articulated by Skutnabb-Kangas (1994; see also Branson & Miller, 1993, 1998; Reagan, in press-b) among others, is grounded in the sociocultural view of deafness. The sociocultural view of deafness leads to an empowerment approach to language rights for the deaf, in which signed language and other supports are called for not as a means to correct a disability, but rather because the deaf, as a cultural and linguistic minority, should be entitled to them as basic human rights (see Nover, 1995). Also at issue here, of course, is the matter of how one defines mother tongue in the context of the deaf child; a matter of no little complexity, to be sure (see Bouvet, 1990, pp. 119–133, for a thorough discussion of this topic). Here, then, *The U.N. Declaration of the Rights of Persons Belonging to National or Ethnic, Religious and Linguistic Minorities* is clearly relevant, although, as Lane and his colleagues have argued, internationally recognized language rights are "almost universally violated when it comes to signed language minorities" (Lane et al., 1996, p. 422; see also Lane, 1984).

Recent efforts in various parts of the United States to legislatively declare ASL a real language, the legal recognition of Swedish Sign Language in Sweden, and the discussion in South Africa about the possibility of South African Sign Language being recognized in the new constitution as a 12th official language in South Africa,[2] are all illustrative of manifestations of this empowerment perspective on language rights for the deaf. Implicit in this empowerment perspective on language rights for the deaf, of course, is a rejection of the compensatory perspective as either a sort of linguistic imperialism, or perhaps even cultural and linguistic genocide (see Skutnabb-Kangas, 1994, 2000a).

Thus far, we have suggested that compensatory and empowerment approaches to language rights for the deaf are representative of basically incompatible views of both deafness and language rights. Although a case might be made for these two perspectives constituting what philosophers of science sometimes call incommensurable paradigms, political practice in the real world is somewhat more complex and confused. This is the case, in part, because resources in many societies tend to be more readily available for disabled groups than they are for cultural and linguistic minorities (and especially for very small cultural and linguistic minorities). Thus, in the case of the deaf it is often politically and financially expedient to accept the status and labels of disability, even when advocating for recognition of the deaf as a nondisabled cultural and linguistic community. In short, there is a generally unarticulated tension with respect to the rights of the deaf. The cost of political recognition as a cultural and linguistic minority group may well be far greater, for the average deaf person, than the benefits of tolerating the paternalism (and even pity) of the hearing majority (see Shapiro, 1993; Wrigley, 1997). Compensatory approaches to language rights, then, may actually in some circumstances be somewhat empowering, even as empowerment approaches may prove to be disempowering—a somewhat odd situation that helps to demonstrate quite clearly how complex the entire matter of language rights really is.

## IMPLICATIONS FOR THE FOREIGN LANGUAGE CLASSROOM

Ultimately, questions of language rights are questions of language policy, and reflect underlying assumptions about the nature of language as well as issues of power, equality, and access in society. As Tollefson (1991) noted:

> The policy of requiring everyone to learn a single dominant language is widely seen as a common-sense solution to the communication problems of multilingual societies. The appeal of this assumption is such that monolingualism is seen as a solution to linguistic inequality. If linguistic minorities learn the dominant languages, so the argument goes, then they will not suffer economic and social inequality. The assumption is an example of an ideology which refers to normally unconscious assumptions that come to be seen as common sense ... such assumptions justify exclusionary policies and sustain inequality. (p. 10)

The desire for simple solutions to complex problems and challenges is perhaps understandable, but it is also dangerous, as the quote with which this chapter began makes clear. Tyranny is always better organized than liberty, but that is no reason to support it. Furthermore, the tendency to address rights issues as pragmatic or empirical matters, as is often the case, is also both misleading and wrong. The question, in short, is not whether instruction in the mother tongue is pedagogically most effective (although the evidence would suggest that it is), any more than whether capital punishment reduces crime—in both cases, fundamental human rights must be understood to remove the question from the empirical realm and move it to the normative realm. Only by placing the questions in the right discourse context can we hope to come to reasonable and justifiable solutions—and, at least in the case of language rights, we have a long way to go before this becomes the norm.

Finally, what does all of this have to do with the foreign language classroom? As we suggested in chapter 3, the foreign language classroom is an ideal place to help students to begin to develop what can be called critical language awareness. In other words, the study of language needs to include not only the communicative and cultural aspects of language, but also the often implicit political and ideological issues related to language (see Blackledge, 2000). Students need to understand the ways in which language is used to convey and protect social status, as well as how it can be used to oppress and denigrate both individuals and groups. Central to the discussion and, indeed, understanding of such issues is an understanding of the nature, purposes, and foundations of language rights. Language rights, like language attitudes, are inevitably going to be either challenged or reinforced in all educational settings, but arguably nowhere more significantly than in the foreign language classroom. The foreign language educator, in short, has a powerful and important role to play in ensuring that students become aware of language rights as a component of human rights, both in their own lives and in the lives of others.

## QUESTIONS FOR REFLECTION AND DISCUSSION

1. In this chapter, it is suggested that language rights are routinely ignored and violated, probably far more than are other human rights, and furthermore, that the most egregious violations of group and individual rights involve language rights. Why do you believe that this might be the case? What can individuals do about this situation?
2. Consider language attitudes in your own community. To what extent and in what ways do these attitudes reflect a positive appreciation of the language rights of others? How do they demonstrate a lack of understanding of language rights?
3. Explain in your own words why the case of Estonia might be considered to be very different from the other cases of violations of language rights described in this chapter. What does this particular case tell us about the nature and status of language rights? About the limits of language rights?
4. Some scholars have argued that language rights constitute only half of the equation, and that individuals and groups must also be understood to have language responsibilities. What do you think that such language responsibilities might be? What are the educational implications of your answer?
5. The issue of the language rights of the deaf is discussed in this chapter. What do you believe are the implications of this discussion for deaf students with regard to studying a foreign language in the context of the public school?

## FOCUS ON THE CLASSROOM

1. What language rights related to their native language do you believe that your students have in the context of the foreign language classroom?
2. What examples of issues of language rights related to the target language are appropriate topics for discussion in the foreign language classroom?
3. How is language used to discriminate against specific groups of people? Can you describe a project that students in a foreign language classroom might undertake to investigate this question?
4. What role, if any, do proponents of U.S. English and similar movements propose for foreign language education?
5. How can foreign language education students contribute to community discussions and understandings of language rights?

## NOTES

1. There are, broadly speaking, two quite different ways to view deafness. The dominant perspective in our society is grounded in the view that deafness is essentially a medical condition, characterized by an auditory deficit—that is, deaf people are people who cannot hear. Such a perspective, which has been labeled the medical or pathological view of deafness, leads naturally to efforts to try to remediate the deficit. In short, this view is premised on the idea that deaf people are not only different from hearing people, but that they are, at least in a physiological sense, inferior to hearing people, in that hearing people can hear and deaf people cannot. If one accepts such a view of deafness, and the myriad assumptions that undergird it, then the only reasonable approach to dealing with deafness is indeed to attempt to remediate the problem—which is, of course, precisely what is done when one focuses on the teaching of speech and lip-reading in education, relies on hearing aids to maximize whatever residual hearing a deaf individual may possess, and seeks to develop medical solutions to hearing impairment (such as cochlear implants). In other words, the medical or pathological view of deafness inevitably leads to efforts to try to help the deaf individual to become as like a hearing person as possible. The alternative perspective for understanding deafness, which has been advocated by a growing number of deaf people as well as by small groups of hearing teachers, linguists, anthropologists, and others involved with the deaf, has been termed the sociocultural perspective on deafness (see Baker & Battison, 1980; Lane, 1984; Neisser, 1983; Reagan, 1990a; Stokoe, 1980; Wilcox, 1989). Basically, the sociocultural view of deafness suggests that for some deaf people, it makes far more sense to understand deafness not as a handicapping condition, let alone as a deficit, but rather, as an essentially cultural condition. Thus, on the account of advocates of this sociocultural view of deafness, the appropriate compari-

# LANGUAGE RIGHTS AS HUMAN RIGHTS

son group for the deaf is not individuals with physical disabilities, and so forth, but rather, would be individuals who are members of other non-dominant cultural and linguistic groups. In short, although the medical view of deafness would lead us to try to correct a deficit, the sociocultural view would lead us to efforts to fight for civil rights (see Shapiro, 1993, pp. 74–104).

2. Recognition of the deaf as a distinctive cultural and linguistic group in South Africa is rapidly developing. For example, early in 1996, the Language Plan Task Group was established by the Minister of Arts, Cultures, Science, and Technology for the purpose of advising him on the development of a coherent National Language Plan for South Africa. Eight subcommittees were appointed and informed a policy document published later that year. During this process, South African Sign Language emerged as a significant topic of discussion. Such was the prominence of the issues related to South African Sign Language that the entire final summit conference, which was attended by a number of deaf delegates, was interpreted in sign language. Further, sign language was explicitly mentioned in five out of eight subcommittee reports of the final report (Language Plan Task Group, 1996). Although there was considerable discussion about the status of South African Sign Language in the constitutional discussions, the constitution that was eventually approved, although recognizing South African Sign Language as a South African language, did not accord it official status.

# 8

# When in Rome (or Pretoria): Language Policy in International Perspective

> Language policy is a form of disciplinary power. Its success depends in part upon the ability of the state to structure into the institutions of society the differentiation of individuals into "insiders" and "outsiders" ... To a large degree, this occurs through the close association between language and nationalism. By making language a mechanism for the expression of nationalism, the state can manipulate feelings of security and belonging ... the state uses language policy to discipline and control its workers by establishing language-based limitations on education, employment, and political participation.
>
> —*James Tollefson* (1991, pp. 207–208)

Language planning and language policy development and implementation play important roles in societies around the world. In 1971, Rubin and Jernudd edited a book entitled, *Can Language be Planned?* That was, and remains, an important question, and one which linguists and policymakers are increasingly confident in answering in the affirmative. As Cooper noted, "Language is the fundamental institution of society, not only because it is the first human institution experienced by the individual, but also because all other institutions are built upon its regulatory patterns ... To plan language is to plan society" (1989, p. 182). And, it is clear, the planning of society is, if anything, an increasingly common phenomenon in both the developed and developing worlds. In fact, the significant question is not whether language can be planned, but rather how and by whom language will be planned.

In this chapter, our focus is basically on the nature of language planning as an applied sociolinguistic activity. We begin with a broad overview of the nature and purposes of language planning and language policy activities in general, including examination of the role of ideology in language policy, and then turn to a discussion of the use (and misuse) of language planning and language policy to achieve social, political, and educational ends. Throughout the chapter, examples of language policies and language planning activities are drawn from a number of significant cases of language planning and language policy implementation in different societies and contexts.

## THE NATURE AND PURPOSES OF LANGUAGE PLANNING

> Language planning refers to deliberate efforts to influence the behavior of others with respect to the acquisition, structure, or functional allocation of their language codes. (Cooper, 1989, p. 45)

Language planning and language policy formulation and implementation have been, and continue to be, important elements of national social and educational policy in many societies, and this has been especially true in the developing world as efforts are made to address the legacy of colonialism and, in many cases, the ongoing presence of considerable cultural and linguistic diversity (see, for example, Mazrui & Mazrui, 1998; Phillipson, 1998; Reagan, 1996; Schiffman, 1996; Weinstein, 1990). Questions of national and official language selection; orthographic selection and spelling standardization; language use in government, judicial, and educational settings; and of language status and power are rarely made easily, and seldom avoid a considerable degree of controversy and conflict. As Altbach (1984) noted, "Language is a key to the intellectual situation in many Third World nations. Language also plays a role in the distribution of knowledge, since the medium through which material is communicated determines accessibility. Many Third World nations are multilingual states in which questions of language policy are often politically volatile" (p. 234). Such controversy is especially common where language policies are concerned with the provision of education, and this is understandable, because, as Kennedy (1983) commented, "The close relationship between use of a language and political power, socioeconomic development, national and local identity and cultural values has led to the increasing realization of the importance of language policies and planning in the life of a nation. Nowhere is this planning more crucial than in education, universally recognized as a powerful instrument of change" (p. iii).

The role of language planning as a component of more general social and educational planning and policy analysis is, in short, an important facet of understanding development in many societies. Language planning as an element of national development strategy can best be understood as the deliberate attempt to change existing language usage, and thus to resolve various types of language problems and controversies (see Christian, 1988; Cobarrubias & Fishman, 1983; Cooper, 1989; Kennedy, 1983; Lambert, 1990; Tollefson, 1991). As Eastman (1983) explained,

"Language planning is the activity of manipulating language as a social resource in order to reach objectives set out by planning agencies which, in general, are an area's governmental, educational, economic, and linguistic authorities" (p. 29).

Language planning activities can focus on issues of language status (status planning), internal development (corpus planning), or on combinations of these two types of language planning activities (see Cobarrubias, 1983b; Williams, 1992, pp. 123–147). *Status planning* refers to efforts by a government or institution to determine what language or languages are to be used in particular spheres of use. The identification of a country's official language, for instance, constitutes status planning, as would a decision about what language should be used in schools. Corpus planning is often a result of status planning; it refers to efforts to standardize, elaborate, and perhaps purify a language selected for use in a particular sphere of language use (see Cluver, 1993b, p. 59).

Language planning activities, both status planning and corpus planning, serve a number of different, although sometimes overlapping, functions: language purification, language revitalization, language reform, language standardization, and modernization (see Eastman, 1983, p. 28; Nahir, 1977). Furthermore, each of these functions of language planning and language policy is reflected and manifested in virtually every sphere of human life: in the political sphere (the language of political debate and discourse, and so on), the judicial sphere (the language of law, as well as the language used by the police and courts), the religious sphere (the language used for worship, as well as the language in which key religious texts are written), the cultural sphere, the commercial and economic sphere (the language of business and industry), the educational sphere (the language of instruction, additional languages studied by pupils, and so forth), and the interpersonal and familial sphere (the language used in the home, with relatives, and so on).

Language purification is a prescriptive effort on the part of policymakers to delimit proper or correct linguistic usage, often based on beliefs about what constitutes the historically pure variety of the language. Such efforts, which generally consist primarily of corpus planning, are often concerned with eliminating foreign or alien usages in both the spoken and written language, and are commonly tied to other manifestations of what might be termed purist or ethnocentric ideologies, although they can also be outgrowths of anticolonialist sentiments and movements. To some extent, one might hypothesize that purist movements are strongest in those instances in which national pride and self-confidence have suffered in some way, though it is also important to note that even languages that have high economic and political status have on occasion been the objects of purist movements (see Jernudd & Shapiro, 1989). For example, there have been numerous efforts in recent years to stop the use of anglicisms in modern French (critically referred to as *Franglais* in French), Although terms like *le week-end* continue to be far more popular in daily speech than the historically preferred *la fin de semaine* (see Ball, 1997, pp. 207–220), and similar phenomena have been noted in Spanish (Mar-Molinero, 1997, pp. 168–170) and German (in which the equivalent of *Franglais* is now *Engleutsch*; Stevenson, 1997, pp. 212–216).[1] Indeed, even in

English there have been such purist efforts, as with the Saxonist movement in the late 19th century, which attempted (generally unsuccessfully) to reform English by replacing foreign terms borrowed from French and Latin roots with terms of Germanic origin (see Baron, 1981).

*Language revitalization* refers to various kinds of activities intended to promote the status and usage of a language that has been, in some sense, previously in decline (or even, in extreme instances, a language that has actually ceased to have native users). As King defined it, language revitalization is "the attempt to add new forms or functions to a threatened language with the ultimate aim of increasing its uses or users" (1999, p. 111). Language revitalization is primarily an example of status planning, although elements of corpus planning (especially in terms of lexical expansion) are also likely to be involved. Examples of the former abound. Swahili in Tanzania is an obvious example to which we shall return shortly, but other cases in the postcolonial world are common as colonial languages are replaced by (or asked to share official status with) previously dominant indigenous languages. The revival of dead languages is considerably rarer, with the best case being offered by the revival of Hebrew as a modern spoken language in Israel (see Nahir, 1988; Sáenz-Badillos, 1993). Other instances of revivals of languages in advanced states of decline also exist. The revival of Irish Gaelic is a well-documented and powerful case in point here (see Hindley, 1990; Ó Riagáin, 1997), which we explore in more detail later in this chapter.

*Language reform* takes place, formally and informally, in many languages accorded official status in the modern world, and includes lexical and orthographic reform as well as occasional syntactic reform. Language reform as a type of language planning activity is, therefore, essentially corpus planning. The reform of written Chinese in the People's Republic of China provides an instance of language reform (see Chen, 1999; Tai, 1988), as do the reforms of Ibo and other indigenous languages in Nigeria (Emenanjo, 1990; Nwachukwu, 1983), Turkish (Dogançay-Aktuna, 1995), and Norwegian (Haugen, 1966), among others. Indeed, there are relatively few languages in the modern world that are used as official languages that have not been subjected to deliberate efforts at language reform (see Cooper, 1989; Kaplan & Baldauf, 1997; Tollefson, 1991).

*Language standardization* involves both status planning, when it refers to the selection of a single variety of a language as the standard language, and corpus planning, when it refers to the codification of the language in a unified variety. Thus, the selection of Kiunguja, the Zanzibar dialect of Swahili, as the national linguistic norm in Tanzania, would constitute an example of language standardization of the status planning type (see Harries, 1983, pp. 127–128), while efforts to create a standardized spelling and grammar for a language would constitute a corpus planning approach to language standardization. Language standardization, it is important to note, can and often does overlap both language reform and lexical modernization in practice.

Last, lexical modernization takes place as efforts are made to increase a language's lexicon to allow it to deal with new technological, political, economic, educational, and social developments and concepts. *Lexical modernization* therefore constitutes a clear instance of corpus planning. All languages, of course, from time to time experience what can be termed lexical gaps; lexical modernization refers specifically to controlled and directed attempts to expand a given language's lexicon in a systematic manner (see Eastman, 1983, pp. 232–237 Nahir, 1977, p. 117). As Jernudd (1977) observed, "A major activity of many language planning agencies ... be they normal language academies, development boards or language committees, is the development of terminologies, particularly in technical fields" (p. 215). Examples of lexical modernization abound; indeed, Fodor and Hagège's multivolume *Language reform: History and future* includes studies of lexical (as well as orthographic and syntactic) modernization efforts in more than 60 different languages (1983/4, 1990). Whereas efforts at lexical modernization are, then, quite common, the extent to which they are effective in mandating lexical usage is somewhat less clear. As Hinnebusch (1979) commented with regard to lexical modernization in Swahili:

> A serious question that has to be asked, however, is whether external planning, planning from the top, has any effect on actual usage. For example, in the list of astronomical terms, *mchota maji* (literally, "water bearer" from *-chota* "dip up" and *maji* "water") is suggested for "Aquarius," but a very popular astrologer in East Africa today uses *ndoo* (literally, "bucket, pail" for that sign; for "Saggitarius" he uses *msuale* (literally, "arrow"), while the suggested list gives *mpiga shaabaha* "shooter of the target" ... (p. 288)

A particularly interesting contemporary case of both official and more informal lexical modernization has been taking place in Russia, as that society undergoes massive social, economic, and political changes in the aftermath of the collapse of the Soviet Union. Examples of new terminology in modern Russian abound; the changes that are taking place in society have led to widespread lexical innovation, borrowing, and creation, as new concepts, practices, technologies, and institutions replace those of the Soviet state (see Ryazanova-Clarke & Wade, 1999). Typical instances of such new lexical items in Russian would include such terms as тонер ("toner"), пейджер, ("pager"), Биг Мак ("Big Mac"), сотеа ("mobile telephone"), копирайт ("copyright"), and маркетинг ("marketing"). Such examples of lexical modernization can be found in all languages. It is important to keep in mind that the need for new terminology to meet new needs in no way indicates any innate deficiency in the language itself; all human languages have lexical gaps, and all human languages have ways of filling those gaps.

## IDEOLOGIES OF LANGUAGE POLICY

Language planning, as an applied sociolinguistic activity, has the potential to function either as a tool for empowerment and liberation, or as a means of oppression and domination. This is the case, in part, because language planning and language

# LANGUAGE POLICY IN INTERNATIONAL PERSPECTIVE

policy activities often involve both implicit and explicit goals and objectives. Furthermore, and closely related to the presence of both implicit and explicit goals and objectives in language planning and language policy, is the fundamentally ideological nature of such activities (see Cobarrubias, 1983a; Joseph & Taylor, 1990; Phillipson, 1992). Cobarrubias (1983a) identified four broadly conceived ideologies of language that guide and orient language policies. As he explained:

> Language ideologies reflect a mode of treatment of one language group with respect to another and ordinarily involve judgments as to what is right or wrong. Also, ideologies involve frames of reference pertaining to an ideal social group that will evolve, at some future time, from the segment of reality to which the ideology is being applied. The ideological aspect related to language-status planning is perhaps the most neglected area of language planning, in spite of the fact that ideologies underlie all forms of status planning. It is because ideologies involve value judgments and direct a certain mode of treatment that status decisions raise ethical issues. (p. 63)

The four ideologies of language identified by Cobarrubias are linguistic assimilation, linguistic pluralism, vernacularization, and internationalization, each of which are now briefly discussed.

*Linguistic assimilation* as an ideology of language is based on the assumption that linguistic (and, presumably, cultural) unity is at the very least desirable in a society, and may actually be necessary to some extent. Thus, language policies grounded in the ideology of linguistic assimilation tend to favor monolingual models of society. An important component of linguistic assimilation is that advocates of such policies are concerned not merely with individuals and groups acquiring competence in a specific, common language, but also with the rejection and replacement of other languages in the society, at least in the public sphere. The ideology of linguistic assimilation also tends, in practice, to encourage a belief in the superiority of the dominant language in a society, and often in practice results in the denial of language rights to speakers of languages other than the dominant language (see Cobarrubias, 1983a, pp. 63–64). In the context of the Third World, language policies based on the ideology of linguistic assimilation were most common during the colonial era. As Cobarrubias noted, "Instances of linguistic assimilation through colonization can be found in Guam, the Philippines under American rule ... and to some degree Puerto Rico prior to the 1952 Constitution" (1983a, p. 64). Educationally, language policies grounded in the ideology of linguistic assimilation will most often entail formal schooling in the selected national language, and the exclusion of other indigenous languages, at least in official settings. Thus, the use of French in francophone Africa in virtually all educational settings (except, notably in traditional Qur'anic schools) would be an example of the ideology of linguistic assimilation in educational practice (see Djité, 1990, 1991; Weinstein, 1980). In such cases, a necessary (and often sufficient) condition for being educated is competence in the dominant language.

Unlike the ideology of linguistic assimilation, that of *linguistic pluralism* emphasizes the language rights of minority groups, and in general tends not only to accept, but to support, language diversity in a society. Linguistic pluralism in practice actually exists in a variety of forms, ranging from relatively weak toleration of diversity to strong support for multiple languages, even to the extent of granting official status to two or more languages in a society. Examples of countries in which official status is granted to more than one language include Nigeria (Afolayan, 1988; Akinnaso, 1989; Akinnaso & Ogunbiyi, 1990), India (Khubchandani, 1983; Srivastava, 1988), South Africa (Alexander, 1989; Reagan, 1987a, 1987b, 1995b; Young, 1988) and Canada (Genesee, 1988; Ricento & Burnaby, 1998), to name just a few, and in each of these cases, educational policy tends to mirror language policy. Whereas policies of linguistic pluralism are often politically the easiest solution for developing societies because they appear to avoid problems related to the domination of less powerful groups by more powerful ones, the trade off that such policies entail is both an economic one and a political one. This is the case because multilingualism will inevitably be more expensive than monolingualism, and because such policies can, in fact, encourage the development of insular pluralistic communities within a society (Bullivant, 1981; see also Beer & Jacob, 1985; Edwards, 1984c).

Often in practice closely related to the ideology of linguistic pluralism is that of *vernacularization*, which entails the selection of one or more indigenous language(s) in a society to serve in an official capacity. Such selection almost always involves considerable language engineering, as discussed earlier, and such engineering inevitably focuses on the educational sphere, with the production of textbooks, curricular materials, matriculation examinations, and so on. Furthermore, vernacularization can focus on a single indigenous language, as in the case of Swahili in Tanzania, or on multiple languages, as has been the case in South Africa (see Louw, 1983/4; Reagan, 1985, 1986b, 1987b, 1995b). As Cobarrubias (1983a) noted,

> Vernacularization involves the restoration and/or elaboration of an indigenous language and its adoption as an official language. There are also several processes of vernacularization which include the revival of a dead language (Hebrew in Israel), the restoration of a classical language (the Arabization process in Syria, Egypt, and Morocco), the promotion of an indigenous language to official status and its eventual standardization (Tagalog in the Philippines and Quechua in Peru). (p. 66)

Finally, the ideology of *internationalization* involves the selection of a language of wider communication, such as English or French, for use as the society's official language. Such selections are quite common throughout the developing world, and almost always reflect the colonial past of a country. Thus, the division between anglophone and francophone Africa largely reflects differences not only in official languages but also in terms of the colonial past (although other ideologies of language also exist in the African context, especially in anglophone Africa, as Nigeria and Tanzania make clear).

# LANGUAGE POLICY IN INTERNATIONAL PERSPECTIVE

In his discussion of the different ideologies of language, Cobarrubias emphasized the diversity of options within each ideology, as well as noting that this taxonomy is in no way an exhaustive one (1983a, p. 63). It should also be noted that these ideologies can occur not only independently, but can also co-occur. Such co-occurrence of different ideologies of language is especially common in the Third World, as can be seen in the inclusion of language and educational policies in francophone Africa under both the ideologies of assimilation and internationalization (see also Reagan, 1985, 1986b).

## THE LANGUAGE PLANNING PROCESS

Language planning efforts can be conceptualized as consisting of four interrelated, and to some extent overlapping, components: (1) the initial fact-finding phase, (2) the establishment and articulation of goals, desired outcomes, and the strategies to be employed in achieving these goals and outcomes, (3) the implementation process, and (4) the evaluation of all aspects of the language planning process (see Reagan, 1983). During the first stage of the language planning process, information about the setting in which the language policy is to be implemented is gathered. Clearly, the more information that is available to the language planner, the better. In any event, two sorts of information must be gathered if the language policy is expected to have a significant and positive impact. The first of these is a clear understanding of the sociolinguistic setting in which the language policy is to be implemented. Especially important in this context are the common patterns of linguistic usage. The second sort of necessary information is that which would provide a proper understanding of other social, economic, and political processes and developments. It is only with a combination of these two kinds of information that a realistic perspective on need determination and assessment of needs and wants can be gained by the language planner.

The second step in the language planning process involves the determination and articulation of goals, strategies, and outcomes. This process will take place on several levels, and will require a variety of skilled personnel. Goals, both linguistic and extralinguistic, will be set based on the assessment of needs and wants determined in the information-gathering phase within the parameters made possible by the political and socioeconomic context. The goals, in turn, will serve to define and delineate the expected (and desired) outcomes of the language policy to be effected. The strategies for achieving these outcomes, which are normally seen as primarily a technical matter, will provide the basis and direction for the implementation of the language policy.

The implementation of the language policy, which is the third step in the language planning process, is in many ways the central focus of much of the language planning literature. This phase entails the mobilization of resources, general finance, personnel management, motivation, and supervision of those concerned both with the management of the language policy program and with its target populations, and preparation, sequencing, and coordination of related aspects of the language policy (such as the development of textbooks, and so forth; Rubin & Jernudd, 1971).

The last step in the process of language planning, and often the most neglected, is that of evaluation. Evaluation of the language policy should take place in two senses—both as an integral, ongoing component of all phases of the language planning process, and as a final cumulative examination of the successes and failures of the language policy (mainly, although not exclusively, in terms of the correlation of goals and outcomes). Insofar as the predicted outcomes are still considered valid ones, the actual outcomes ought to be, as a consequence of evaluation, brought continually closer to the articulated goals of the language policy.

The model of the process of language planning presented here is essentially a normative one, which is to say that this is how language planners and policymakers would generally advocate that policies related to language be made. However, as our earlier discussion of the development and implementation of manual sign codes made clear, such a model all too often does not actually describe or reflect reality. In fact, language policies and related language planning decisions are frequently made solely or primarily on the basis of short-term political expediency, misguided assumptions and beliefs, and a range of extralinguistic factors. It is also true, however, that language policies and language planning activities are quite often unsuccessful (sometimes spectacularly so), often precisely because of the way in which they were designed and implemented, as we see in the following section of this chapter.

## EVALUATING LANGUAGE POLICIES

An important point that is often minimized, or even overlooked entirely, in discussions of language planning is that such activity is profoundly political in nature (see McKay 1993; Pennycook 1994, 1998; Phillipson 1992; van Dijk, 1995). Language planning involves public decisions about language, its use, status and development—decisions that have overwhelming significance socially, economically, educationally, and politically for society and the individual. Language planning cannot be separated from such concerns, nor indeed, would it be appropriate to try to do so. Language planning efforts are, in short, inevitably ideological and political in nature, and this fact must be taken into account in trying to understand them (see Tollefson, 1991, pp. 22–42).

The philosopher Kerr (1976) suggested four tests that any good public policy must pass. These four tests, and the fundamental questions that they seek to raise, are:

1. The desirability test: Is the goal of the policy one that the community as a whole believes to be desirable?

2. The justness test: Is the policy just and fair? That is, does it treat all people in an equitable and appropriate manner?
3. The effectiveness test: Is the policy effective? Does it achieve its objectives?
4. The tolerability test: Is the policy resource-sensitive? Is it viable in the context in which it is to be effected?

These four tests are quite useful in evaluating language policies, and can serve as a working model for analyzing different language planning processes, providing us with a series of questions that can be used in evaluating different language policy options (and, indeed, can be used in evaluating other sorts of social and educational policies as well).

At this point, we turn to a somewhat more in-depth exploration of two specific examples of language policy development and implementation: first, the case of post-apartheid South Africa, and second, the case of Irish in Ireland.

## THE CASE OF POST-APARTHEID SOUTH AFRICA

One of the more exciting and promising events of the late 20th century was the end of apartheid and the establishment of a truly democratic society in South Africa. The post-apartheid period in South Africa has been one in which political, social, and economic change has taken place on an incredibly widespread scale as the society attempts to redress the harms and injustices perpetuated by the apartheid regime. Given the historic importance of language policy and language planning activities in South African society, it is hardly surprising that this is an area that has received extensive attention by the new government (see de Klerk & Barkhuizen, 1998; Mtuze, 1993; Reagan, 2000a). This fact alone would make the South African case worth a careful and thorough reexamination, but in fact there are even broader reasons for focusing on issues of language policy in contemporary South Africa. As Blommaert (1996) noted:

> The 1990s ... have been marked by a renewed interest in language planning. The historical changes in South Africa triggered a new enthusiasm among language scholars, and almost automatically drove them into the direction of language planning issues because of the nature of the political-ideological debate surrounding the end of apartheid. Issues of national and subnational identity, of culture and language, featured prominently in almost any debate on the future of South Africa, and the new Republic set an important precedent by allowing eleven languages to be used as official languages instead of the usual one, two or four of most other African states. Here was a country which championed multilingualism as a symbol of political and cultural pluralism. (p. 203)

The South African case raises a number of important issues of concern for those interested in language policy and language planning: issues of multilingualism, linguistic diversity, linguistic integration, linguistic equity, and language rights. Furthermore, South Africa is fascinating for those interested in matters of language because it is characterized by elements of both the developed and the developing worlds, and thus, to some extent, provides us with a microcosm of the broader international issues related to language. By far the wealthiest and most developed of all the nations of Africa, South Africa has a well-developed infrastructure that in many ways parallels those of western Europe and North America, a large and well-educated professional work force, and significant natural resources, including a very modern and productive agricultural sector. At the same time, South Africa is a society with fairly extensive linguistic diversity, a low literacy rate, serious problems of social and economic inequity, limited resources that are insufficient for meeting the expectations of most people in the society, and a rapidly growing population for which its infrastructure is nowhere near adequate. From a linguistic perspective, South Africa is a reasonably diverse society in which English plays a key role both as a native language of some South Africans and as a common lingua franca for others, but is by no means demographically a majority language in the society.

In the years since the 1994 election, South Africa has begun seriously and thoughtfully to address many of the challenges related to language and language policy that will face virtually all societies in the next century. Its experiences in this regard are both telling and significant, and have far broader implications for other societies. In this section of the chapter, recent developments in South Africa with respect to language policy are explored, and possible lessons for efforts to promote linguistic diversity in multilingual settings are identified.

South African society is characterized by extensive diversity. The society is multiracial, multicultural, multireligious, and multilingual. Indeed, the diversity present in contemporary South Africa is arguably nowhere manifested more clearly than in the case of language. In addition to Afrikaans and English, which during the apartheid era served as the country's official languages, nine indigenous African languages and five Indian languages are spoken. The situation is further complicated by the presence of a number of immigrant languages, languages used primarily or exclusively for religious purposes (Arabic, Hebrew, and Sanskrit), sign languages, and various kinds of nonstandard languages and language varieties. Despite this high degree of linguistic diversity, which is of course far from uncommon elsewhere in the developing world, however, South Africa also shares a number of linguistic characteristics with the world's so-called developed nations. The country's linguistic diversity includes a language of wider communication, English, which is widely spoken throughout the country, and by at least some members of all of the different ethnolinguistic groups. There is a high level and degree of bilingualism and even multilingualism, reflecting the educational level of the population as well as the extensive intergroup contact that continues, in spite of the legacy of apartheid, to characterize South African society (see Kaschula & Anthonissen, 1995). And, although still far too low to be acceptable, and certainly skewed disproportionately toward certain groups at the expense of others, the literacy rate in South Africa is impressive when compared with that of virtually any other African society (e.g., National Education Policy Investigation, 1993b, pp. 69–70; Pretorius & Lemmer, 1998; Prinsloo & Breier, 1996).

Language and the *taalstryd*, or language struggle, has been a central point of disagreement and debate throughout the history of South Africa, especially (though by no means exclusively) in the educational sphere (see Hartshorne, 1987, 1992). Under the apartheid regime, the language medium question was most controversial in Black education, where the policy of initial mother tongue instruction was widely denounced as an attempt to retribalize Black South Africans (see Alexander, 1989). To some extent, though, it must be remembered that the mother tongue policy was in fact a reflection of the historical taalstryd, which took place in the White community of South Africa in the 19th and early 20th centuries, as that struggle deeply influenced White perceptions and government policy with regard to language policies in education. This earlier taalstryd, had focused in part on the rights of Afrikaners to educate their children in their mother tongue, in the face of ongoing efforts at anglicization (see Reagan, 1986a, 1986b, 1986c; Steyn 1980, 1987). Although the tensions between English and Afrikaans were never eliminated, government policies of what might be termed active official bilingualism, coupled with English and Afrikaans speakers attending their own-medium schools, worked to mitigate what tensions existed between the two groups.

Language remained a highly controversial issue in Black education throughout the apartheid era, however (Alexander, 1989; Hartshorne, 1987; Heugh, 1987a, 1987b; Marivate, 1993; Ndebele, 1987; Reagan, 1984, 1986a, 1986b; Reagan & Ntshoe, 1987). Somewhat ironically, it was the Nationalist government that supported mother tongue schooling for Blacks, whereas Blacks, for the most part, opposed such schooling. It is this irony that provides, at least in part, a key to understanding the apartheid era (and, indeed, much of the post-apartheid) debate on language policy in South African education (Heugh, 1995; Reagan, 1986a, 1986d, 1998). The apartheid regime consistently favored mother tongue schooling for Blacks (and, in fact, for almost all children in the country), but for arguably quite different reasons than those used to defend mother tongue instruction for White children (see Hartshorne, 1987, 1992; Reagan, 1998). It is clear that mother tongue programs for Blacks were not only consistent with the ideology of apartheid, but that they functioned as one of the pillars of apartheid in perpetuating both racial and ethnolinguistic divisions in South African society (see Reagan, 1987b). Mother tongue schooling for Blacks was employed from the passage of the Bantu Education Act of 1953 to the end of the apartheid era to support the social and educational goals of Verwoerdian-style apartheid (Thompson, 1985). The apartheid regime used such programs to reinforce ethnic and tribal identity among Black schoolchildren, seeking to divide and conquer by encouraging ethnolinguistic divisions within the Black community (Hartshorne, 1987, 1992; Heugh, 1985; for a discussion of this phenomenon in other colonial settings, see Mansour, 1993, pp. 58–61). As Barnard perceptively noted:

*Moedertaalonderwys* ... is not the Afrikaans term for mother-tongue instruction. It is a political concept which has its roots in the dogma of Christian National Education. According to this dogma, each "race" or *"volk"* has its own identity which sets it apart from all others ... Surely one has to wonder and become suspicious when there is this insistence on the part of the authorities to force upon all children, against the wishes of their parents, a particular language ... What is being attempted is certainly not mother-tongue education in the interests of the children but the enforcement of *"moedertaalonderwys"* as an instrument of social control and subjugation, as a means to an end ... (Quoted in Heugh, 1987b, pp. 143–144)

Given this historical background, it is easy to understand the resistance to mother-tongue education, as well as to mandatory instruction in Afrikaans (see Reagan, 1985, 1987a), found in many parts of the Black community during the apartheid era. Indeed, schooling designed to emphasize ethnic and cultural differences all too often falls prey to this sort of pluralist dilemma. As the Australian scholar Bullivant (1981) observed, programs designed and intended to encourage ethnic identification, including various kinds of multicultural education programs in many western societies, "are ideal methods of controlling knowledge/power, while appearing through symbolic political language to be acting solely from the best of motives in the interests of the ethnic groups themselves" (p. 291). This was clearly the case in South Africa, although few Blacks were taken in by the rhetoric of pluralism. Unfortunately, the legacy of apartheid includes suspicions about mother-tongue instruction in any form, which has led to on-going tensions with respect to educational language policy in post-apartheid South Africa. As Kamwangamalu (1997) observed:

as a result of apartheid policies, for the Black people in South Africa mother-tongue education has been synonymous with inferior education. Consequently, they have tended to resist such education and to opt, instead, for English-medium education. However, as the literature shows, English-medium education has tended to be elitist and has failed to promote literacy in South Africa, much as it has failed in the rest of the continent ... mother-tongue education might become an alternative to English-medium education provided that it is "cleansed" of the stigma it has been carrying since the heyday of apartheid ... (p. 249)

In the aftermath of the 1994 election, the Government of National Unity, as well as the new constitution, recognized 11 official languages, rejecting the historical bilingual policy (which reflected only the linguistic diversity of White South Africa) with a multilingual policy more accurately reflecting the reality of South African society (see Department of National Education, 1997). Further, *The Reconstruction and Development Programme* of the African National Congress (1994) called for the development of "all South African languages and particularly the historically neglected indigenous languages" (1994, p. 71). It is important to note here that this commitment to multilingualism did not entail maintaining all public and private sector services in all 11 official languages, which would have

# LANGUAGE POLICY IN INTERNATIONAL PERSPECTIVE 119

been almost certain to prove cost prohibitive. Such a scenario would have assumed that past models of bilingualism would be superimposed on current realities—that is, that the absolute equality of English and Afrikaans sought by the apartheid regime (primarily as a component of Afrikaner political ideology) would be the model for the language policy to be pursued by the democratic government of South Africa with respect to all 11 official languages. This, of course, need not be the case, and in fact has quite clearly not been the case in contemporary South Africa. Rather, the focus of the new constitution with respect to official languages and issues of language rights is intended to be as inclusive as possible, and supportive of multilingualism, but also pragmatically and economically feasible (see Constitutional Assembly, 1997; Department of National Education, 1997). The challenge that the new constitution attempts to meet is to ensure individual language rights (no small matter in a nation in which roughly half the population do not speak English) and to symbolically emphasize the multilingual and multicultural nature of the society, and at the same time allocating resources in a economically and politically responsible manner. Although one could see such efforts on the part of the government as disingenuous and even misleading, given the de facto dominant status of English in South Africa (see Verhoef, 1998a, 1998b), such a view is not really merited by the realities of the situation. Indeed, the government has made a significant commitment to the promotion of multilingualism in South Africa, and is in fact engaged in a very much up-hill battle to do so in the context of the immense economic and social power of English (see Barkhuisen & Gough, 1996; Chick & Wade, 1997; Chisanga & Kamwangamalu, 1997; Heugh, 1993), as we shall see.

With the end of the apartheid era and the election of a democratic government in South Africa, language policy in general, and in education in particular, has inevitably received considerable attention as the institutions of South African society are transformed (for detailed discussions of contemporary language policy in South Africa, see Beukes, 1991a, 1991b, 1992, 1996; Beukes & Barnard, 1994; Chick, 1992; Cluver, 1992; Desai, 1991, 1994; Heugh, 1995; Kashoki, 1993; Pieterse, 1991; Prinsloo & Malan, 1988; Prinsloo, Peeters, Turi, & van Rensburg, 1993; Reagan, 1990c, 1995b; Ridge, 1996; Schuring, 1991; Swanepoel & Pieterse, 1993). One powerful example of this concern with language policy, especially in the educational sphere, is *A Policy Framework for Education and Training*, which is a discussion document issued by the Education Department of the African National Congress, and which sets out proposals related to issues of education and training (African National Congress, 1995). Included in this document are four lessons that are identified as being of the utmost importance in order that the "cycle of language oppression be broken" in South African society in general, and in education in particular (African National Congress, 1995, p. 62). The four lessons identified in *A Policy Framework for Education and Training* include:

1. Language policy in education should be the subject of a nation-wide consultative process, to ensure that proposed changes in policy have the broad

consent of the language communities which will be directly affected by them.

2. No person or language community should be compelled to receive education through a language of learning they do not want.
3. No language community should have reason to fear that the education system will be used to suppress its mother tongue.
4. Language restrictions should not be used to exclude citizens from educational opportunities. (ANC, 1995, p.66)

To ensure that these lessons are reflected in any language policy to be developed in South Africa, the African National Congress discussion document goes on to identify three general principles upon which educational language policy should be based. These principles include the right of the individual to choose which language or languages to study and to use as a language of learning (medium of instruction), the right of the individual to develop the linguistic skills in the language or languages of his or her choice (which are necessary for full participation in national, provincial, and local life), and the necessity to promote and develop South African languages that were previously disadvantaged and neglected (African National Congress, 1995, p. 63). It seems clear, then, that both the lessons to be learned from past experience and the general principles on which educational language policies are to be based are reflective, in large part, of concerns about past practices in South Africa, and are intended to be consistent with the goal of a democratic and nonracial language policy, as well as with the constitutional recognition of the equality of the 11 official languages of South Africa.

An excellent example of the sort of approach to language policy formulation envisioned by the African National Congress is the National Education Policy Investigation's work on language (National Education Policy Investigation, 1992a, 1992b, 1993a, 1993b). The National Education Policy Investigation was a project undertaken by the National Education Co-ordinating Committee between 1990 and 1992, which explored policy options in the educational sphere "within a value framework derived from the ideals of the broad democratic movement" (National Education Policy Investigation, 1992b, p. vi). The National Education Policy Investigation sought to set the stage for on-going, and indeed protracted and extensive, debates about educational policy issues. Indeed, at one point in the mid-1990s, more than 60 separate committees around the country were involved in discussions of national language policy. The focus of the National Education Policy Investigation (1992b) can clearly be seen in the final concluding paragraph of the language report, which argued that:

Any [language policy] option that is chosen can have an empowering or a disempowering effect on learners, depending on its suitability for the particular school's context, on how it is implemented, and on how it relates to the national language policy of the country. There is no one policy that is ideal for all schools. Language policy for education needs, therefore, to be flexible without being so laissez faire as to allow the perpetuation of present discriminatory policies or ill-informed choices of alternatives to them. (p. 93)

Current efforts now underway in South Africa are moving in accord with this advice, and it is clear that the government has had the expectation that, as a consequence, the educational language policies that are in the process of being developed are far more likely to receive broad popular support than have past policies (see Reagan, 1995b). Perhaps the most outstanding example of this has been the reception of the final report of the Language Plan Task Group (LANGTAG). This group was created in 1995 by Ngubane, the Minister of Arts, Culture, Science, and Technology, with the explicit task of devising a national language plan for South Africa. The final LANGTAG report, issued in August 1996, clearly attempted to achieve the following objectives, which Ngubane identified:

1. All South Africans should have access to all spheres of South African society by developing and maintaining a level of spoken and written language which is appropriate for a range of contexts in the official language(s) of their choice.
2. All South Africans should have access to the learning of languages other than their mother tongue.
3. The African languages, which have been disadvantaged by the linguicist policies of the past, should be developed and maintained.
4. Equitable and widespread language services should be established. (p. 7)

In short, what is occurring with respect to language policy in the contemporary South African context, at least from the perspective of the government, is an on-going effort to both democratize the language planning process and to ensure the protection of language rights for all South Africans. More specifically, the government is engaged in a multifaceted effort in the sphere of language policy and language planning, including not only status and corpus planning, but also language attitude planning and the articulation and implementation of protections for individual language rights.

Status planning has already taken place in terms of the selection of the country's 11 official languages, as well as in the on-going development of language medium policies in the educational sphere (Beukes, 1992). Further, one of the more interesting and unusual aspects of the status planning process in the South African case has been the inclusion of the status of South African Sign Language in the discussions and debates about language policy (see Penn 1992, 1993; Penn & Reagan 1990, 1995, 1999; Reagan & Penn 1997). Unlike such discussions related to ASL in the U.S. context, the South African debate did not evolve around questions of whether South African Sign Language is a real language, but rather, simply around what its constitutional status should be. Although ultimately not included as an official language in the new constitution, South African Sign Language does nevertheless include constitutional recognition and support—and in fact the significance of its exclusion as an official language would seem to be primarily symbolic in nature, since the language and educational rights cf the deaf individual are clearly protected by the constitution (Constitutional Assembly, 1997; see also Office of the Deputy President, 1997).

Corpus planning is an area in which South Africa has had extensive experience. The support and development of Afrikaans as an official language in South Africa was an incredibly powerful example of corpus planning (see Steyn, 1992, 1998), but even in terms of African languages, there have been long-term efforts at corpus planning. As Kloss noted in 1978:

> Committees have been working for some twenty years on languages like Southern Sotho, Pedi, Zulu, and Tsonga, to create scientific vocabularies in those languages with a view to the production of school books in them at the upper secondary level ... In South Africa, more qualified scholars, White and Black, are working on this "linguistic engineering" than in all the rest of Africa. Even Swahili is well behind the South African languages in educational development, in spite of its easy lead in political status ... (p. 21)

Although true, Kloss' comments ignored an important aspect of the corpus planning efforts during the apartheid period. A more critical (and accurate) view of these efforts was provided by the African National Congress, which observed:

> The languages of the people are not permitted to be developed by them in their own way. Ignorant and officious White professors sit on education committees as arbiters of African languages and books without consultation with the people concerned. The grotesque spectacle is seen of the White government of South Africa posing as a "protector" of so-called Bantu culture and traditions of which they know nothing ... (quoted in Heugh, 1987a, pp. 210–211)

Perhaps the central difference between contemporary corpus planning efforts and those of the past is to be found not so much in particular decisions or policies, but rather in the advent of democratic language planning activities grounded in the communities in which the affected languages are actually used (see, for example, Department of Arts, Culture, Science, and Technology, 1997; Mtintsilana & Morris, 1988).

Beyond status and corpus planning, however, a significant focus of contemporary language planning activities in South Africa is on what might be termed language attitude planning (Finchilescu & Nyawose, 1998; Louw-Potgieter & Louw, 1991; Verhoef, 1998b). Language attitude planning in the South African context actually has both an articulated and an unarticulated purpose. The articulated purpose is to raise consciousness about the multilingual nature of South African society, to increase toleration and acceptance of language differences, and to encourage the growth of individual bilingualism and multilingualism in the country's languages (see Beukes, 1996; Heugh, Siegrhn & Plüddemann, 1995; King & van den Berg, 1992; Mawasha, 1996; Verhoef, 1998a). The unarticulated but nevertheless powerful purpose of language attitude planning in contemporary South Africa is to attempt to address the concerns about the future of specific languages in the country—most notably Afrikaans (see Brink, 1984; Cluver, 1993a; Combrink, 1991; Kriel, 1998; Maartens, 1994; van Rensburg, 1993, 1997; Webb, 1992), but also European languages (see Department of Education and Culture, House of Assembly, 1992; B. Smit, 1993, 1996; U. Smit, 1994; Strike, 1996) and sincere worries about the future of many of the African languages (Baai, 1992; Msimang, 1992; Mutasa, 1996; see also Robinson, 1996). Indeed, changing common, negative attitudes about the African languages in South Africa is one of the greater challenges faced by language planners in the new regime, as indeed has been the case in many other postindependence countries (see Rahman, 1996, 1998; Ramanathan, 1999; Sarinjeive, 1997, 1999; Schiffman, 1996; Schmied, 1991; Schuring, 1991). Hardly surprisingly, it has been in the educational sphere where such efforts face the greatest resistance, due both to the historical significance of mother tongue schooling and the very real practical advantages of English (see Barkhuisen & Gough, 1996; Chick & Wade, 1997; Chisanga & Kamwangamalu, 1997; Heugh, 1993; Ndebele, 1987; Peirce, 1989; Tollefson, 2000).

Finally, the establishment and promotion of language rights has been an on-going concern of the post-apartheid South African government (see Co-ordinating Committee on the National Action Plan, 1998; Department of Arts, Culture, Science, and Technology, 1999; Desai, 1994). This concern with language rights in South Africa has in many ways paralleled a growing international interest in language rights, as we saw in chapter 7, and in the South African case, such matters have demonstrably been taken seriously both in terms of constitutional and legal policy and in terms of practice (see Mamdani, 2000; Musker, 1997). And yet, whereas all this may sound quite promising, and is certainly a dramatic improvement on the apartheid past, it is by no means the whole story. What seems to be taking place in contemporary South African society is that the linguistic market has created a context in which competence in English is the primary criterion for economic success and social mobility, and that this context has been clearly recognized and acted upon by the population (see Gaganakis, 1992). The result has been a decline in the teaching and learning of most other languages (see Reagan, 2000a; Strike, 1996) in the country,[2] and an incredible growth in the teaching of English. To be sure, this growth has also inspired increased emphasis on critical language awareness in the teaching of English (see Fairclough, 1989, 1992, 1995; Janks, 1991, 1997; Janks & Ivanič, 1992), and the clear success of English in the marketplace has raised serious ideological concerns both in South African and elsewhere (Bamgbose, Banjo, & Thomas, 1997; de Kadt, 1996; Holborow, 1999; Krishnaswamy & Burde, 1998; Lowenberg, 1995; Mansoor, 1993; Phillipson & Skutnabb-Kangas, 1996). Nevertheless, perhaps the clearest lesson that contemporary South Africa has to teach us has to do with the overwhelming dominance of English, a dominance supported by both economic factors and by tacit government acquiescence in the face of considerable linguistic diversity. It is interesting that this has been the case even given strongly articulated language policies that encourage and support multilingualism. Issues of linguistic toleration, language rights, and the relationship of language to ethnic identity notwithstanding, the economic return on competence in English is effectively overwhelming efforts to encourage competence in other languages (see also Mazrui & Mazrui, 1998; Pennycook, 1994, 2000; Phillipson, 1992; Phillipson & Skutnabb-Kangas, 1995). English medium schooling is rapidly becoming the dominant model in much of South Africa, the study of other languages (European, Afrikaans, and even indigenous African languages) has substantially declined and is continuing to do so (see Reagan, 2000a), publications and other kinds of media are increasingly dominated by English, and even in Parliament and government circles, the language of daily operation tends to be English. Although neither Afrikaans nor most of the indigenous African languages are in any immediate danger, language shift toward English is clearly taking place at an accelerated rate, and the number of spheres in which languages other than English can be used is rapidly declining. What is constitutionally a multilingual society is in fact a diglossic one in which English is the high variety and other languages are low varieties (see Kamwangamalu, 1998). In short, what the South African case appears to demonstrate at this point in time is the incredible power of the English language, and, in fact, the threat that such power poses to virtually all other languages, especially in multilingual environments.

## THE CASE OF IRISH

Language is intrinsically tied to individual and group identity, and this means that issues related to language will inevitably incite strong emotional and psychological reactions in some cases (see Piron, 1994; Reagan, 1992). One way in which such reactions can be understood is by examining what might be termed the mythology of particular languages—that is, the set of beliefs a linguistic community holds about its language, as well as the symbolism of the language (and of the use of the language) for its community of users. In this part of the chapter, we examine the historical and contemporary status of Irish, as well as the mythology and symbolism of language for the case of Irish.

The effort to revitalize the Irish language is in many ways a paradigmatic case for an examination of the role of mythology and symbolism in language planning and language policy, since from the rise of the Irish revival movement in the mid-19th century there has been a close linkage between the Irish language movement and ideological and political forces in the country (see Edwards, 1984a; Hindley, 1990). Furthermore, the case of Irish is relatively well documented in the language planning literature (see Edwards, 1984a, 1984b; Gruenais, 1986; Hindley, 1990; Macnamara, 1971; Maguire, 1991; O'Cinneide, Keane, & Cawley,

1985; Ó Domhnalláin, 1977; Ó Dubhghaill, 1987; Ó Riagáin, 1988), and Irish is often cited in discussions about the evaluation of the effectiveness of particular language planning activities (see Fishman, 1991, pp. 122–148; Macnamara, 1971; Paulston, 1994, pp. 79–90; Rubin, 1971). This interest in the lessons of the Irish case for evaluation is in fact central to our focus here, because the reason that the Irish case is of such interest to language planners generally is that the articulated goals of the movement, and of the Irish government since the 1920s, can be argued to be in fact somewhat different from the real policy goals—or, at the very least, to have changed over the course of the 20th century in some significant ways (see Macnamara, 1971, pp. 83–84; Paulston, 1994). In essence, the rhetoric surrounding the Irish language movement is suggestive of an effort to increase the use and status of Irish in daily life, while the reality appears to focus more on its limited use as a symbol of national identity. Even the role of Irish as a symbol of national identity is unusual, though, as Edwards (1985) commented, "There exists, today, a strong Irish identity which does not involve Irish, in a communicative sense, for the vast majority. At the same time, the language continues to serve a symbolic function for many" (p. 64).

In other words, Irish functions not as a communicative symbol, but rather as an emblematic symbol, for most Irish people today. As Paulston (1994) argued, "people may perceive of Irish as having a very high symbolic value for the nation, without at the same time being willing or able to use it in daily discourse" (p. 86). This emblematic symbolism distinguishes the case of Irish rather dramatically from most other examples of national languages that perform symbolic functions. In short, the mythological and symbolic value of Irish in Ireland is of far greater significance than is its functional value.

An essential component of understanding the role of Irish in contemporary Irish society is a familiarity with the history of the language. Irish is a Celtic language, originally brought to Ireland by the invading Gaels around 300 B.C. (see Ó Siadhail, 1989, pp. 1–2), later spreading to Scotland and the Isle of Man (where it became distinct from Irish, ultimately evolving into Scots Gaelic and Manx by the 17th century). The early history of the Irish language is one of growing success; indeed, by the sixth century A.D. Irish was an established literary language (see Hindley, 1990, pp. 3–4; Ó Huallacháin, 1991, pp. 1–3, 1994; Wardhaugh, 1987, p. 90). As Edwards (1985) noted:

> In the so-called "Golden Age" of the sixth to the ninth centuries, Ireland was the only Western European country whose vernacular was seen to be suitable for education and literature. By the eighth century, Irish had largely replaced Latin as a religious medium and was cultivated by the monastic orders. (p. 53)

This situation began to change gradually with the Anglo-Norman invasion of Ireland in 1172 and the establishment of the Pale along the eastern coast (and including Dublin) as an English and Norman French-speaking enclave. However, the initial patterns of language shift were not so much from Irish to English as the other way around—the English settlers were largely Gaelicized, becoming *Hibernis ipsis Hiberniores* (more Irish than the Irish), as the 1366 Statutes of Kilkenny, which focused on preventing English settlers from adopting Irish ways, make clear (Hudson-Edwards, 1990, p. 63; Paulston, 1994, pp 80–81). It was only with the Tudors that this tendency began to change, encouraged by the suppression and exile of the Irish aristocracy, the implementation of the plantation system in the North, and later, the devastation of the Great Famine in the 19th century (1846–1848) and the establishment of the National School System (which excluded Irish) in 1831 (see Edwards, 1984b; Hechter, 1975; Hudson-Edwards, 1990). In any event, the 19th century witnessed the language shift away from Irish and toward English that by mid-century, was largely an accomplished fact, with declining percentages of monolingual speakers of Irish and a growing percentage of Irish-English bilinguals—a bilingualism that was, for the most part, "usually a way-station on the road to English only" (Edwards, 1985, p. 54).

It was in this demographic context that the movement for the maintenance and revival of the Irish language emerged. Although initially not tied directly to the movement for Irish independence, the movement for the restoration of Irish *"did play an important role in the revolutionary movement and many of its members became political leaders in the Free State"* (Edwards, 1985, p. 55). With the establishment of the Irish Free State in 1921, the Irish language movement found itself in a position unmatched by any of the other Celtic languages (which had also experienced 19th century romantic, nationalistic movements aimed at language preservation)—Irish alone had the power of a state behind it. Indeed, from the establishment of the Free State, Irish has constitutionally been the national and first official language of the country. With this background in mind, we turn now to a discussion of the ways in which language policy and language planning have been used in the Irish state to promote Irish.

An interesting feature of the 19th century movement for the revival of Irish was that the people most committed to the language tended not to be themselves native speakers of Irish, but were, rather, educated, upper middle-class individuals for whom Irish was an acquired language (see Edwards, 1985, p. 55; Romaine, 1994, p. 94; Wardhaugh, 1987, pp. 92–93)—an aspect of the language situation in Ireland that has remained true to a significant extent to the present, and one that has had important implications for language policy in the country.

From the establishment of the Free State to the present, Irish language policy, in addition to a general concern with language standardization (see Ó Baoill, 1988), has been focused in three distinct areas: education, the *Gaeltacht*, and official life (Dorian, 1988; Edwards, 1985). The thread that holds language policy in these three areas together is the commitment to the maintenance and, to the extent possible, the extension of the use of Irish.

The most significant emphasis in Irish language planning and language policy since 1921 has been in the educational sphere. Early in the Irish language movement, and even among some language advocates today, there have been calls for the revival of Irish as the common, everyday language of the country, as part of a more general de-Anglicizing of Irish society—an objective that obviously entailed a large role for the educational system, given the fact that as recently as the 1926 Census only 18% of the population could speak Irish. Indeed, one of the central purposes of national education was to be the revival of the Irish language, as Coolahan (1981) noted:

> Another very potent force ... concentrated on the need for curricular reform, in particular the allotting of a much more central role to the Irish language with an Irish emphasis in courses in history, geography, music, etc. Inspired by the ideology of cultural nationalism it was held that the schools ought to be the prime agents in the revival of the Irish language and native tradition which it was held were the hallmarks of nationhood and the basis for independent statehood. Many people held that the schools in the nineteenth century had been a prime cause of the decline of the Irish language; under a native Irish government the process would have to be reversed. (p. 38)

Language policy in education has been concentrated largely in the primary grades, although Irish remains a compulsory subject in secondary schools and, until the mid-1970s, a pass was required in Irish to receive a school Leaving Certificate (Edwards, 1985, p. 57). There is an extensive literature related to educational and pedagogical issues concerning the teaching and learning of Irish, much of it concentrating on problems in Irish language instruction. As Edwards (1985) indicated, these problems include:

> Standards are allegedly low, in both teaching quality and student proficiency. Pupils who have studied Irish for a dozen years cannot speak it. Teachers are critical of both oral competence and grammatical skill, and there are discontinuities of emphasis between primary and secondary levels ... there is a special piquancy here—Irish is a second language to most children, but it is a rather special one, at least in the eyes of many. (p. 57)

The 1985 *Language in the Curriculum/Teanga Sa Churaclam* discussion paper of the Curriculum and Examinations Board, for example, included a serious discussion of many of these issues, and focused clearly on the tension between the poor quality of much Irish instruction and the general support among the Irish population for the teaching of the language in Irish schools, even at the same time noting that, "only one-third of the public rates Irish as one of the most important subjects for children to learn in school" (Curriculum and Examinations Board, 1985, p. 28).

Despite the concerns about the quality of Irish instruction, however, it is important to note that the emphasis in Irish education has, in actual fact, been moderately successful. The 1986 Census identifies slightly in excess of 31% of the population as Irish speaking (though, of course, virtually all of these individuals are bilingual), with the total number of Irish speakers in Ireland continuing to rise. Given the limited pragmatic opportunities for use of the language, this increase in the number of bilingual speakers is actually quite impressive.

The *Gaeltacht* encompasses those primarily rural areas of western Ireland that remain largely Irish speaking, and which have been specially designated by the Government to receive "a greater degree of state aid toward their economic and social development than is provided to other rural areas" (Commins, 1988, p. 11). In other words, the *Gaeltacht* is the area in which the largest concentrations of native speakers of Irish are to be found, and the Government has, since independence, sought to maintain and protect these areas (Dorian, 1988; Fishman, 1991, pp. 124–126). There is, however, a fundamental paradox with respect to the *Gaeltacht*, which remains among the poorer parts of Ireland. The paradox is, essentially, that:

> the Gaeltacht is vital to the language but, because of its socioeconomic situation, is constantly encroached upon by English-language influences. If nothing is done, it will continue to shrink; if things *are* done, an artificial enclave may be created. Further, special measures may actually expedite English influence. In such a situation, can a language survive in anything like its usual unselfconscious state? (Edwards, 1985, p. 58)

The implications of this paradox for the survival of the Irish language have been made quite clear by Hindley (1990), in his book *The Death of the Irish Language*, in which he argued that:

> There is no room for honest doubt that the Irish language is now dying. The only doubt is whether the generation of children now in a handful of schools in Conamara, Cloch Chionnaola and Gaoth Dobhair, and Corca Dhuibhne are the last generation of first-language native speakers or whether there will be one more. The reasons ... relate primarily to economic forces which have promoted the modernization of the Gaeltacht economy and the mobilization of its people, involving them intimately in much wider and constant social and economic relationships that are encompassed by the language. (p. 248)

A further problem is posed by the geography of the *Gaeltacht* itself although in 1800 virtually all of Ireland could be said to constitute a unified *Gaeltacht*, today the *Gaeltacht* is a geographically fragmented region, with pockets of Irish speakers separated from one another by significant distances, and surrounded by areas in which English is the dominant language (Dorian, 1988; Fishman, 1991).

Nonetheless, the maintenance of the *Gaeltacht* has been, and remains, a key element in Irish language policy, and is perhaps the clearest area in which one can see the overlap of social, economic, and language policies in the country. This is hardly surprising because, as Lewis (1980) observed, the "*Fíor Ghaeltacht* is the home of the Irish language at present and its main if not its only hope for the future" (Lewis, 1980, p. 95).

As the national and first official language of Ireland, Irish obviously has a role to play in official life—but, this having been said, it is somewhat difficult to actually pin that role down. Until the mid-1970s, Civil Service positions required a nominal knowledge of Irish, but even this requirement has now been largely abandoned. To be sure, there remains a significant educational commitment to the teaching of Irish, government services are provided in Irish, signage is, to some extent, bilingual (although even in the *Gaeltacht*, English tends to prevail), government publications are issued in both Irish and English, and certain Irish terms are used even in English for distinctive Irish political institutions (for instance, the Irish Prime Minister is called the *Taoiseach*, the Parliament is called the *Dáil*, and so on). However, although there is clearly a place for Irish in official life, that place is somewhat amorphous, as can be seen in the fact that the Irish government, on joining the European Community, chose not to request that Irish—the country's national and first language constitutionally, as noted earlier—be adopted by the European Union, as would (at least arguably) have been its right. In other words, there appear to be practical and pragmatic limits to the use and status of Irish in official life.

We turn now to a discussion of the mythology of the Irish language in contemporary Irish society. It is clear that Irish has little economic value, even in Ireland, and furthermore, that what economic value it does have (for civil servants, and so on) is largely one that is artificially maintained. Also, the language fulfills no particular communicative or pragmatic function, especially given the fact that virtually all speakers of Irish are fully bilingual in English, a world language of wider communication. The situation in which Irish finds itself, in short, is that:

> Irish has little more than a symbolic, ceremonial function in Ireland today. Some knowledge of Irish is or has been required at times to practice law, for police work, to be a career soldier, and to be a civil servant. Irish is hardly ever used in business and commerce and even the Church finds little occasion for using it. Most Irish feel no need of any kind for the language and exist quite satisfactorily without it. There is no reason to believe that they are going to discover that they will need Irish in the future; their own particular variety of English serves them perfectly well. (Wardhaugh, 1987, p. 94)

The picture is further complicated by the nature of the population who are speakers of Irish. Excluding the relatively small numbers of native language speakers of Irish, the vast majority are in fact second language users of the language who have acquired their competence in school. These speakers of the language:

> are an unrepresentative, though influential, sector of educated Irish society. Outside native Irish-speaking districts, fluent Irish is a fairly reliable indicator of middle-class status, while the working class remain ignorant of the language. The new bilinguals constitute a network, largely urban and middle class, not a community, and only a small number of them might be expected to pass the language on to the next generation. As one Irish person said, "although we are all *for* Irish as we are for cheaper bus fares, heaven, and the good life, nobody of the masses is willing to make the effort." The urban middle class can in a sense afford the luxury of using Irish since they are comfortable in their status as English speakers, but it was this very

group who jettisoned the language in their effort to obtain socio-economic security at a time when everyone spoke Irish. (Romaine, 1994, p. 42).

This is an important point: In most parts of Ireland, speakers of Irish constitute an informal network rather than a linguistic community per se. The language, in other words, functions as an emblematic marker of nationalist identity, but even in this respect, its utility is limited as most Irish people would agree that competence in Irish is not a necessary condition for being Irish (however desirable a condition it might be considered to be).

Irish, then, functions increasingly as a marginalized symbol rather than as a functional language, gaining support not for its utility, in even limited spheres of use, but rather for what might be termed its romantic appeal. The decline of the language in the *Gaeltacht* will have negative consequences even in this limited sphere, though, as Hindley (1990) observed:

> Much of the romantic appeal of the language will die with the Gaeltacht, for there is no doubt that going to learn Irish there, among native speakers in their (usually) beautiful and exotic environment, is far more attractive than learning it in the classroom, lecture theatre, or study in some English-speaking town ... The romantic-nationalist element is thus psychologically vital to maintain a flow of future learners and the death of the Gaeltacht would remove its sole material prop. (p. 253)

Just as there is a mythology associated with and supporting the Irish language, so too is there a mythology in Ireland with respect to the English language. And, just as there is something of a tension between the support of the majority of the people in Ireland for the maintenance of Irish even in the face of the lack of use of the language, so there is a tension between the common view of English as the killer or murderer of Irish (see Edwards, 1986) and the widespread and highly effective use of English as the native language of the vast majority of the Irish population. In short, the very ambivalence that colors attitudes about Irish is also reflected in the attitudes about English.

## LANGUAGE POLICY AND THE FOREIGN LANGUAGE EDUCATOR

Our discussion thus far might lead one to believe that issues of language planning and language policy take place only at the national and international levels. If this were in fact the case, there would still be compelling reasons for foreign language educators to be interested in and concerned with such undertakings. However, in reality language policies exist on all levels of society—and one of the places in which they are actually most powerful is in the context of the school (see, for instance, Lambert, 1994). All schools have language policies, although these policies may be implicit or explicit, and all teachers are involved in the implementation of these language policies. As Corson (1999) explained,

# LANGUAGE POLICY IN INTERNATIONAL PERSPECTIVE

School language policies are viewed by many in education as an integral and necessary part of the administration and curriculum practice of schools. A language policy . . . identifies areas of the school's scope of operations and program where language problems exist that need the commonly agreed approach offered by a policy. A language policy sets out what the school intends to do about these areas of concern and includes provisions for follow-up, monitoring, and revision of the policy itself ... (p. 1)

The decision about the language (or languages) to be used as the medium of instruction in the school is a language policy decision, as are decisions about what other languages are to be taught, how language will be taught, the relative significance of different languages in the school context, and so on. For the foreign language educator, this means that our very existence as a profession depends on language policies. The need for students to study a foreign language as a component of their general education is, then, part of the language policy discourse and practice in any school. Which foreign languages to be taught is likewise a language policy decision.

Beyond such direct concerns, though, language policy should also be of concern to foreign language educators in terms of our efforts to promote the sort of critical language awareness in students discussed briefly in chapter 7. Among the key concepts that critical language awareness approaches to language and language study seek to convey to students are the following:

- People have the power to shape the conventions the underlie discourse, just as much as any other social practices.
- Although we tend to accept the way language is, and the way discourses operate, they are changing all the time.
- Forms of discourse receive their value according to the positions of their users in systems of power relations.
- Struggles over the control of discourse are the main ways in which power is obtained and exercised in modern societies. (Corson, 1999, p. 143–144)

In addition, such concepts are manifested in efforts to promote social awareness of discourse, critical awareness of language variety, and practice for change. In short, it is clear that language planning and language policies can and do serve a variety of quite different ends. Language planning can serve as a tool for empowering groups and individuals, for creating and strengthening national bonds and ties, and for maximizing educational and economic development, but it can also be used (and has been used) to maintain and perpetuate oppression, social class discrimination, and social and educational inequity (see Fairclough, 1989; Pennycook, 1994, 1998; Skutnabb-Kangas, 2000a, 2000b). Language planning efforts, if they are to be defensible, must entail the active involvement and participation of those for whom they are intended. Only when emerging in such a context can language planning efforts contribute to the creation of more just, humane and legitimate social and educational policies. As Tollefson (1991) argued quite powerfully, "the foundation for rights is *power* and ... constant *struggle* is necessary to sustain language rights" (p. 167). It is just such an understanding that we need to promote and encourage in our students.

## QUESTIONS FOR REFLECTION AND DISCUSSION

1. Consider the role of language planning and language policy with respect to the language that you wish to teach. What governmental organizations can you identify that are involved in such activities? What private organizations do you know about that are engaged in language planning and language policy? How important are formal efforts at language planning and language policy formulation and implementation in the case of the language that you wish to teach?
2. Consider the implicit and explicit language policies in a school setting with which you are familiar. Using the four policy tests proposed by Kerr, evaluate these policies. Based on your evaluation, what changes do you believe would be appropriate in these policies?
3. What do you believe the implications of critical language awareness are for actual teaching practice in the foreign language classroom? What would constitute evidence that the foreign language teacher is concerned with promoting such critical language awareness in his or her students?
4. The two case studies discussed in this chapter (language policy in post-apartheid South Africa, and the case of Irish) are very different in a number of ways, both from each other and from the contemporary U.S. context. And yet, both cases have important implications for language policy in the U.S. context, especially with respect to educational language policies. Identify and discuss three important lessons from each of the case studies that would be important for us to understand in evaluating and improving language policies in U.S. public schools.
5. Cooper (1989, p. 45) argued that, "Language planning refers to deliberate efforts to influence the behavior of others with respect to the acquisition, structure, or functional allocation of their language codes." To what extent, then, do you believe that all second and foreign language education is language planning?

## FOCUS ON THE CLASSROOM

1. What are examples of educational language policies in your state? In your school district? In your school? In your own classroom?

# LANGUAGE POLICY IN INTERNATIONAL PERSPECTIVE

2. In what ways do you believe language purism has influenced the content of foreign language classes and textbooks?
3. When students in foreign language classes mix their native language and the target language, is this an example of lexical modernization? Why or why not?
4. What differences might one expect to find in foreign language classes in societies that encourage linguistic assimilation and in societies that encourage linguistic pluralism? In your own experience, which of these more accurately represents what we find in the U.S. case? Why? What are the pedagogical implications of this?
5. In what ways does the case of South Africa have relevance for your students? What are the implications of your answer for both the content and methodologies used in the foreign language classroom?

## NOTES

1. The phenomenon of language purism is especially important in the context of foreign language education. For an insightful and compelling discussion of this issue, see Dennis Baron's (1982) *Grammar and Good Taste: Reforming the American Language*.
2. It is interesting to note here that the decline in interest in studying the African languages in the South African context has been taking place even as there has been a dramatic improvement in the pedagogical quality of teaching materials and textbooks for many of these languages. This has been especially true in the cases of Xhosa (see Munnik, 1994; Pinnock, 1994; Zotwana, 1991) and Zulu (see Nxumalo & Cioran, 1996), although high quality Sesotho (see Mokoena, 1998) materials have also been developed and texts and materials for other languages are in production. In addition, multimedia programs are being produced (most notably by the Multimedia Education Project of the University of Cape Town; see Dowling, 1998).

# 9

# Toward a Critical Foreign Language Pedagogy

> It is all too easy to underestimate the power of language ... because almost every human being knows and uses one or more languages, we have let that miracle be trivialized ... We forget, or are unaware of, the power that language has over our minds and our lives; we use that power ourselves as casually as we use the electric power in our homes, with scarcely a thought given to its potential to help or harm. We make major decisions about language on the most flimsy and trivial—and often entirely mistaken—grounds.
>
> —*Elgin* (2000, p. 239)

Language, we believe, matters. Knowledge of language matters, as does knowledge about language. Attitudes and beliefs about language matter, as well. And yet, for the most part people in our society are not only monolingual, but also know very little about language and linguistics. Whereas a knowledge of mathematics or history, for instance, would be almost universally accepted as among the characteristics of an educated person, the same, at least in the United States, cannot be said to be true for either knowledge of a second language or for knowledge *about* language. This is the case not only for the general public, but even for many of those who spend their lives teaching and learning languages. Such ignorance is not simply sad, either; it, too, makes a difference. As Osborn (2000) noted:

> If a student has a bad experience in high school biology, s/he may well not like science for the remainder of life ... s/he may think that frogs are disgusting, insects appalling, and botanical studies quite boring. S/he may even think that biologists are strange individuals. But it is quite likely that the experience will not translate into some sociologically relevant bias. This assurance is much weaker if one has negative experiences in a foreign language class. (p. 15)

# TOWARD A CRITICAL FOREIGN LANGUAGE PEDAGOGY

Thus, the foreign language educator has an incredibly complex and daunting task. Traditionally, we have recognized that it is our job not only to teach students the linguistic basics of the target language, but also to provide them with an introduction to the cultures, literatures, and indeed, the worlds of the speakers of the target language. Our focus over the course of the 19th and 20th centuries has undergone a series of changes, moving first from a purely linguistic emphasis, as would be the case with a grammar-translation approach to language teaching, to one in which included the high culture of the target language, to more recent efforts to present the many different cultures and literatures associated with the target language. We have also become increasingly concerned, of course, with ensuring that foreign language classes are more communicative in both nature and objectives. Although it would not be unreasonable for us to suggest that our job as foreign language educators is quite sufficiently complex already, the fact of the matter is that we do need to reconsider the functions and purposes of foreign language education for most of our students.

To be sure, foreign language educators have long pointed to the role of foreign language study in helping students to understand the grammar of their own language. All too few students come to us with any solid understanding of traditional grammatical terminology, for instance, and it is quite common to hear students and others assert that everything they know about formal English grammar they learned in a foreign language class.[1] Such knowledge has considerable value, and should not be undervalued, although one might well suggest that students should have learned such things before they enter the foreign language classroom. However, it is clear that there is much about languages in general that educated persons should know and understand that goes far beyond such basic knowledge, and it is with this larger puzzle that we are concerned here. In essence, what we are suggesting is that the foreign language classroom is in many ways an ideal place for students to learn about what might be called the metalinguistics of human language in general, and of both their native language and the target language in particular.

## THE METALINGUISTIC CONTENT OF THE FOREIGN LANGUAGE CLASSROOM

What, then, is this metalinguistic content that students should learn? In recent years, a number of educational scholars have begun to articulate this metalinguistic knowledge base, in terms of what students should learn and with respect to what classroom teachers (teachers of language and others) need to know (see Andrews, 1998, 2001; Benesch, 2001; Byrnes, Kiger, & Manning, 1997; Ovando, 2001; Pennycook, 2001; Reagan, 1997a; van Lier, 1995, 1996). Although a complete outline of such knowledge is neither possible nor appropriate here, it is useful for us to identify in general terms some of the core ideas and concepts that would have to be included in the articulation and implementation of such a metalinguistic knowledge base. The following items, then, are intended to provide a sort of guiding framework or outline for the more complete articulation of this metalinguistic knowledge base:

- The social context of language use
- The nature and outcomes of language contact
- The nature and implications of code-switching and code-mixing
- Bilingualism and multilingualism as individual and social norms
- An awareness of the ecology of language(s)
- Ideology and language
- The relationship between language and power
- Realistic understanding of the nature and extent of language diversity in different societies
- Language attitudes
- Issues of language standardization
- Issues of linguistic purism
- The nature and implications of linguistic variation
- The concept of linguistic legitimacy
- Language rights and language responsibilities
- The nature and process of language change
- The interrelationship of languages and language families
- The historical development of languages
- Language acquisition and language learning
- The relationship between language and culture
- The nature of literacy, and the concept of multiple literacies
- Language differences versus language pathologies
- The nature and uses of language policy and language planning
- Critical language awareness

Each of these topics, of course, might easily be expanded into one or more books in its own right. We take it as a given that readers of this volume, by this point, have at least a general understanding of what each of these topics is all about, and, even more important, about why it is included on this list.

## THE ROLE OF PORTFOLIOS AND TEACHER NARRATIVES

It is important to encourage teachers to begin to explore their own roles in regard to the development of an emancipatory foreign language pedagogy. Teachers can move from the elements discussed in this volume, such as critical reflection, curricular nullification, and the inclusion of metalinguistic content in language classrooms, to discover and discuss with other teachers and scholars changes that can be implemented in the field. These changes may include specific strategies or methods, but may ultimately involve a fundamental transformation of our approach to language education. To reach this zenith of the teachers' involvement in shaping a critical paradigm, and in establishing the parameters of discussion in the field, it is imperative that teacher educators encourage the use of tools with which practitioners can express their practice, and ultimately, their praxis.

Teaching, as we discussed, includes an exceptionally complex set of tasks. Reflective practice is beneficial for those who wish to examine their own activities, challenge their prejudices, and evaluate their planning in regard to stated or implicit goals. Yet, by finding vehicles to express their reflection with each other, teachers would additionally improve teaching practice. We suggest that two forms of such expression, teaching portfolios (see Lyons, 1998) and teacher narratives (see Preskill & Jacobvitz, 2001), will be invaluable in this end.

## WHAT DO TWO WHITE GUYS KNOW, ANYWAY?

Recent critical scholarship has made it increasingly clear that one's context and position have important and powerful impacts on how one constructs reality (see, for example, Applebaum, 2000; Brady & Kanpol, 2000; Howard, 1996; Larson & Ovando, 2001; McLaren & Muñoz, 2000; Sleeter & McLaren, 1995). Gender, race, ethnicity, language, and so on, are not merely elements or factors in how one sees the world, but rather, constitute the fundamental scaffolding within which and from which one organizes experience and knowledge. This makes it essential that an author identify and position him or herself, so that readers will understand the social, cultural, economic, and linguistic context in which his or her arguments and insights occur. We do not believe that there is any sort of deterministic connection between an individual's background and his or her beliefs, commitments, and actions, but there is clearly a relationship that needs to be understood. We believe that such personal positioning is important, and, having presented a fairly complex set of arguments about contemporary foreign language education in the United States, now turn to a brief commentary on our own backgrounds. In our case, we are both White males, native speakers of two different varieties of American English, who have chosen to spend our lives studying and learning other languages and cultures. Although our strongest languages are German and Russian, between us we have also studied, albeit to varying degrees of proficiency, Afrikaans, ASL, Anglo-Saxon, Danish, Dutch, Esperanto, French, Italian, Latin, Serbian, Spanish, Xhosa, and Zulu. We recognize that our understanding of the teaching and learning of foreign languages has been colored not only by race, ethnicity, and gender, but also by our personal and professional interests in human language, as well as by our experiences in learning and living with other human languages and cultures. At the same time, though, we believe that whereas one's perspective is inevitably restricted by background and experience, this cannot be used as a justification for ignoring injustice and oppression. An important part of critical reflection is the need for us all to be aware of and sensitive to the many different kinds of oppression that surround us. As educators, we must not only be cognizant of oppression, but must use our teaching practice to challenge such oppression, and to help our students learn to do the same. In short, we are all faced with the rather daunting task identified by Sleeter (1996) with respect to the preparation of future teachers: "How ... does one involve a class of male and female white students from mainly middle class backgrounds in a critique of various forms of oppression and at the same time help them to construct for themselves insights grounded in emancipation of *other people?"* (p. 416).

## CONCLUSION

In concluding this chapter and the volume, we believe that it is important to stress that we are not suggesting that foreign language educators cease to teach the target language, nor in fact are we suggesting that such teaching is not merely worthwhile in its own right, but invaluable. We strongly believe that foreign language education can and should play a central role in every individual's education. What we are suggesting, though, is that as foreign language educators we need to continue our efforts to move beyond what might be called technicist concerns about the teaching of foreign languages. Debates and discussions about alternative teaching methodologies certainly have value, but we must also address the social, cultural, political, and ideological contexts in which we teach, and in which languages are used.

Bolgar, in addressing the decline in the study of classics, wrote that:

> Two things emerge forcibly from any serious consideration of what one might call "the Latin problem." The first is that some considerable change in teaching method is inevitable if the subject is to survive. The second is that the majority of the profession—and particularly its older members—are bound to feel opposed to this change, which will demand great sacrifices on their part. We are faced, through no fault of our own, with a situation where our only alternative to hard work and hard thinking is to watch our subject dwindle till it disappears from the curriculum and leaves us stranded. The testing moment has arrived for classical studies. We must prove that they are fortifying, that they strengthen man's power to deal with the problems of life. We must prove their worth or see them perish. (quoted in Smith, 1977, p. 81)

The future for foreign language study in the United States is by no means as grim as was the future of classics when this was written. Happily, classicists have responded admirably to the changes about which Bolgar was concerned, and the study of the classical languages, and especially of Latin, is once again relatively popular. The challenge before us now is to advocate the study of foreign languages not only for the reasons that we historically offered, but to expand our efforts to include increasing student understanding and awareness of language, broadly conceived, as an outcome

# TOWARD A CRITICAL FOREIGN LANGUAGE PEDAGOGY

of the study of foreign languages. Language study, in short, must become a core element in the teaching of critical perspectives for life in a democratic society.

## QUESTIONS FOR REFLECTION AND DISCUSSION

1. In the quote with which this chapter opens, Elgin (2000) wrote about "the power that language has over our minds and our lives." What do you think that she means by this power? How is it manifested in daily life? What are the possible misuses of such power?
2. What do the authors mean by the metalinguistic content of the foreign language curriculum? Would such content be part of the formal curriculum, or part of the hidden curriculum? To what extent do you believe that foreign language classes are already teaching metalinguistic content?
3. Select five specific items from the metalinguistic knowledge base identified in this chapter. How might you incorporate each of these items in an introductory level foreign language course? In an intermediate level language course?
4. What do you think that the authors mean when they refer to technicist issues in foreign language education? How does this concept fit with notions of critical pedagogy and reflective practice as you understand them?
5. When Osborn (2000, p. 15), in his discussion of the effects of high school teaching on students' life outcomes, noted that in the case of biology, "the experience will not translate into some sociologically relevant bias" but furthermore, that "this assurance is much weaker if one has negative experiences in a foreign language class," what does he mean? What does this point tell you about the significance of foreign language education as a component of a general education?

## FOCUS ON THE CLASSROOM

1. Examine the list of metalinguistic content presented in this chapter. Identify points in your existing curriculum (or in a foreign language textbook) where these points might be treated in the classroom.
2. Why might a foreign language teacher have his or her students write their own language autobiographies at the start of a language course? How might such an assignment be integrated with other subject areas?
3. How can the foreign language educator assist his or her students in identifying their own unarticulated beliefs about language? Their own linguistic biases?

4. Do classroom foreign language teachers have a moral or ethical responsibility to the native speakers of the target language? If so, what is that responsibility?
5. Design an instructional activity that encourages students to construct their own definition of culture. How might you use this activity in a foreign language classroom?

## NOTE

1. Although such beliefs are widespread in the general public and among foreign language teachers, it should be noted that they are, at best, misguided and misinformed. The idea that studying a second language would assist the student in understanding the grammar of his or her own language appears to date back to about 1000 A.D., when Aelfric of Eynsham produced a grammar of Latin written in Anglo-Saxon, and explicitly argued that the work would function as a guide to Anglo-Saxon grammar. As the classicist Smith (1977) cogently noted, "thus began ... the quarrel which general linguists and teachers of English have with Latin teachers who claim to be teaching English grammar. Grammatical categories, they object, are valid only for the language from whose study they are derived, and should not be imposed on other languages. Latin and Greek were sufficiently similar for Latin to be amenable to the categories of Greek grammar, but Anglo-Saxon has, formally speaking, only four noun cases to Latin's six, and no passive conjugation at all; whereas English has nothing of either, except a genitive. So far from a knowledge of Latin grammar being transferable to the understanding of English, it only causes false assumptions and confusion" (pp. 30–31).

# References

Achard, P. (1993). *La sociologie du langage.* [The sociology of lanaguage.] Paris: Presses Universitaires de France.
Ackerman, D. (1989). Intellectual and practical criteria for successful curriculum integration. In H. Jacobs (Ed.), *Interdisciplinary curriculum* (pp. 25–38). Alexandria, VA: Association for Supervision and Curriculum Development.
African National Congress. (1994). *The reconstruction and development programme: A policy framework.* Johannesburg, South Africa: Author.
African National Congress. (1995). *A policy framework for education and training* (Discussion document). Braamfontein, South Africa: Author, Education Department.
Afolayan, A. (1988). Bilingualism and bilingual education in Nigeria. In C. Paulston (Ed.), *International handbook of bilingualism and bilingual education* (pp. 345–358). Westport, CT: Greenwood Press.
Aikman, S. (1999). Sustaining indigenous languages in southeastern Peru. *International Journal of Bilingual Education and Bilingualism, 2,* 198–213.
Akinnaso, F. (1989). One nation, four hundred languages: Unity and diversity in Nigeria's language policy. *Language Problems and Language Planning, 13,* 133–146.
Akinnaso, F., & Ogunbiyi, I. (1990). The place of Arabic in language education and language planning in Nigeria. *Language Problems and Language Planning, 14,* 1–19.
Alexander, N. (1989). *Language policy and national unity in South Africa/Azania.* Cape Town, South Africa: Buchu Books.
Alexander, R. (2000). *Intensive Bulgarian: A textbook and reference grammar* (Vol. Two). Madison: University of Wisconsin Press.
Allen, H., & Linn, M. (Eds.). (1986). *Dialect and language variation.* Orlando, FL: Academic Press.
Almond, B. (1993). Rights. In P. Singer (Ed.), *A companion to ethics* (pp. 259–269). Oxford, England: Basil Blackwell.
Altbach, P. (1984). The distribution of knowledge in the third world: A case study in neocolonialism. In P. Altbach & G. Kelly (Eds.), *Education and the colonial experience* (2nd Rev. ed.; pp. 229–251). New Brunswick, NJ: Transaction.
Altbach, P., Kelly, G., Petrie, H., & Weis, L. (Eds.) (1991). *Textbooks in American society: Politics, policy, and pedagogy.* Albany: State University of New York Press.
Andrews, L. (1998). *Language exploration and awareness: A resource book for teachers* (2nd ed.). Mahwah, NJ: Lawrence Erlbaum Associates.
Andrews, L. (2001). *Linguistics for L2 teachers.* Mahwah, NJ: Lawrence Erlbaum Associates.
Annamalai, E. (1986). Language rights and language planning. *New Language Planning Newsletter, 1,* 1–3.
Anward, J. (1997). Parameters of institutional discourse. In B. Gunnarsson, P. Linell, & B. Nordberg (Eds.), *The construction of professional discourse* (pp. 127–150). New York: Longman.
Anyon, J. (1979). Ideology and United States social studies textbooks. *Harvard Educational Review, 49,* 361–386.
Apple, M. (1979). *Ideology and curriculum.* Boston: Routledge & Kegan Paul.

# REFERENCES

Apple, M. (1990). *Ideology and curriculum* (2nd ed.). New York: Routledge.
Apple, M. (1995). *Education and power* (2nd ed.). New York: Routledge.
Apple, M. (1996). *Cultural politics and education.* New York: Teacher's College Press.
Apple, M., & Christian- Smith, L. (1991). The politics of the textbook. In M. Apple & L. Christian-Smith (Eds.), *The politics of the textbook* (pp. 1–21). New York: Routledge.
Apple, M., & Weiss, L. (Eds.). (1983). *Ideology and practice in schooling.* Philadelphia: Temple University Press.
Applebaum, B. (2000). Wanted: White, anti-racist identities. *Educational Foundations, 14,* 5–18.
Augarde, T. (Ed.). (1991). *The Oxford dictionary of modern quotations.* Oxford, England: Oxford University Press.
Auld, W. (1988). *La fenomeno Esperanto.* [The Esperanto phenomenon.] Rotterdam: Universala Esperanto-Asocio.
Baai, Z. (1992). Towards a more communicative approach to the teaching of African languages, particularly Xhosa, as second languages. *Southern African Journal of Applied Language Studies, 1,* 60–68.
Bahan, B. (1992). American Sign Language literature: Inside the story. In *Deaf studies: What's up? Conference proceedings* (pp. 153–164). Washington, DC: College for Continuing Education, Gallaudet University.
Bailey, G., & Maynor, N. (1987). Decreolization? *Language in Society, 16,* 449–473.
Bailey, G., & Maynor, N. (1989). The divergence controversy. *American Speech, 64,* 12–39.
Baker, C., & Battison, R. (Eds.). (1980). *Sign language and the deaf community: Essays in honor of William C. Stokoe.* Silver Spring, MD: National Association of the Deaf.
Baldauf, R. (1993). Fostering bilingualism and national development through school second language study. *Journal of Multilingual and Multicultural Development, 14,* 121–134.
Ball, R. (1997). *The French-speaking world: A practical introduction to sociolinguistic issues.* London: Routledge.
Ball, S. (Ed.). (1990). *Foucault and education: Disciplines and knowledge.* London: Routledge.
Bamgbose, A., Banjo, A., & Thomas, A. (Eds.). (1997). *New Englishes: A West African perspective.* Trenton, NJ: Africa World Press.
Banks, J. (1994). *An introduction to multicultural education.* Boston: Allyn & Bacon.
Barkhuizen, G., & Gough, D. (1996). Language curriculum development in South Africa: What place for English? *TESOL Quarterly, 30,* 453–471.
Baron, D. (1981). *Going native: The regeneration of Saxon English* (American Dialect Society, No. 69). University: University of Alabama Press.
Baron, D. (1982). *Grammar and good taste: Reforming the American language.* New Haven, CT: Yale University Press.
Baron, D. (1990). *The English-only question: An official language for Americans?* New Haven, CT: Yale University Press.
Barrow, R., & Woods, R. (1988). *An introduction to philosophy of education* (3rd ed.). London: Routledge.
Bartlett, L. (1990). Teacher development through reflective teaching. In J. Richards & D. Nunan (Eds.), *Second language teacher education* (pp. 202–214). Cambridge, England: Cambridge University Press.
Bartolomé, L. (1998). *The misteaching of academic discourses: The politics of language in the classroom.* Boulder, CO: Westview Press.
Barzun, J. (1954). *Teacher in America.* Garden City, NY: Doubleday.
Baugh, J. (1983). *Black street speech: Its history, structure and survival.* Austin: University of Texas Press.
Baugh, J. (1988). Review of *Twice as less: Harvard Educational Review, 58,* 395–404.
Baynton, D. (1996). *Forbidden signs: American culture and the campaign against sign language.* Chicago: University of Chicago Press.
Beardsmore, H. (1993a). European models of bilingual education: Practice, theory and development. *Journal of Multilingual and Multicultural Development, 14,* 103–120.

# REFERENCES

Beardsmore, H. (Ed.). (1993b). *European models of bilingual education.* Clevedon, UK: Multilingual Matters.
Beer, W., & Jacob, J. (Eds.). (1985). *Language policy and national unity.* Totowa, NJ: Rowman & Allanheld.
Belka, R. (2000). Is American Sign Language a 'foreign' language? *Northeast Conference on the Teaching of Foreign Languages Review, 48,* 45–52.
Benesch, S. (2001). *Critical English for academic purposes: Theory, politics, and practice.* Mahwah, NJ: Lawrence Erlbaum Associates.
Bennet, J. (1996, December 25). Administration rejects Black English as a second language. *The New York Times,* p. A-22.
Benseler, D., Lohnes, W., & Nollendorfs, V. (Eds.). (1988). *Teaching German in America: Prolegomena to a history.* Madison: University of Wisconsin Press.
Benson, P., Grundy, P., Itakura, H., & Skutnabb-Kangas, T. (Eds.). (in press). *Access to language rights.* Amsterdam: John Benjamins.
Berliner, D. (1986). In pursuit of the expert pedagogue. *Educational Researcher, 15,* 5–13.
Beukes, A. (1991a). Language teaching and the politics of language. *Journal for Language Teaching, 25,* 89–100.
Beukes, A. (1991b). The politics of language in formal education: The position of Afrikaans. *Journal for Language Teaching, 25,* 64–78.
Beukes, A. (1992). Moedertaalonderrig in 'n demokratiese Suid-Afrika. [Mother tongue instruction in a democratic South Africa.] *Per Linguam, 8,* 42–51.
Beukes, A. (1996). New horizons in language laws and language rights: Multilingualism in the new South Africa. In *XIV World Congress of the Fédération Internationale des Traducteurs Proceedings* (Vol. 2, pp. 609–622). Melbourne, Australia: The Australian Institute of Interpreters and Translators.
Beukes, A., & Barnard, M. (Eds.). (1994). *Proceedings of the 'Languages for All' Conference: Towards a Pan South African language board.* Pretoria, South Africa: CSIR Conference Centre.
Beyer, L., & Apple, M. (Eds.). (1988). *The curriculum: Problems, politics and possibilities.* Albany: State University of New York Press.
Bezberezhyeva, Y. (1998). My language is not my enemy. In *Estonia and Russia: More cheese from New Zealand?* (EuroUniversity Series, International Relations, Vol. 1, pp. 31–32). Tallinn, Estonia: The Olof Palme International Center, The EuroUniversity, and the Institute of International and Social Studies.
Biron, C. (1998). Bringing the standards to life: Points of departure. *Foreign Language Annals, 31,* 584–594.
Blackledge, A. (2000). *Literacy, power and social justice.* Stoke on Trent, Staffordshire, England: Trentham.
Blommaert, J. (1996). Language planning as a discourse on language and society: The linguistic ideology of a scholarly tradition. *Language Problems and Language Planning, 20,* 199–222.
Blyth, C. (1997). A constructivist approach to grammar: Teaching teachers to teach aspect. *The Modern Language Journal, 81,* 50–66.
Boseker, B. (1994). The disappearance of American Indian languages. *Journal of Multilingual and Multicultural Development, 15,* 147–160.
Boulter, C. (1997). Discourse and conceptual understanding in science. In B. Davies & D. Corson (Eds.), *Encyclopedia of language and education, Vol. 3: Oral discourse and education* (pp. 239–248). Dordrecht, Netherlands: Kluwer.
Bourdieu, P., Passeron, J., & de Saint Martin, M. (1994). *Academic discourse.* Stanford, CA: Stanford University Press.
Bouvet, D. (1990). *The path to language: Bilingual education for deaf children.* Clevedon, UK: Multilingual Matters.
Bowers, C., & Flinders, D. (1990). *Responsive teaching: An ecological approach to classroom patterns of language, culture, and thought.* New York: Teachers College Press.

# REFERENCES

Brady, J., & Kanpol, B. (2000). The role of critical multicultural education and feminist critical thought in teacher education: Putting theory into practice. *Educational Foundations, 14*, 39–50.

Bragg, L. (Ed.). (2001). *DEAF WORLD: A historical reader and primary sourcebook*. New York: New York University Press.

Braine, G. (Ed.). (1999). *Non-native educators in English language teaching*. Mahwah, NJ: Lawrence Erlbaum Associates.

Branson, J., & Miller, D. (1993). Sign language, the deaf and the epistemic violence of mainstreaming. *Language and Education, 7*, 21–41.

Branson, J., & Miller, D. (1998). Achieving human rights: Educating deaf immigrant students from non-English-speaking families in Australia. In A. Weisel (Ed.) *Issues unresolved* (pp. 88–100). Washington, DC: Gallaudet University Press.

Brecht, R., & Walton, A. (1994). National strategic planning in the less commonly taught languages. In R. Lambert (Ed.), *Foreign language policy* (pp. 190–212). Thousand Oaks, CA: Sage.

Brink, A. (1984). The future of Afrikaans. *Leadership SA, 3*, 29–36.

Brosh, H. (1993). The influence of language status on language acquisition: Arabic in the Israeli setting. *Foreign Language Annals, 26*, 347–358.

Brosh, H. (1997). The sociocultural message of language textbooks: Arabic in the Israeli setting. *Foreign Language Annals, 30*, 311–326.

Bullivant, B. (1981). *The pluralist dilemma in education: Six case studies*. Sydney, Australia: George Allen & Unwin.

Burling, R. (1973). *English in black and white*. New York: Holt, Rinehart and Winston.

Butters, R. (1989). *The death of Black English: Divergence and convergence in black and white vernaculars*. Frankfort, Germany: Peter Lang.

Byrnes, D., Kiger, G., & Manning, M. (1997). Teachers' attitudes about language diversity. *Teaching and Teacher Education, 13*, 637–644.

California State University. (1987). *CSU School and College Review* 6, special edition on Freshman Admissions.

Cameron, D. (1995). *Verbal hygiene*. London: Routledge.

Campbell, G. (1995). *Concise compendium of the world's languages*. London: Routledge.

Case, C., Lanier, J., & Miskel, C. (1986). The Holmes Group report: Impetus for gaining professional status for teachers. *Journal of Teacher Education, 37*, 36–43.

Cenoz, J., & Genesee, F. (Eds.). (1998). *Beyond bilingualism: Multilingualism and multilingual education*. Clevedon, UK: Multilingual Matters.

Chambers, J. (Ed.). (1983). *Black English: Educational equity and the law*. Ann Arbor, MI: Karoma.

Chambers, J., & Trudgill, P. (1980). *Dialectology*. Cambridge, England: Cambridge University Press.

Chambliss, J. (1987). *Educational theory as theory of conduct*. Albany: State University of New York Press.

Chastain, K. (1976). *Developing second-language skills: Theory to practice* (2nd ed.). Chicago: Rand McNally.

Chen, P. (1999). *Modern Chinese: History and sociolinguistics*. Cambridge, England: Cambridge University Press.

Chick, J. (1992). Language policy in education. In R. McGregor & A. McGregor (Eds.), *McGregor's education alternatives* (pp. 271–292). Kenwyn, South Africa: Juta.

Chick, J., & Wade, R. (1997). Restandardisation in the direction of a new English: Implications for access and equity. *Journal of Multilingual and Multicultural Development, 18*, 271–284.

Chisanga, T., & Kamwangamalu, N. (1997). Owning the other tongue: The English language in Southern Africa. *Journal of Multilingual and Multicultural Development, 18*, 89–99.

Chomsky, N. (1988). *Language and problems of knowledge: The Managua lectures*. Cambridge, MA: MIT Press.

# REFERENCES

Christian, D. (1988). Language planning: The view from linguistics. In F. Newmeyer (Ed.), *Linguistics: The Cambridge survey* (Vol. 4, pp. 193–209). Cambridge, England: Cambridge University Press.

Christison, M. (1998). An introduction to multiple intelligence theory and second language learning. In J. Reid (Ed.), *Understanding learning styles in the second language classroom* (pp. 1–14). Upper Saddle River, NJ: Prentice-Hall.

Clachar, A. (1998). Differential effects of linguistic imperialism on second language learning: Americanisation in Puerto Rico versus Russification in Estonia. *International Journal of Bilingual Education and Bilingualism, 1*, 100–118.

Cleary, L., & Linn, M. (Eds.). (1993). *Linguistics for teachers.* New York: McGraw-Hill.

Cluver, A. (1992). Language planning models for a post-apartheid South Africa. *Language Problems and Language Planning, 16*, 105–136.

Cluver, A. (1993a). The decline of Afrikaans. *Language Matters: Studies in the Languages of Southern Africa, 24*, 15–46.

Cluver, A. (1993b). *A dictionary of language planning terms.* Pretoria, South Africa: University of South Africa.

Clyne, M., Fernandez, S., Chen, I., & Summo-O'Connell, R. (1997). *Background speakers: Diversity and its management in LOTE programs.* Belconnen, Australia: Language Australia.

Cobarrubias, J. (1983a). Ethical issues in status planning. In J. Cobarrubias & J. Fishman (Eds.), *Progress in language planning* (pp. 41–85). Berlin: Mouton.

Cobarrubias, J. (1983b). Language planning: The state of the art. In J. Cobarrubias & J. Fishman (Eds.), *Progress in language planning* (pp. 3–26). Berlin: Mouton.

Cobarrubias, J., & Fishman, J. (Eds.). (1983). *Progress in language planning: International perspectives.* Berlin: Mouton.

Cobb, P. (1994). Where is the mind? Constructivist and socioculturalist perspectives on mathematical development. *Educational Researcher, 23*, 13–20.

Cobb, P. (1996). Where is the mind? A coordination of sociocultural and cognitive constructionist perspectives. In C. Fosnot (Ed.), *Constructivism* (pp. 34–52). New York: Teacher's College Press.

Cobern, W. (1993). Contextual constructivism: The impact of culture on the learning and teaching of science. In K. Tobin (Ed.), *The practice of constructivism in science education* (pp. 51–69). Hillsdale, NJ: Lawrence Erlbaum Associates.

Cohen, H. (2000). A farewell to Esperanto? *Lingua Franca (May/June)*, 57–62.

Cohen, L. (1994). *Train go sorry: Inside a deaf world.* Boston: Houghton Mifflin.

Collier, V. (1987). Age and rate of acquisition of second language for academic purposes. *TESOL Quarterly, 21*, 617–641.

Collier, V. (1989). How long? A synthesis of research on academic achievement in a second language. *TESOL Quarterly, 23*, 509–531.

Combrink, J. (1991). Die toekomstige status en funksies van Afrikaans. [The future status and functions of Afrikaans.] *Tydskrif vir Geesteswetenskappe, 31*, 101–112.

Commins, P. (1988). Socioeconomic development and language maintenance in the Gaeltacht. In P. Ó Riagáin (Ed.), *Language planning in Ireland* (pp. 11–28). Berlin, Germany: deGruyter.

Condon, M., Clyde, J., Kyle, D., & Hovda, R. (1993). A constructivist basis for teaching and teacher education: A framework for program development and research on graduates. *Journal of Teacher Education, 44*, 273–278.

Confrey, J. (1995). How compatible are radical constructivism, sociocultural approaches, and social constructivism? In L. Steffe & J. Gale (Eds.), *Constructivism in education* (pp. 185–225). Hillsdale, NJ: Lawrence Erlbaum Associates.

Connelly, F., & Clandinin, D. (1990). Stories of experience and narrative inquiry. *Educational Researcher, 19*, 2–14.

Constitutional Assembly. (1997). *The constitution of the Republic of South Africa, 1996: Annotated version.* Wynburg, South Africa: Author.

Coolahan, J. (1981). *Irish education: History and structure*. Dublin, Ireland: Institute of Public Administration.
Cooper, D. (1975). *Knowledge of language*. New York: Humanities Press.
Cooper, J. (Ed.). (1990). *Classroom teaching skills* (4th ed.). Lexington, MA: Heath.
Cooper, J. (1993). *Literacy: Helping children construct meaning* (2nd ed.). Boston: Houghton Mifflin.
Cooper, R. (1989). *Language planning and social change*. Cambridge, England: Cambridge University Press.
Co-ordinating Committee on the National Action Plan. (1998). *The National Action Plan for the Promotion and Protection of Human Rights*. Houghton, South Africa: Author.
Corson, D. (1999). *Language policy in schools: A resource for teachers and administrators*. Mahwah, NJ: Lawrence Erlbaum Associates.
Corson, D. (2001). *Language diversity and education*. Mahwah, NJ: Lawrence Erlbaum Associates.
Coulombe, P. (1993). Language rights, individual and communal. *Language Problems and Language Planning, 17*, 140–152.
Craig, B. (1995). Boundary discourse and the authority of language in the second-language classroom: A social-constructionist approach. In J. Alatis, C. Straehle, B. Gallenberger, & M. Ronkin (Eds.), *Georgetown University round table on languages and linguistics 1995: Linguistics and the education of language teachers* (pp. 40–54). Washington, DC: Georgetown University Press.
Crawford, J. (1992a). *Hold your tongue: Bilingualism and the politics of 'English only.'* Reading, MA: Addison-Wesley.
Crawford, J. (Ed.). (1992b). *Language loyalties: A source book on the official English controversy*. Chicago: University of Chicago Press.
Crawford, J. (2000). *At war with diversity: U.S. language policy in an age of anxiety*. Clevedon, UK: Multilingual Matters.
Crookall, D., & Oxford, R. (1988). Review essay. *Language Learning, 31*, 128–140.
Crystal, D. (1991). *A dictionary of linguistics and phonetics* (3rd ed.). Oxford, England: Basil Blackwell.
Crystal, D. (2000). *Language death*. Cambridge, England: Cambridge University Press.
Cummins, J. (1980). The construct of language proficiency in bilingual education. In J. Alatis (Ed.), *Georgetown University round table on languages and linguistics: Issues in bilingual education* (pp. 81–103). Washington, DC: Georgetown University Press.
Cummins, J. (1981). Age on arrival and immigrant second language learning in Canada: A reassessment. *Applied Linguistics, 2*, 132–149.
Cummins, J. (1984). *Bilingualism and special education*. Clevedon, UK: Multilingual Matters.
Cummins, J. (1994). Knowledge, power, and identity in teaching English as a second language. In F. Genesee (Ed.), *Educating second language children* (pp. 33–58). Cambridge, England: Cambridge University Press.
Curriculum and Examinations Board. (1985). *Language in the curriculum: A Curriculum and Examinations Board Discussion Paper/Teanga Sa Churaclam: Pléphápéar ón mBord Curaclaim agus Scrúduithe*. Dublin, Ireland: The Curriculum and Examinations Board.
Curtain, H., & Pesola, C. (1994). *Languages and children, making the match: Foreign language instruction for an early start, grades K-8* (2nd ed.). White Plains, NY: Longman.
Davis, R., Maher, C. & Noddings, N. (Eds.). (1990). *Constructivist views on the teaching and learning of mathematics*. Reston, VA: National Council of Teachers of Mathematics.
Davison, D., Miller, K., & Methany, D. (1995). What does integration of science and mathematics really mean? *School Science and Mathematics, 95*, 226–230.
Degenaar, J. (1987). Nationalism, liberalism, and pluralism. In J. Butler, R. Elphick, & D. Walsh (Eds.), *Liberalism in South Africa* (pp. 236–249). Cape Town, South Africa: David Philip.
de Kadt, E. (1996). Language and apartheid: The power of minorities. *Alternation: Journal of the Centre for the Study of Southern Africa, 3*, 184–194.

# REFERENCES

de Klerk, V., & Barkhuizen, G. (1998). Language policy in the SANDF: A case of biting the bullet? *Language Problems and Language Planning, 22*, 215–236.
Demos, J. (1970). *A little commonwealth: Family life in Plymouth Colony.* New York: Oxford University Press.
Department of Arts, Culture, Science, and Technology. (1997). *Standardising the designation of government departments* (Language Planning Report #5.5). Pretoria, South Africa: Government Printer.
Department of Arts, Culture, Science, and Technology. (1999). *Marketing linguistic human rights* (Language Planning Report #5.7). Pretoria, South Africa: Government Printer.
Department of Education and Culture, House of Assembly. (1992). *An investigation into the position of French and German in the Republic of South Africa.* Pretoria, South Africa: Government Printer.
Department of National Education. (1997). *South Africa's new language policy: The facts.* Pretoria, South Africa: Government Printer.
Desai, Z. (1991). Democratic language planning and the transformation of education in post-apartheid South Africa. In E. Unterhalter, H. Wolpe, & T. Botha (Eds.), *Education in a future South Africa* (pp. 112–122). Houghton, South Africa: Heinemann.
Desai, Z. (1994). Praat or speak but don't theta: On language rights in South Africa. In D. Barton (Ed.), *Sustaining local literacies* (pp. 19–29). Clevedon, UK: Multilingual Matters.
DeStefano, J. (Ed.). (1973). *Language, society and education: A profile of Black English.* Worthington, OH: Charles A. Jones.
Dewey, J. (1910). *How we think.* Boston: Heath.
Dewey, J. (1933). *How we think: A restatement of the relations of reflective thinking to the educative process* (2nd Rev. ed.). Lexington, MA: Heath.
Dewey, J. (1938). *Logic: The theory of inquiry.* New York: Henry Holt.
Dewey, J. (1943). *The child and the curriculum / The school and society.* Chicago: University of Chicago Press. (Original works published in 1902 and 1900)
Dewey, J. (1976). The relationship of thought and its subject matter. Reprinted in J. Boydston (Ed.), *John Dewey: The middle works, Vol. 2 (1902–1903)* (pp. 298–315). Carbondale, IL: Southern Illinois University Press. (Original work published 1903)
Dewey, J. (2000). My pedagogic creed. Reprinted in R. Reed & T. Johnson (Eds.), *Philosophical documents in education* (2nd ed.; pp. 92–100). New York: Longman. (Original work published 1897)
Dicker, S. (1996). *Languages in America: A pluralistic view.* Clevedon, UK: Multilingual Matters.
Dillard, J. (1972). *Black English: Its history and usage in the United States.* New York: Vintage.
Dillard, J. (Ed.). (1975). *Perspectives on Black English.* The Hague, Netherlands: Mouton.
Djité, P. (1990). Les langues africaines dans la nouvelle francophonie. [The African languages in the new francophonie.] *Language Problems and Language Planning, 14*, 20–32.
Djité, P. (1991). Langues et développement en Afrique. [Languages and development in Africa.] *Language Problems and Language Planning, 15*, 121–138.
Dogançay-Aktuna, S. (1995). An evaluation of the Turkish language reform after 60 years. *Language Problems and Language Planning, 19*, 221–249.
Donna, S. (2000). *Teach business English.* Cambridge, England: Cambridge University Press.
Dorian, N. (1988). The Celtic languages in the British Isles. In C. Paulston (Ed.), *International handbook of bilingualism and bilingual education* (pp. 109–139). New York: Greenwood.
Dowling, T. (1998). *Speak Xhosa with us/Thetha isiXhosa Nathi* [CD-ROM program.] Cape Town, South Africa: Mother Tongues Multimedia Development, in association with the University of Cape Town Multimedia Education Project.
Driver, R., Asoko, H., Leach, J., Mortimer, E., & Scott, P. (1994). Constructing scientific knowledge in the classroom. *Educational Researcher, 23*, 5–12.
Duffy, T., & Jonassen, D. (Eds.). (1992). *Constructivism and the technology of instruction: A conversation.* Hillsdale, NJ: Lawrence Erlbaum Associates.
Eastman, C. (1983). *Language planning: An introduction.* San Francisco, CA: Chandler & Sharp.

Eco, U. (1995). *The search for the perfect language.* Oxford, Englanc: Basil Blackwell.
Edmondson, W., & Karlsson, F. (Eds.). (1990). *SLR '87: Papers from the Fourth International Symposium on sign language research.* Hamburg, Germany: Signum Press.
Edwards, J. (1984a). Irish: Planning and preservation. *Journal of Multilingual and Multicultural Development, 5,* 267–275.
Edwards, J. (1984b). Irish and English in Ireland. In P. Trudgill (Ed.), *Language in the British Isles* (pp. 480–498). Cambridge, England: Cambridge University Press.
Edwards, J. (Ed.). (1984c). *Linguistic minorities, policies and pluralism.* London: Academic Press.
Edwards, J. (1985). *Language, society and identity.* Oxford, England: Basil Blackwell.
Edwards, J. (1986). Did English murder Irish? *English Today, 6,* 7–10.
Edwards, J. (1994). *Multilingualism.* London: Routledge.
Edwards, J., & MacPherson, L. (1987). Views of constructed languages, with special reference to Esperanto: An experimental study. *Language Problems and Language Planning, 11,* 283–304.
Elgin, S. (2000). *The language imperative.* Cambridge, MA: Perseus Books.
Emenanjo, E. (Ed.). (1990). *Multilingualism, minority languages and language policy in Nigeria.* Agbor, Nigeria: Center Books, in collaboration with the Linguistic Association of Nigeria.
Emmorey, K., & Reilly, J. (Eds.). (1995). *Language, gesture, and space.* Hillsdale, NJ: Lawrence Erlbaum Associates.
Everson, M. (1993). Research in the less commonly taught languages. In A. O. Hadley (Ed.), *Research in language learning* (pp. 198–228). Lincolnwood, IL: National Textbook Company, in conjunction with the American Council on the Teaching of Foreign Languages.
Fairclough, N. (1989). *Language and power.* New York: Longman.
Fairclough, N. (Ed.). (1992). *Critical language awareness.* New York: Longman.
Fairclough, N. (1995). *Critical discourse analysis: The critical study of language.* New York: Longman.
Faltis, C. (1997). Bilingual education in the United States. In J. Cummins & D. Corson (Eds.), *Encyclopedia of language and education, Vol. 5: Bilingual education* (pp. 189–197). Dordrecht, Netherlands: Kluwer.
Fantini, A., & Reagan, T. (1992). *Esperanto and education: Toward a research agenda.* Washington, DC: Esperantic Studies Foundation.
Fensham, P., Gunstone, R., & White, R. (Eds.). (1994). *The content of science: A constructivist approach to its teaching and learning.* London: Falmer Press.
Fettes, M. (1992). *A guide to language strategies for First Nations communities.* Ottawa, Canada: Assembly of First Nations.
Fettes, M. (1994). Linguistic rights in Canada: Collisions or collusions? A conference report. *Bulletin of the Canadian Centre for Linguistic Rights, 1,* 18–20.
Fettes, M. (1998). Life on the edge: Canada's aboriginal languages under official bilingualism. In T. Ricento & B. Burnaby (Eds.), *Language and politics in the United States and Canada* (pp. 117–149). Mahwah, NJ: Lawrence Erlbaum Associates.
Finchilescu, G., & Nyawose, G. (1998). Talking about language: Zulu students' views on language in the new South Africa. *South African Journal of Psychology, 28,* 53–61.
Fischer, R., & Lane, H. (Eds.). (1993). *Looking back: A reader on the history of deaf communities and their sign languages.* Hamburg, Germany: Signum Press.
Fischer, S., & Siple, S. (Eds.). (1990). *Theoretical issues in sign language research: Vol. 1, Linguistics.* Chicago: University of Chicago Press.
Fishman, J. (1991). *Reversing language shift: Theoretical and empirical foundations of assistance to threatened languages.* Clevedon, UK: Multilingual Matters.
Fitzgibbons, R. (1981). *Making educational decisions: An introduction to philosophy of education.* New York: Harcourt Brace.
Fodor, I., & Hagege, C. (Eds.). (1983/4). *Language reform: History and future, Vols. 1-3.* Hamburg, Germany: Buske Verlag.

# REFERENCES

Fodor, I., & Hagege, C. (Eds.). (1990). *Language reform: History and future, Vol. 5.* Hamburg, Germany: Buske Verlag.
Forman, G., & Pufall, P. (Eds.). (1988). *Constructivism in the computer age.* Hillsdale, NJ: Lawrence Erlbaum Associates.
Forster, P. (1982). *The Esperanto movement.* The Hague, Netherlands: Mouton.
Forster, P. (1987). Some social sources of resistance to Esperanto. In *Serta Gratvlatoria in Honorem Juan Régulo, II (Esperantismo;* pp. 203–211). La Laguna: University de La Laguna.
Fosnot, C. (1989). *Enquiring teachers, enquiring learners: A constructivist approach to teaching.* New York: Teacher's College Press.
Fosnot, C. (1993). Preface. In J. G. Brooks & M. Brooks (Eds.), *The case for constructivist classrooms* (pp. vii–viii). Alexandria, VA: Association for Supervision and Curriculum Development.
Fosnot, C. (Ed.). (1996a). *Constructivism: Theory, perspectives, and practice.* New York: Teacher's College Press.
Fosnot, C. (1996b). Constructivism: A psychological theory of learning. In C. Fosnot (Ed.), *Constructivism* (pp. 8–33). New York: Teacher's College Press.
Frank, H. (1987). Propedeutika valoro de la internacia lingvo. [The propedeutic value of the international language.] In *Serta Gratvlatoria in Honorem Juan Reglo, II (Esperantismo;* pp. 213–222). La Laguna: University de La Laguna.
Franklin, P., Laurence, D., & Welles, E. (Eds.). (1999). *Preparing a nation's teachers: Models for English and foreign language programs.* New York: Modern Language Association of America.
Frawley, W. (1997). *Vygotsky and cognitive science: Language and the unification of the social and computational mind.* Cambridge, MA: Harvard University Press.
Freire, P. (1973). *Education for critical consciousness.* New York: Seabury Press.
Freire, P. (1974). *Pedagogy of the oppressed.* New York: Seabury Press.
Freire, P. (2000). From *Pedagogy of the oppressed.* In R. Reed & T. Johnson (Eds.), *Philosophical documents in education* (2nd ed.; pp. 188–198). New York: Longman. (Original work published 1972)
Frishberg, N. (1988). Signers of tales: The case for literary status of an unwritten language. *Sign Language Studies, 59,* 149–170.
Fromkin, V., & Rodman, R. (1993). *An introduction to language* (5th ed.). Fort Worth, TX: Harcourt Brace Jovanovich.
Gaganakis, M. (1992). Language and ethnic group relations in non-racial schools. *English Academy Review, 9,* 46–55.
Gardner, H. (1983). *Frames of mind: The theory of multiple intelligences.* New York: Basic Books.
Gardner, H. (1991). *The unschooled mind: How children think and how schools should teach.* New York: Basic Books.
Gardner, H. (1993). *Multiple intelligences: The theory in practice.* New York: Basic Books.
Gardner, R. (1985). *Social psychology and language learning: The role of attitudes and motivation.* London: Edward Arnold.
Gee, J. (1996). *Social linguistics and literacies: Ideology in discourse* (2nd ed.). London: Taylor & Francis.
Gehlker, M., Gozzi, M., & Zeller, I. (1999). Teaching the Holocaust in the foreign language classroom. *Northeast Conference on the Teaching of Foreign Languages Review, 46,* 20–29.
Genesee, F. (1988). The Canadian second language immersion program. In C. Paulston (Ed.), *International handbook of bilingualism and bilingual education* (pp. 163–183). New York: Greenwood.
Gergen, K. (1982). *Towards transformation in social knowledge.* New York: Springer-Verlag.
Gergen, K. (1995). Social construction and the educational process. In L. Steffe & J. Gale (Eds.), *Constructivism in education* (pp. 17–39). Hillsdale, NJ: Lawrence Erlbaum Associates.

Gerwin, D., & Osborn, T. (in press). Challenging the monovocal narrative: Interdisciplinary units in the foreign language classroom. In T. Osborn (Ed.), *The future of foreign language education in the United States.* Westport, CT: Bergin and Garvey.

Giroux, H. (Ed.). (1991). *Postmodernism, feminism, and cultural politics: Redrawing educational boundaries.* Albany, NY: State University of New York Press.

Giroux, H. (1992a). *Border crossings: Cultural workers and the politics of education.* New York: Routledge.

Giroux, H. (1992b). Educational leadership and the crisis of democratic government. *Educational Researcher, 21,* 8–11.

Giroux, H. (1994). Doing cultural studies: Youth and the challenge of pedagogy. *Harvard Educational Review, 64,* 278–308.

Giroux, H. (1997a). *Pedagogy and the politics of hope: Theory, culture and schooling.* Boulder, CO: Westview Press.

Giroux, H. (1997b). Rewriting the discourse of racial identity: Toward a pedagogy and politics of whiteness. *Harvard Educational Review, 67,* 285–320.

Glenny, M. (1996). *The fall of Yugoslavia: The Third Balkan War* (3rd ed.). New York: Penguin.

Glossop, R. (1988). International child-to-child correspondence using Esperanto. *Gifted International, 5,* 81–84.

Gollnick, D., & Chinn, P. (1994). *Multicultural education in a pluralistic society* (4th ed.). New York: Merrill.

Gomes de Matos, F. (1985). The linguistic rights of language learners. *Language Planning Newsletter, 11,* 1–2.

González, R., & Melis, I. (Eds.). (2001a). *Language ideologies: Critical perspectives on the official English movement, Vol. I, Education and the social implications of official language.* Mahwah, NJ: Lawrence Erlbaum Associates.

González, R., & Melis, I. (Eds.). (2001b). *Language ideologies: Critical perspectives on the official English movement, Vol. II, History, theory, and policy.* Mahwah, NJ: Lawrence Erlbaum Associates.

Goodlad, J. (1994). *Educational renewal: Better teachers, better schools.* San Francisco, CA: Jossey-Bass.

Goodlad, J. (1997). *In praise of education.* New York: Teacher's College Press.

Goodman, N. (1992). *Introduction to sociology.* New York: HarperPerennial.

Goodman, T. (1978). Esperanto: Threat or ally? *Foreign Language Annals, 11,* 201–203.

Goswami, D., & Stillman, P. (Eds.). (1987). *Reclaiming the classroom: Teacher research as an agency for change.* Portsmouth, NH: Heinemann.

Green, T. (1971). *The activities of teaching.* New York: McGraw-Hill.

Gregor, D. (1976). Der kulturelle Welt des Esperanto. [The cultural world of Esperanto.] In R. Haupenthal (Ed.), *Plansprachen* (pp. 297–304). Darmstad, Germany: Wissenschaftliche Buchgesellschaft.

Gregory, S. (1992). The language and culture of deaf people: Implications for education. *Language and Education, 6,* 183–197.

Gregory, S., & Hartley, G. (Eds.). (1991). *Constructing deafness.* London: Pinter Publishers, in association with the Open University.

Grennon Brooks, J., & Brooks, M. (1993). *The case for constructivist classrooms.* Alexandria, VA: Association for Supervision and Curriculum Development.

Grenoble, L., & Whaley, L. (Eds.). (1998). *Endangered languages: Current issues and future prospects.* Cambridge, England: Cambridge University Press.

Gruenais, M. (1986). Irish-English: No model; a case. *Language Problems and Language Planning, 10,* 272–281.

Guérard, A. (1922). *A short history of the international language movement.* London: T. F. Unwin.

Gunnarsson, B. (1997). Language for special purposes. In G. Tucker & D. Corson (Eds.), *Encyclopedia of language and education, Vol. 4: Second language education* (pp. 105–117). Dordrecht, Netherlands: Kluwer.

# REFERENCES

Gunnarsson, B., Linell, P., & Nordberg, B. (Eds.). (1997). *The construction of professional discourse.* New York: Longman.
Guntermann, G. (Ed.). (1993). *Developing language teachers for a changing world.* Lincolnwood, IL: National Textbook Company, in conjunction with the American Council on the Teaching of Foreign Languages.
Gutman, A. (1987). *Democratic education.* Princeton: Princeton University Press.
Hadley, A. (1993). *Teaching language in context* (2nd ed.). Boston: Heinle & Heinle.
Hale, T. (1999). Francophone African literature and the hexagon: Building bridges for the new millennium. *The French Review, 72,* 444–455.
Hamel, E. (1995a). Indigenous education in Latin America: Policies and legal frameworks. In T. Skutnabb-Kangas & R. Phillipson (Eds.), *Linguistic human rights* (pp. 271–287). Berlin, Germany: deGruyter.
Hamel, E. (1995b). Linguistic rights for Amerindian peoples in Latin America. In T. Skutnabb-Kangas & R. Phillipson (Eds.), *Linguistic human rights* (pp. 289–303). Berlin, Germany: deGruyter.
Hamm, C. (1989). *Philosophical issues in education: An introduction.* New York: Falmer Press.
Harries, L. (1983). The nationalisation of Swahili in Kenya. In C. Kennedy (Ed.), *Language planning and language education* (pp. 118–128). London: George Allen & Unwin.
Hartshorne, K. (1987). Language policy in African education in South Africa, 1910–1985, with particular reference to the issue of medium of instruction. In D. Young (Ed.), *Bridging the gap between theory and practice in English second language teaching* (pp. 62–81). Cape Town, South Africa: Maskew Miller Longman.
Hartshorne, K. (1992). *Crisis and challenge: Black education, 1910–1990.* Cape Town, South Africa: Oxford University Press.
Haugen, E. (1966). *Language conflict and language planning: The case of modern Norwegian.* Cambridge, MA: Harvard University Press.
Hawkesworth, C. (1998). *Colloquial Croatian and Serbian: The complete course for beginners.* London: Routledge.
Heath, S. (1983). *Ways with words: Language, life, and work in communities and classrooms.* Cambridge, England: Cambridge University Press.
Hechter, M. (1975). *Internal colonialism: The Celtic fringe in British national development, 1536–1966.* Berkeley, CA: University of California Press.
Henning, E. (1995). Problematising the discourse of classroom management from the view of social constructivism. *South African Journal of Education, 15,* 124–129.
Hernandez, R. (1996, December 26). Never mind teaching Ebonics: Teach proper English. *The Hartford Courant,* p. A-21.
Hernández-Chávez, E. (1995). Language policy in the United States: A history of cultural genocide. In T. Skutnabb-Kangas & R. Phillipson (Eds.), *Linguistic human rights* (pp. 141–158). Berlin, Germany: deGruyter.
Herriman, M., & Burnaby, B. (Eds.). (1996). *Language policies in English-dominant countries.* Clevedon, UK: Multilingual Matters.
Heugh, K. (1985). The relationship between nationalism and language in education in the South African context. In D. Young (Ed.), *UCT papers in language education* (pp. 35–70). Cape Town, South Africa: University of Cape Town, Language Education Unit, Department of Education.
Heugh, K. (1987a). Trends in language medium policy for a post-apartheid South Africa. In D. Young (Ed.), *Language: Planning and medium in education* (pp. 206–220). Rondebosch, South Africa: Language Education Unit (UCT) and SAALA.
Heugh, K. (1987b). *Underlying ideology of language medium policies in multilingual societies.* Unpublished Master's Phil. thesis, University of Cape Town, South Africa.
Heugh, K. (1993). The place of English in relation to other languages in South Africa. *Per Linguam, 9,* 210.
Heugh, K. (1995). Disabling and enabling: Implications of language policy trends in South Africa. In R. Mesthrie (Ed.), *Language and social history* (pp. 329–350). Cape Town, South Africa: David Philip.

Heugh, K., Siegrühn, A., & Plüddemann, P. (Eds.). (1995). *Multilingual education for South Africa.* Johannesburg: Heinemann.
Hindley, R. (1990). *The death of the Irish language.* London: Routledge.
Hinnebusch, T. (1979). Swahili. In T. Shopen (Ed.), *Languages and their status* (pp. 209–293). Philadelphia: University of Pennsylvania Press.
Hirst, P. (1974). *Knowledge and the curriculum.* London: Routledge & Kegan Paul.
Hitler, A. (1940). *Mein Kampf: Complete and unabridged.* New York: Reynal & Hitchcock.
Hoffmeister, R. (1990). ASL and its implications for education. In H. Bornstein (Ed.), *Manual communication* (pp. 81–107). Washington, DC: Gallaudet University Press.
Holborow, M. (1999). *The politics of English: A Marxist view of language.* London: Sage.
Holmes, S. (1996, December 30). Voice of inner city streets is defended and criticized. *The New York Times,* A-9.
Hornberger, N. (1999). Maintaining and revitalising indigenous languages in Latin America: State planning vs. grassroots initiatives. *International Journal of Bilingual Education and Bilingualism, 2,* 159–165.
Howard, G. (1996). Whites in multicultural education: Rethinking our role. In J. Banks (Ed.), *Multicultural education, transformative knowledge, and action: Historical and contemporary perspectives* (pp. 323–334). New York: Teacher's College Press.
Hudson, R. (1996). *Sociolinguistics* (2nd ed.). Cambridge, England: Cambridge University Press.
Hudson-Edwards, A. (1990). Language policy and linguistic toleration in Ireland. In K. Adams & D. Brink (Eds.), *Perspectives on official English* (pp. 63–81). Berlin, Germany: deGruyter.
Hymes, D. (1996). *Ethnography, linguistics, narrative inequality: Toward an understanding of voice.* London: Taylor and Francis.
Irwin, J. (1987). *What is a reflective–analytical teacher?* Unpublished manuscript, University of Connecticut, School of Education, at Storrs.
Irwin, J. (1996). *Empowering ourselves and transforming schools: Educators making a difference.* Albany: State University of New York Press.
Jacobowitz, E. (1992). American Sign Language literature: Curriculum considerations. In *Deaf studies for educators: Conference proceedings* (pp. 76–82). Washington, DC: Gallaudet University Press, College for Continuing Education.
Jacobs, H. (Ed.). (1989). *Interdisciplinary curriculum: Design and implementation.* Alexandria, VA: Association for Supervision and Curriculum Development.
Jacobs, R. (1996). Just how hard is it to learn ASL? The case for ASL as a truly foreign language. In C. Lucas (Ed.), *Multicultural aspects of sociolinguistics in deaf communities* (pp. 183–226). Washington, DC: Gallaudet University Press.
Janks, H. (1991). A critical approach to the teaching of language. *Educational Review, 43,* 191–199.
Janks, H. (1997). Critical discourse analysis as a research tool. *Discourse: Studies in the Politics of Education, 18,* 329–342.
Janks, H., & Ivanič, R. (1992). Critical language awareness. In N. Fairclough (Ed.), *Critical language awareness* (pp. 305–331). New York: Longman.
Janton, P. (1993). *Esperanto: Language, literature, and community.* (H. Tonkin, Ed.; H. Tonkin, J. Edwards, & K. Weiner-Johnson, Trans.). Albany: State University of New York Press.
Jarvis, G. (1980). The value of second-language learning. In F. Grittner (Ed.), *Learning a second language: Seventy-ninth yearbook of the National Society for the Study of Education, Part II* (pp. 26–43). Chicago: National Society for the Study of Education, distributed by the University of Chicago Press.
Jernudd, B. (1977). Linguistic sources for terminological innovation: Policy and opinion. In J. Rubin, B. Jernudd, J. Das Gupta, J. Fishman, & C. Ferguson (Eds.), *Language planning processes* (pp. 215–236). The Hague, Netherlands: Mouton.
Jernudd, B., & Shapiro, M. (Eds.). (1989). *The politics of language purism.* Berlin, Germany: deGruyter.

# REFERENCES

Johnson, R., Liddell, S., & Erting, C. (1989). *Unlocking the curriculum: Principles for achieving access in deaf education* (Gallaudet Research Institute Working Paper 89-3). Washington, DC: Gallaudet University Press.
Johnson, S. (1998). *Exploring the German language.* London: Arnold.
Jordan, D. (1987). Esperanto and Esperantism: Symbols and motivations in a movement for linguistic equality. *Language Problems and Language Planning, 11,* 104–125.
Joseph, J., & Taylor, T. (Eds.). (1990). *Ideologies of language.* London: Routledge.
Kafai, Y., & Resnick, M. (Eds.). (1996). *Constructivism in practice: Designing, thinking, and learning in a digital world.* Mahwah, NJ: Lawrence Erlbaum Associates.
Kagan, O., & Rifkin, B. (Eds.). (2000). *The learning and teaching of Slavic languages and cultures.* Bloomington, IN: Slavica.
Kamii, C., Manning, M. & Manning, G. (Eds.). (1991). *Early literacy: A constructivist foundation for whole language.* Washington, DC: National Education Association.
Kamwangamalu, N. (1997). Multilingualism and education policy in post-apartheid South Africa. *Language Problems and Language Planning, 21,* 234–253.
Kamwangamalu, N. (1998). 'We-codes', 'they-codes', and 'codes-in-between': Identities of English and codeswitching in post-apartheid South Africa. *Multilingua: Journal of Cross-Cultural and Interlanguage Communication, 17,* 277–296.
Kaplan, R., & Baldauf, R. (1997). *Language planning: From theory to practice.* Clevedon, UK: Multilingual Matters.
Kaschula, R., & Anthonissen, C. (1995). *Communicating across cultures in South Africa: Toward a critical language awareness.* Johannesburg, South Africa: Witwatersrand University Press.
Kashoki, M. (1993). Some thoughts on future language policy for South Africa. *African Studies, 52,* 141–162.
Kaufman, D., & Grennon Brooks, J. (1996). Interdisciplinary collaboration in teacher education: A constructivist approach. *TESOL Quarterly, 30,* 231–251.
Keeskes, I., & Papp, T. (2000). *Foreign language and mother tongue.* Mahwah, NJ: Lawrence Erlbaum Associates.
Keiny, S. (1994). Constructivism and teachers' professional development. *Teaching and Teacher Education, 10,* 157–167.
Kennedy, C. (Ed.). (1983). *Language planning and language education.* London: George Allen & Unwin.
Kerr, D. (1976). *Educational policy: Analysis, structure, and justification.* New York: McKay.
Khubchandani, L. (1983). *Plural languages, plural cultures.* Honolulu, HI: University of Hawaii Press.
Killion, J., & Todnem, G. (1991). A process for personal theory building. *Educational Leadership, 48,* 14–16.
Kincheloe, J., Slattery, P., & Steinberg, S. (2000). *Contextualizing teaching: Introduction to education and educational foundations.* New York: Longman.
King, K. (1999). Inspecting the unexpected: Language status and corpus shifts as aspects of Quichua language revitalization. *Language Problems and Language Planning, 23,* 109–132.
King, K. (2000). Language ideologies and heritage language education. *International Journal of Bilingual Education and Bilingualism, 3,* 167–184.
King, M., & van den Berg, O. (1992). *One nation, many languages: What policy for schools?* Pietermaritzburg, South Africa: Centaur Publications, in association with the Independent Examinations Board.
Klee, C. (1998). Communication as an organizing principle in the national standards: Sociolinguistic aspects of Spanish language teaching. *Hispania, 81,* 339–351.
Kloss, H. (1978). *Problems of language policy in South Africa.* Vienna, Austria: Wilhelm Braumüller.
Knowlson, J. (1975). *Universal language schemes in England and France, 1600–1800.* Toronto: University of Toronto Press.

# REFERENCES

Kochman, T. (Ed.). (1972). *Rappin' and stylin' out: Communication in black urban America.* Urbana: University of Illinois Press.

Kochman, T. (1981). *Black and white styles in conflict.* Chicago: Univers ty of Chicago Press.

Kramer, C. (1999a). *Macedonian: A course for beginning and intermediate students.* Madison: University of Wisconsin Press.

Kramer, C. (1999b). Official language, minority language, no language at all: The history of Macedonian in primary education in the Balkans. *Language Prcblems and Language Planning, 23,* 233–250.

Kramsch, C. (1993). *Context and culture in language teaching.* Oxford: Oxford University Press.

Krashen, S, & Terrell, T. (1983). *The natural approach.* Oxford: Pergarr on Press.

Kriel, M. (1998). Taal en identiteitskrisis, en die alternatiewe Afrikaans musiekbeweging. [Language and identity-crisis in the alternative Afrikaans music movement.] *South African Journal of Linguistics, 16,* 16–26.

Krishnaswamy, N., & Burde, A. (1998). *The politics of Indians' English: Linguistic colonialism and the expanding English empire.* Delhi: Oxford University Press.

Kroll, S., & Zahirovič, D. (1998). *Bosnian-English–English-Bosnian dictionary.* New York: Hippocrene.

Kumaravadivelu, B. (1994). The postmethod condition: (E)merging strategies for second–foreign language teaching. *TESOL Quarterly, 28,* 27–48.

Kyle, J., & Woll, B. (1985). *Sign language: The study of deaf people and their language.* Cambridge, England: Cambridge University Press.

Labov, W. (1972a). *Language in the inner city: Studies in the Black English vernacular.* Philadelphia: University of Pennsylvania Press.

Labov, W. (1972b). *Sociolinguistic patterns.* Philadelphia: University of Pennsylvania Press.

Labov, W. (1978). *The study of nonstandard English.* Urbana, IL: National Council of Teachers of English.

Labov, W. (1993). Recognizing Black English in the classroom. In L. Cleary & M. Linn (Eds.), *Linguisitics for teachers* (pp. 149–173). New York: McGraw-Hill.

Ladwig, J. (1996). *Academic distinctions: Theory and methodology in the sociology of school knowledge.* New York: Routledge.

Lakoff, G., & Johnson, M. (1980). *Metaphors we live by.* Chicago: University of Chicago Press.

Lakoff, R. (2000). *The language war.* Berkeley, CA: University of California Press.

Lambert, R. (1990). *Language policy: An international perspective.* Washington, DC: Johns Hopkins University, National Foreign Language Center.

Lambert, R. (Ed.). (1994). *Foreign language policy: An agenda for change.* Thousand Oaks, CA: Sage.

Lampe, J. (2000). *Yugoslavia as history: Twice there was a country* (2nd ed.). Cambridge, England: Cambridge University Press.

Lane, H. (1984). *When the mind hears: A history of the deaf.* New York: Rardom House.

Lane, H. (1992). *The mask of benevolence: Disabling the deaf community.* New York: Knopf.

Lane, H., Hoffmeister, R., & Bahan, B. (1996). *A journey into the DEAF-WORLD.* San Diego, CA: DawnSign Press.

Lanehart, S. (1998). African American Vernacular English and education: The dynamics of pedagogy, ideology and identity. *Journal of English Linguistics, 26,* 122–136

Lanehart, S. (1999). African American Vernacular English. In J. Fishman (Ed.), *Handbook of language and ethnic identity* (pp. 211–225). Oxford, England: Oxford University Press.

Language Plan Task Group. (1996). *Towards a national language plan for South Africa: Final report of the Language Plan Task Group (LANGTAG).* Pretoria, South Africa: Government Printer.

Lantolf, J. (2000). Introducing sociocultural theory. In J. Lantolf (Ed.), *Sociocultural theory and second language learning* (pp. 1–26). Oxford, England: Oxford University Press.

Large, A. (1985). *The artifical language movement.* Oxford, England: Basil Blackwell.

Larson, C., & Ovando, C. (2001). *The color of bureaucracy: The politics of equity in multicultural school communities.* Belmont, CA: Wadsworth.

# REFERENCES

Lauristin, M., & Vihalemm, P. (Eds.). (1997). *Return to the western world: Cultural and political perspectives on the Estonian post-communist transition* (pp. 279–297). Tartu: Tartu University Press.

Lee, G. (Ed.). (1967). *Crusade against ignorance: Thomas Jefferson on education.* New York: Teacher's College Press.

Lee, P. (1996). *The Whorf theory complex: A critical reconstruction.* Philadelphia: John Benjamins.

Leon-Smith, G. (1987). *The role of Esperanto in the teaching of modern languages.* London: Esperanto-Asocio de Britujo.

Lessow-Hurley, J. (1996). *The foundations of dual language instruction* (2nd ed.). New York: Longman.

Lewis, E. (1980). *Bilingualism and bilingual education: A comparative study.* Albuquerque, NM: University of New Mexico Press.

Lillo-Martin, D. (1991). *Universal grammar and American Sign Language: Setting the null argument parameters.* Dordrecht, Netherlands: Kluwer.

Lins, U. (1990). *La danĝera lingvo: Studo pri la persekutoj kontraŭ Esperanto.* [The dangerous language: A study on the persecution of Esperanto.] Moscow: Progreso.

Lippi-Green, R. (1997). *English with an accent: Language, ideology and discrimination in the United States.* London: Routledge.

Lipton, G. (1992). *Practice handbook to elementary foreign language programs* (2nd ed). Lincolnwood, IL: National Textbook Company.

Liskin-Gasparro, J. (1982). *ETS oral proficiency testing manual.* Princeton, NJ: Educational Testing Service.

Littlewood, W. (1984). *Foreign and second language learning: Language acquisition research and its implications for the classroom.* Cambridge, England: Cambridge University Press.

Lodge, R., Armstrong, N., Ellis, Y., & Shelton, J. (1997). *Exploring the French language.* London: Arnold.

Lomas, C., & Osora, A. (Eds.). (1999). *El enfoque comunicativo de la enseñanza de la lengua.* [The communicative focus in language teaching.] Buenos Aires: Paidós.

Lonning, R., & DeFranco, T. (1997). Integration of science and mathematics: a theoretical model. *School Science and Mathematics, 97,* 18–25.

Lonning, R., DeFranco, T. & Weinland, T. (1998). Development of theme-based, interdisciplinary, integrated curriculum: A theoretical model. *School Science and Mathematics, 98,* 312–318.

Louw, J. (1983/4). The development of Xhosa and Zulu as languages. In I. Fodor & C. Hagège (Eds.), *Language reform, Vol. 2* (pp. 371–392). Hamburg, Germany: Buske Verlag.

Louw-Potgieter, J., & Louw, J. (1991). Language planning: Preferences of a group of South African students. *South African Journal of Linguistics, 9,* 96–99.

Low, W. (1992). Colors of ASL ... A world expressed: ASL poetry in the curriculum. In *Deaf studies for educators: Conference proceedings* (pp. 53–59). Washington, DC: College for Continuing Education, Gallaudet University.

Lowenberg, P. (1995). Language and the institutionalization of ethnic inequality: Malay and English in Malaysia. In C. Schäffner & A. Wenden (Eds.), *Language and peace* (pp. 161–172). Amsterdam: Harwood Academic Publishers.

Lubensky, S., & Jarvis, D. (Eds.). (1984). *Teaching, learning, acquiring Russian.* Columbus, OH: Slavica.

Lucas, C. (Ed.). (1989). *The sociolinguistics of the deaf community.* San Diego, CA: Academic Press.

Lucas, C. (Ed.). (1990). *Sign language research: Theoretical issues.* Washington, DC: Gallaudet University Press.

Lucas, C. (Ed.). (1995). *Sociolinguistics in deaf communities.* Washington, DC: Gallaudet University Press.

Lucas, C. (Ed.). (1996). *Multicultural aspects of sociolinguistics in deaf communities.* Washington, DC: Gallaudet University Press.

# REFERENCES

Lucas, C., & Valli, C. (1992). *Language contact in the American deaf community.* San Diego, CA: Academic Press.

Luelsdorff, P. (1975). *A segmental phonology of Black English.* The Hague, Netherlands: Mouton.

Luke, A. (1988). *Literacy, textbooks and ideology.* Philadelphia: Falmer Press.

Lyons, N. (Ed.). (1998). *With portfolio in hand: Validating the new teacher professionalism.* New York: Teacher's College Press.

Maartens, J. (1994). Teaching Afrikaans as emancipatory discourse. In R. Botha, M. Kemp, C. le Roux, & W. Winckler (Eds.), *Taalwetenskap vir die taalprofessies/Linguistics for the language professions, 2* (pp. 298–208). Stellenbosch, South Africa: University of Stellenbosch, Department of General Linguistics.

Macedo, D. (2000). The colonialism of the English only movement. *Educational Researcher, 29,* 15–24.

MacMillan, M. (1982). Henri Bourassa on the defence of language rights. *Dalhousie Review, 62,* 413–430.

Macnamara, J. (1971). Successes and failures in the movement for the restoration of Irish. In J. Rubin & B. Jernudd (Eds.), *Can language be planned?* (pp. 65–94). Honolulu, HI: The University Press of Hawaii.

Magadla, L. (1996). Constructivism: A practitioner's perspective. *South African Journal of Higher Education, 10,* 83–88.

Magner, T. (1984). Ruminations of teaching Russian. In S. Lubensky & D. Jarvis (Eds.), *Teaching, learning, acquiring Russian* (pp. 11–17). Columbus, OH: Slavica.

Maguire, G. (1991). *Our own language: An Irish initiative.* Clevedon, UK: Multilingual Matters.

Mamdani, M. (Ed.). (2000). *Beyond rights talk and culture talk.* Cape Town, South Africa: David Philip.

Mansoor, S. (1993). *Punjabi, Urdu, English in Pakistan: A sociolinguistic study.* Lahore, Pakistan: Vanguard.

Mansour, G. (1993). *Multilingualism and nation-building.* Clevedon, UK: Multilingual Matters.

Marinova-Todd, S., Marshall, D., & Snow, C. (2000). Three misconceptions about age and L2 learning. *TESOL Quarterly, 34,* 9–34.

Marivate, C. (1993). Language and education, with special reference to the mother-tongue policy in African schools. *Language Matters: Studies in the Languages of Southern Africa, 24,* 91–105.

Markarian, R. (1964). *The educational value of Esperanto teaching in the schools.* Rotterdam, Netherlands: Universala Esperanto-Asocio.

Mar-Molinero, C. (1997). *The Spanish-speaking world: A practical introduction to sociolinguistic issues.* London: Routledge.

Mar-Molinero, C. (2000). *Politics of language in the Spanish-speaking world.* London: Routledge.

Marr, T. (1999). Neither the state nor the grass roots: Language maintenance and the discourse of the Academia Mayor de la Lengua Quechua. *International Journal of Bilingual Education and Bilingualism, 2,* 181–197.

Martel, A. (2000). Paradoxes of plurilingualism. For better? For worse? And beyond? In R. Phillipson (Ed.), *Rights to language: Equity, power, and education* (pp. 151–159). Mahwah, NJ: Lawrence Erlbaum Associates.

Martin-Jones, M., & Romaine, S. (1986). Semilingualism: A half-baked theory of communicative competence. *Applied Linguistics, 7,* 26–38.

Matras, Y. (1990). *Some problems of Kurdish orthography: Summary of thesis.* Hamburg: University of Hamburg, Department of Linguistics.

Mawasha, A. (1996). Teaching African languages to speakers of other South African languages: Operationalising the new democratic language policy in South Africa. *Journal for Language Teaching, 30,* 35–41.

# REFERENCES

Maxwell, B. (1997, January 2). Miss Bonaparte wouldn't approve! *The New Britain Herald*, p. B-2.
Maxwell, D. (1988). On the acquisition of Esperanto. *Studies in Second Language Acquisition, 10*, 51–61.
Mazrui, A., & Mazrui, A. (1998). *The power of Babel: Language and governance in the African experience*. Oxford, England: James Currey.
McKay, S. (1993). *Agendas for second language literacy*. Cambridge, England: Cambridge University Press.
McLaren, P. (1989). *Life in schools*. New York: Longman.
McLaren, P., & Giroux, H. (1997). Writing from the margins: Geographies of identity, pedagogy, and power. In P. McLaren, *Revolutionary Multiculturalism* (pp. 16–41). Boulder, CO: Westview Press.
McLaren, P., & Leonard, P. (Eds.). (1993). *Paulo Freire: A critical encounter*. New York: Routledge.
McLaren, P., & Muñoz, J. (2000). Contesting whiteness: Critical perspectives on the struggle for social justice. In C. Ovando & P. McLaren (Eds.), *The politics of multiculturalism and bilingual education: Students and teachers caught in the cross fire* (pp. 23–49). Boston, MA: McGraw-Hill.
McRae, K. (1978). Bilingual language districts in Finland and Canada: Adventures in the transplanting of an institution. *Canadian Public Policy, 4*, 331–351.
McWhorter, J. (1998). *The word on the street: Fact and fable about American English*. New York: Plenum.
Measures, E., Quell, C., & Wells, G. (1997). A sociocultural perspective on classroom discourse. In B. Davies & D. Corson (Eds.), *Encyclopedia of language and education, Vol. 3: Oral discourse and education* (pp. 21–29). Dordrecht, Netherlands: Kluwer.
Merrill, M. (1992). Constructivism and instructional design. In T. Duffy & D. Jonassen (Eds.), *Constructivism and the technology of instruction* (pp. 99–114). Hillsdale, NJ: Lawrence Erlbaum Associates.
Metzger, M. (Ed.). (2000). *Bilingualism and identity in deaf communities*. Washington, DC: Gallaudet University Press.
Miller, S., & Fredericks, M. (1988). Uses of metaphor: A qualitative case study. *International Journal of Qualitative Studies in Education, 1*, 263–272.
Mintzes, J., Wandersee, J., & Novak, J. (Eds.). (1997). *Teaching science for understanding: A human constructivist view*. San Diego: Academic Press.
Mokoena, A. (1998). *Sesotho made easy*. Pretoria, South Africa: J. L. van Schaik.
Moll, L. (Ed.). (1990). *Vygotsky and education: Instructional implications and applications of sociocultural psychology*. Cambridge, England: Cambridge University Press.
Moore, J. (1980). The structure of Esperanto. *Babel: Journal of the Australian Federation of Modern Language Teacher's Association, 16*, 25–27.
Msimang, C. (1992). The future status and function of Zulu in the new South Africa. *South African Journal of African Languages, 12*, 139–143.
Mtintsilana, P., & Morris, R. (1988). Terminology in African languages in South Africa. *South African Journal of African Languages, 8*, 109–113.
Mtuze, M. (1993). The language practitioner in a multilingual South Africa. *South African Journal of African Languages, 13*, 47–52.
Mufwene, S. (Ed.). (1993). *Africanisms in Afro-American language varieties*. Athens: The University of Georgia Press.
Mufwene, S., Rickford, J., Bailey, G., & Baugh, J. (Eds.). (1998). *African American English: Structure, history and use*. London: Routledge.
Munnik, A. (1994). *Learn Xhosa*. Pietermaritzburg, South Africa: Shuter & Shooter.
Musker, P. (Ed.). (1997). *Multilingual learning: Working in multilingual classrooms*. Cape Town, South Africa: Maskew Miller Longman.
Mutasa, D. (1996). Constraints on the promotion of African languages to the level of English, French and Portuguese. *South African Journal of Linguistics* (Suppl. 32), 23–34.

Nahir, M. (1977). The five aspects of language planning. *Language Problems and Language Planning, 1*, 107–124.
Nahir, M. (1988). Language planning and language acquisition: The 'great leap' in the Hebrew revival. In C. Paulston (Ed.), *International handbook of bilingualism and bilingual education* (pp. 275–295). New York: Greenwood.
Nash, G., Crabtree, C., & Dunn, R. (1997). *History on trial: Culture wars and the teaching of the past.* New York: Knopf.
National Council of Teachers of Mathematics. (1991). *Professional standards for teaching mathematics.* Reston, VA: Author.
National Education Policy Investigation. (1992a). *Post-secondary education.* Cape Town, South Africa: Oxford University Press.
National Education Policy Investigation. (1992b). *Report of the National Educational Policy Investigation Language Research Group.* Cape Town, South Africa: Oxford University Press.
National Education Policy Investigation. (1993a). *Education planning, systems, and structure.* Cape Town, South Africa: Oxford University Press.
National Education Policy Investigation. (1993b). *The Framework Report.* Cape Town, South Africa: Oxford University Press.
National Standards in Foreign Language Education Project. (1996). *Standards for foreign language learning: Preparing for the 21st century.* Lawrence, KS: Allen Press.
Natsis, J. (1999). Legislation and language: The politics of speaking French in Louisiana. *The French Review, 73*, 325–331.
Nattinger, J. (1993). Communicative language teaching: A new metaphor. In L. Cleary & M. Linn (Eds.), *Linguistics for teachers* (pp. 599–612). New York: McGraw-Hill.
Ndebele, N. (1987). The English language and social change in South Africa. *The English Academy Review, 4*, 1–16.
Neisser, A. (1983). *The other side of silence: Sign language and the deaf community in America.* New York: Knopf.
Nelson, K. (1996). *Language in cognitive development: The emergence of the mediated mind.* Cambridge, England: Cambridge University Press.
Nettle, D. (1999). *Linguistic diversity.* Oxford, England: Oxford University Press.
Nettle, D., & Romaine, S. (2000). *Vanishing voices: The extinction of the world's languages.* Oxford, England: Oxford University Press.
Nicaise, M., & Barnes, D. (1996). The union of technology, constructivism, and teacher education. *Journal of Teacher Education, 47*, 205–212.
Nieto, S. (1996). *Affirming diversity: The sociopolitical context of multicutural education* (2nd ed.). New York: Longman.
Noddings, N. (1990). Constructivism in mathematics education. In R. Davis, C. Maher, & N. Noddings (Eds.), *Constructivist views on the teaching and learning of mathematics* (pp. 7–18). Reston, VA: National Council of Teachers of Mathematics.
Norlander-Case, K., Reagan, T., & Case, C. (1999). *The professional teacher: The preparation and nurturance of the reflective practitioner.* San Francisco, CA: Jossey-Bass.
Norris, D. (1993). *Serbo-Croat: A complete course for beginners.* London: Hodder Headline.
Nover, S. (1995). Politics and language: American Sign Language and English in deaf education. In C. Lucas (Ed.), *Sociolinguistics in deaf communities* (pp. 109–163). Washington, DC: Gallaudet University Press.
Nuessel, F. (2000a). *The Esperanto language.* New York: Legas.
Nuessel, F. (2000b). The use of metaphor to comprehend and explicate scientific theory. In P. Perron, L. Sbrochhi, P. Colilli, & M. Danesi (Eds.), *Semiotics as a bridge between the humanities and the sciences* (pp. 479–500). New York: Legas.
Nwachukwu, P. (1983). *Towards an Igbo literary standard.* London: Kegan Paul, Trench, Trubner.
Nxumalo, T., & Cioran, S. (1996). *Funda IsiZulu!–Learn Zulu! An introduction to Zulu.* Cape Town, South Africa: Juta.

# REFERENCES

Nyikos, M., & Hashimoto, R. (1997). Constructivist theory applied to collaborative learning in teacher education: In search of ZPD. *The Modern Language Journal, 81*, 506–517.
Ó Baoill, D. (1988). Language planning in Ireland: The standardization of Irish. In P. Ó Riagáin (Ed.), *Language planning in Ireland* (pp. 109–126). Berlin: deGruuyter.
O'Cinneide, M., Keane, M., & Cawley, M. (1985). Industrialization and linguistic change among Gaelic-speaking communities in the west of Ireland. *Language Problems and Language Planning, 9*, 3–16.
Ó Domhnalláin, T. (1977). Ireland: The Irish language in education. *Language Problems and Language Planning, 1*, 83–95.
Ó Dubhghaill, A. (1987). An Ghaeilge sa Bhunscoil ar Bhruach na Nóchaidí: Modh Múinte Eile mar Réiteach? *Oideas, 31*, 38–51.
Office of Deputy President T. M. Mbeki. (1997). *White Paper on an Integrated National Disability Strategy.* Pretoria, South Africa: Author.
Ó Huallacháin, C. (1991). *The Irish language in society.* Coleraine, N. Ireland: University of Ulster.
Ó Huallacháin, C. (1994). *The Irish and Irish: A sociolinguistic analysis of the relationship between a people and their language.* Baile Átha Cliath, Ireland: Irish Franciscan Provincial Office.
Okrand, M. (1992). *The Klingon dictionary.* New York: Pocket Books.
Olivier, P. (1993). Language rights and human rights. In K. Prinsloo, Y. Peeters, J. Turi, & C. van Rensburg (Eds.), *Language, law and equality* (pp. 128–137). Pretoria, South Africa: University of South Africa.
Olszewski, L. (1996, December 19). Oakland schools OK Black English: Ebonics to be regarded as different, not wrong. *The San Francisco Chronicle*, pp. A-1, A-19.
Ó Riagáin, P. (Ed.). (1988). *Language planning in Ireland (International Journal of the Sociology of Language* 70). Berlin: deGruyter.
Ó Riagáin, P. (1997). *Language policy and social reproduction: Ireland, 1893–1993.* Oxford, England: Calrendon Press.
Orr, E. (1987). *Twice as less: Black English and the performance of black students in mathematics and science.* New York: Norton.
Ortony, A. (Ed.). (1980). *Metaphor and thought.* Cambridge, England: Cambridge University Press.
Osborn, T. (1998a). *The concept of 'foreignness' in U.S. secondary language curricula: A critical philosophical analysis.* Unpublished doctoral dissertation, University of Connecticut, Storrs.
Osborn, T. (1998b). Providing access: Foreign language learners and genre theory. *Foreign Language Annals, 31*, 40–47.
Osborn, T. (1999). Reflecting on *foreignness:* The challenges of a new millennium. *New York State Association of Foreign Language Teachers Annual Meeting Series, 16*, 21–24.
Osborn, T. (2000). *Critical reflection and the foreign language classroom.* Westport, CT: Bergin & Garvey.
Osborn, T. (in press). Making connections and comparisons: Integrating foreign language with other core curricula. *Northeast Conference of the Teaching of Foreign Languages Review.*
Osborn, T., & Reagan, T. (1998). Why Johnny can't *hablar, parler* or *sprechen:* Foreign language education and multicultural education. *Multicultural Education, 6*, 2–9.
Ó Siadhail, M. (1989). *Modern Irish: Grammatical structure and dialectal variation.* Cambridge, England: Cambridge University Press.
Ovando, C. (2001). Language diversity and education. In J. Banks & C. Banks (Eds.), *Multicultural education* (pp. 268–291). New York: Wiley.
Overfield, D. (1997). From the margins to the mainstream: Foreign language education and community-based learning. *Foreign Language Annals, 30*, 485–491.
Ozolins, U. (1994). Upwardly mobile languages: The politics of language in the Baltic states. *Journal of Multilingual and Multicultural Development, 15*, 161–169.
Padden, C., & Humphries, T. (1988). *Deaf in America: Voices from a culture.* Cambridge, MA: Harvard University Press.

Parker, S. (1997). *Reflective teaching in the postmodern world: A manifesto for education in postmodernity.* Buckingham, England: Open University Press.
Partridge, M. (1972). *Serbo-Croat: Practical grammar and reader.* Belgrade, Yugoslavia: Izdavaki Zavod Jugoslavija.
Paulston, C. (1994). *Linguistic minorities in multilingual settings: Implications for language policies.* Amsterdam: John Benjamins.
Payne, J. (1990). Iranian languages. In B. Comrie (Ed.), *The world s major languages* (pp. 514–522). Oxford, England: Oxford University Press.
Peirce, B. (1989). Toward a pedagogy of possibility in the teaching of English internationally: People's English in South Africa. *TESOL Quarterly, 23*, 401–420.
Penn, C. (1992). The sociolinguistics of South African Sign Language. In R. Herbert (Ed.), *Language and society in Africa* (pp. 277–284). Johannesburg, South Africa: Witwatersrand University Press.
Penn, C. (1993). Signs of the times: Deaf language and culture in South Africa. *South African Journal of Communication Disorders, 31*, 6–11.
Penn, C., & Reagan, T. (1990). How do you sign 'apartheid'? The politics of South African Sign Language. *Language Problems and Language Planning, 14*, 91–103.
Penn, C., & Reagan, T. (1995). On the other hand: Implications of the study of South African Sign Language for the education of the deaf in South Africa. *South African Journal of Education, 15*, 92–96.
Penn, C., & Reagan, T. (1999). Linguistic, social and cultural perspectives on sign language in South Africa. *Indian Journal of Applied Linguistics, 25*, 49–69.
Pennycook, A. (1994). *The cultural politics of English as an international language.* New York: Longman.
Pennycook, A. (1998). *English and the discourses of colonialism.* London: Routledge.
Pennycook, A. (2000). The social politics and cultural politics of language classrooms. In J. Hall & W. Eggington (Eds.), *The sociopolitics of English language teaching* (pp. 89–103). Clevedon, UK: Multilingual Matters.
Pennycook, A. (2001). *Critical applied linguistics: A critical introduction.* Mahwah, NJ: Lawrence Erlbaum Associates.
Perry, T., & Delpit, L. (Eds.). (1998). *The real Ebonics debate: Power, language, and the education of African American children.* Boston, MA: Beacon Press.
Peters, C. (2000). *Deaf American literature: From carnival to the canon.* Washington, DC: Gallaudet University Press.
Peters, R. (1966). *Ethics and education.* London: George Allen & Unwin.
Peters, R. (Ed.). (1967). *The concept of education.* London: Routledge & Kegan Paul.
Peters, R. (Ed.). (1973). *The philosophy of education.* Oxford, England: Oxford University Press.
Phillips, J. (1998). Media for the message: Technology's role in the Standards. *CALICO Journal, 16*, 25–36.
Phillipson, R. (1992). *Linguistic imperialism.* Oxford: Oxford University Press.
Phillipson, R. (1998). Language policies: Towards a multidisciplinary approach. In M. Fettes & S. Bolduc (Eds.), *Al lingva demokratio/Towards linguistic democracy/Vers la démocratie linguistique: Proceedings of the Nitobe Symposium of International Organizations* (pp. 95–97). Rotterdam, Netherlands: Universala Esperanto-Asocio.
Phillipson, R. (Ed.). (2000). *Rights to language: Equity, power and education.* Mahwah, NJ: Lawrence Erlbaum Associates.
Phillipson, R., Rannut, M., & Skutnabb-Kangas, T. (1995). Introduction. In T. Skutnabb-Kangas & R. Phillipson, in conjunction with M. Rannut (Eds.), *Linguistic human rights* (pp. 1–22). Berlin: deGruyter.
Phillipson, R., & Skutnabb-Kangas, T. (1995). Linguistic rights and wrongs. *Applied Linguistics, 16*, 483–504.
Phillipson, R., & Skutnabb-Kangas, T. (1996). English only worldwide or language ecology? *TESOL Quarterly, 30*, 429–452.

# REFERENCES

Piaget, J. (1976). *Psychologie et epistémologie.* [Psychology and epistemology.] Paris: Editions Gonthier.
Piaget, J. (1979). *L'epistémologie génétique* [Genetic epistemology.] (3rd ed.). Paris: Presses Universitaires de France.
Piaget, J. (1986). *Logique et connaissance scientifique.* [Logic and scientific knowledge.] Paris: Gallimard.
Piaget, J. (1993). *Le jugement et le raisonnement chez l'enfant* [The judgment and reasoning of the child.] (8th ed.). Paris: Delachaux & Niestle.
Piaget, J. (1996). *La construction du réel chez l'enfant* [The child's construction of reality.] (6th ed.). Neuchatel: Delachaux & Niestle.
Pieterse, H. (1991). Taalbeplanningsmodelle vir Suid-Afrika. [Language planning models for South Africa.] *Tydskrif vir Geesteswetenskappe, 31,* 87–100.
Pinnock, P. (1994). *Xhosa: A cultural grammar for beginners.* Cape Town, South Africa: African Sun Press.
Piron, C. (1994). *Psychological reactions to Esperanto* (Esperanto Documents 42–A). Rotterdam, Netherlands: Universal Esperanto Association.
Ponayi, M. (1967). *The tacit dimension.* Garden City, NY: Anchor.
Posner, R. (1996). *The Romance languages.* Cambridge, England: Cambridge University Press.
Preskill, S., & Jacobvitz, R. (2001). *Stories of teaching: A foundation for educational renewal.* Upper Saddle River, NJ: Prentice-Hall.
Pretorius, F., & Lemmer, E. (Eds.). (1998). *South African education and training: Transition in a democratic era.* Johannesburg, South Africa: Hodder & Stoughton.
Prillwitz, S., & Vollhaber, T. (Eds.). (1990a). *Current trends in European sign language research.* Hamburg, Germany: Signum Press.
Prillwitz, S., & Vollhaber, T. (Eds.). (1990b). *Sign language research and application.* Hamburg, Germany: Signum Press.
Prinsloo, K., & Malan, C. (1988). Cultures in contact: Language and the arts in South Africa. In H. Marais (Ed.), *South Africa* (pp. 257–281). Pinetown, South Africa: Owen Burgess.
Prinsloo, K., Peeters, Y., Turi, J., & van Rensburg, C. (Eds.). (1993). *Language, law and equality: Proceedings of the Third International Conference of the International Academy of Language Law.* Pretoria, South Africa: University of South Africa.
Prinsloo, M., & Breier, M. (Eds.). (1996). *The social uses of literacy: Theory and practice in contemporary South Africa.* Amsterdam: John Benjamins.
Pullum, G. (1991). *The great Eskimo vocabulary hoax and other irreverent essays on the study of language.* Chicago: University of Chicago Press.
Quick, M. (1989). Does anyone here speak Esperanto? *Gifted Child Today* (May/June), 15–16.
Rahman, T. (1996). British language policies and imperialism in India. *Language Problems and Language Planning, 20,* 91–115.
Rahman, T. (1998). *Language and politics in Pakistan.* Karachi, Pakistan: Oxford University Press.
Rainer, J., & Guyton, E. (1994). Developing a constructivist teacher education program: The policy-making stage. *Journal of Teacher Education, 45,* 140–146.
Ramanathan, V. (1999). 'English is here to stay': A critical look at institutional and educational practices in India. *TESOL Quarterly, 33,* 211–231.
Rannut, M. (1995). Beyond linguistic policy: The Soviet Union versus Estonia. In T. Skutnabb-Kangas & R. Phillipson (Eds.), *Linguistic human rights* (pp. 179–208). Berlin: deGruyter.
Reagan, T. (1983). The economics of language: Implications for language planning. *Language Problems and Language Planning, 7,* 148–161.
Reagan, T. (1984). Language policy, politics and ideology: The case of South Africa. *Issues in Education, 2,* 155–164.
Reagan, T. (1985). 'Taalideologie' en taalbeplanning. ["Language ideology" and language planning.] *South African Journal of Linguistics, 3,* 45–59.

Reagan, T. (1986a). Considerations on liberation and oppression: The place of English in black education in South Africa. *Journal of Thought, 21*, 91–99.

Reagan, T. (1986b). 'Language ideology' in the language planning process: Two African case studies. *South African Journal of African Languages, 6*, 94–97.

Reagan, T. (1986c). Taalbeplanning in die Suid-Afrikaanse onderwys: 'n oorsig. [Language planning in South African education: An overview.] *South African Journal of Linguistics, 4*, 32–55.

Reagan, T. (1986d). The role of language policy in South African education. *Language Problems and Language Planning, 10*, 1–13.

Reagan, T. (1987a). Ideology and language policy in education: The case of Afrikaans. In H. du Plessis & T. du Plessis (Eds.), *Afrikaans en taalpolitiek* (pp. 133–139). Pretoria, South Africa: Haum.

Reagan, T. (1987b). The politics of linguistic apartheid: Language policies in black education in South Africa. *Journal of Negro Education, 56*, 299–312.

Reagan, T. (1988). Multiculturalism and the deaf: An educational manifesto. *Journal of Research and Development in Education, 22*, 1–6.

Reagan, T. (1989). Nineteenth-century conceptions of deafness: Implications for contemporary educational practice. *Educational Theory, 39*, 39–46.

Reagan, T. (1990a). Cultural considerations in the education of deaf children. In D. Moores & K. Meadow-Orlans (Eds.), *Research in educational and developmental aspects of deafness* (pp. 74–84). Washington, DC: Gallaudet University Press.

Reagan, T. (1990b). The development and reform of sign languages. In I. Fodor & C. Hagège (Eds.), *Language reform: History and future, Vol. 5* (pp. 253–267). Hamburg, Germany: Buske Verlag.

Reagan, T. (1990c). Responding to linguistic diversity in South Africa: The contribution of language planning. *South African Journal of Linguistics, 8*, 178–184.

Reagan, T. (1992). The deaf as a linguistic minority: Educational considerations. In T. Hehir & T. Latus (Eds.), *Special education at the century's end* (pp. 305–320). Cambridge, MA: Harvard Educational Review.

Reagan, T. (1995a). Language and the skills of oracy in traditional African education. *Journal of Research and Development in Education, 28*, 106–112.

Reagan, T. (1995b). Language planning and language policy in South Africa: A perspective on the future. In R. Mesthrie (Ed.), *Language and social history* (pp. 319–328). Cape Town, South Africa: David Philip.

Reagan, T. (1996). The contribution of language planning and language policy to the reconciliation of unity and diversity in the post-Cold War era. In K. Müller (Ed.), *Language status in the post-Cold War era* (pp. 59–66). Lanham, MD: University Press of America and Center for Research and Documentation on World Language Problems.

Reagan, T. (1997a). The case for applied linguistics in teacher education. *Journal of Teacher Education, 48*, 185–195.

Reagan, T. (1997b). When is a language not a language? Challenges to 'linguistic legitimacy' in educational discourse. *Educational Foundations, 11*, 5–28.

Reagan, T. (1998). Multilingualism and language competition in contemporary South Africa: A case study of the role of language rights in nation-building. In J. Levitt, L. Ashley, & W. Finke (Eds.), *Language and communication in the new century* (pp. 149–196). East Rockaway, NY: Cummings & Hathaway.

Reagan, T. (1999). Constructivist epistemology and second/foreign language pedagogy. *Foreign Language Annals, 32*, 413–425.

Reagan, T. (2000a). A South African perspective: Second language teaching and learning in the university. In J. Rosenthal (Ed.), *Handbook of undergraduate second language education* (pp. 253–275). Mahwah, NJ: Lawrence Erlbaum Associates.

Reagan, T. (2000b). But does it *count?* Reflections on 'signing' as a foreign language. *Northeast Conference on the Teaching of Foreign Languages Review, 48*, 16–26.

# REFERENCES

Reagan, T. (in press-a) 'Knowing' and 'learning' a foreign language: Epistemological reflections on classroom practice. In T. Osborn (Ed.), *The future of foreign language education in the United States.* Westport, CT: Greenwood.

Reagan, T. (in press-b). Language rights and the deaf: Compensatory and empowerment approaches in language policy. In P. Benson, P. Grundy, H. Itakura, & T. Skutnabb-Kangas (Eds.), *Access to language rights.* Amsterdam: John Benjamins.

Reagan, T., Case, C., & Brubacher, J. (2000). *Becoming a reflective educator: How to build a culture of inquiry in the schools* (2nd ed.). Thousand Oaks, CA: Corwin.

Reagan, T., & Ntshoe, I. (1987). Language policy and black education in South Africa. *Journal of Research and Development in Education, 20,* 1–18.

Reagan, T., & Osborn, T. (1998). Power, authority, and domination in foreign language education: Toward an analysis of educational failure. *Educational Foundations, 12,* 45–62.

Reagan, T., & Penn, C. (1997). Language policy, South African Sign Language, and the deaf: Social and educational implications. *Southern African Journal of Applied Language Studies, 5,* 1–13.

Rée, J. (1999). *I see a voice: Deafness, language and the senses—A philosophical history.* New York: Metropolitan Books.

Reid, J. (Ed.). (1998). *Understanding learning styles in the second language classroom.* Upper Saddle River, NJ: Prentice-Hall.

Rhodes, N., & Branaman, L. (1999). *Foreign language instruction in the United States: A national survey of elementary and secondary schools.* McHenry, IL: Delta Systems, for the Center for Applied Linguistics.

Ricento, T., & Burnaby, B. (Eds.). (1998). *Language and politics in the United States and Canada: Myths and realities.* Mahwah, NJ: Lawrence Erlbaum Associates.

Richards, J. (1998). *Beyond training: Perspectives on language teacher education.* Cambridge, England: Cambridge University Press.

Richards, J., & Lockhart, C. (1994). *Reflective teaching in second language classrooms.* Cambridge, England: Cambridge University Press.

Richardson, D. (1988). *Esperanto: Learning and using the international language.* El Cerrito, CA: Esperanto League for North America, in cooperation with Orcas Publishing.

Richardson, V. (Ed.). (1997a). *Constructivist teacher education: Building a world of new understandings.* London: Falmer Press.

Richardson, V. (1997b). Constructivist teaching and teacher education: Theory and practice. In V. Richardson (Ed.), *Constructivist teacher education* (pp. 3–14). London: Falmer Press.

Richmond, I. (1993). Esperanto literature and the international reader. In I. Richmond (Ed.), *Aspects of internationalism* (pp. 103–118). Lanham, MD: University Press of American and Center for Research and Documentation on World Language Problems.

Rickford, J., & Rickford, R. (2000). *Spoken soul: The story of Black English.* New York: Wiley.

Ridge, S. (1996). Language policy in a democratic South Africa. In M. Herrman & B. Burnaby (Eds.), *Language policies in English-dominant countries* (pp. 15–34). Clevedon, UK: Multilingual Matters.

Robinson, C. (1996). Winds of change in Africa: Fresh air for African languages? Some preliminary reflections. In H. Coleman & L. Cameron (Eds.), *Change and language* (pp. 166–182). Clevedon, UK: Multilingual Matters, in association with the British Association for Applied Linguistics.

Romaine, S. (1994). *Language in society: An introduction to sociolinguistics.* Oxford: Oxford University Press.

Rouchdy, A. (Ed.). (1992). *The Arabic language in America.* Detroit, MI: Wayne State University Press.

Rubin, J. (1971). Evaluation and language planning. In J. Rubin & B. Jernudd (Eds.), *Can language be planned?* (pp. 217–252). Honolulu: The University Press of Hawaii.

Rubin, J., & Jernudd, B. (Eds.). (1971). *Can language be planned? Sociolinguistic theory and practice for developing nations.* Honolulu: University Press of Hawaii.

Ruíz, R. (1991). The empowerment of language minority students. In C. Sleeter (Ed.), *Empowerment through multicultural education* (pp. 217–227). Albany: State University of New York Press.
Rutherford, S. (1993). *A study of American deaf folklore.* Silver Spring, MD: Linstok Press.
Ryazanova-Clarke, L., & Wade, T. (1999). *The Russian language today.* London: Routledge.
Sáenz-Badillos, A. (1993). *A history of the Hebrew language.* Cambridge, England: Cambridge University Press.
Safford, P., & Safford, E. (1996). *A history of childhood and disability.* New York: Teachers College Press.
Samway, K., & McKeon, D. (1999). *Myths and realities: Best practices for language minority students.* Portsmouth, NH: Heinemann.
Sarason, S. (1990). *The predictable failure of educational reform.* San Francisco: Jossey-Bass.
Sarinjeive, D. (1997). Realities and ideologies of English and 'other' Englishes. *Journal for Language Teaching, 31*, 68–76.
Sarinjeive, D. (1999). The mother-tongue, English and student aspirations and realities. *Journal for Language Teaching, 33*, 128–140.
Scheffer, I. (1960). *The language of education.* Springfield, IL: Thomas.
Scheffler, I. (1979). *Beyond the letter: A philosophical inquiry into ambiguity, vagueness and metaphor in language.* London: Routledge & Kegan Paul.
Schein, J. (1989). *At home among strangers: Exploring the deaf community in the United States.* Washington, DC: Gallaudet University Press.
Schiffman, H. (1996). *Linguistic culture and language policy.* London: Routledge.
Schlyter, B. (1998). New language laws in Uzbekistan. *Language Problems and Language Planning, 22*, 143–181.
Schmied, J. (1991). *English in Africa: An introduction.* London: Longman.
Schneider, E. (1989). *American earlier Black English: Morphological and syntactic variables.* Tuscaloosa: The University of Alabama Press.
Schön, D. (1983). *The reflective practitioner: How professionals think in action.* New York: Basic Books.
Schön, D. (1987). *Educating the reflective practitioner.* San Francisco: Jossey-Bass.
Schorr, J. (1997, January 2). Give Oakland's schools a break. *The New York Times*, p. A-19.
Schmitt, N. (2000). *Vocabulary in language teaching.* Cambridge, England: Cambridge University Press.
Schuring, G. (1991). Language policies in Africa and their relevance to a future South Africa. In D. van Vuuren, N. Wiehahn, N. Rhoodie, & M. Wiechers (Eds.), *South Africa in the nineties* (pp. 617–647). Pretoria, South Africa: Human Sciences Research Council.
Schwandt, T. (1994). Constructivist, interpretivist approaches to human inquiry. In N. Denzin & Y. Lincoln (Eds.), *Handbook of qualitative research* (pp. 118–137). Thousand Oaks, CA: Sage.
Scott, J. (1998). The serious side of Ebonics humor. *Journal of English Linguistics, 26*, 137–155.
Scott, R. (1972). A proposed framework for analyzing deviance as a property of social order. In R. Scott & J. Douglas (Eds.), *Theoretical perspectives on deviance* (pp. 9–36). New York: Basic Books.
Shanahan, D. (1998). Culture, culture and 'culture' in foreign language teaching. *Foreign Language Annals, 31*(3), 451–458.
Shapiro, J. (1993). *No pity: People with disabilities forging a new Civil Rights movement.* New York: Times.
Sherwood, B. (1982). The educational value of Esperanto. In R. Eichloz & V. Eichloz (Comps.), *Esperanto en la moderna mondo/Esperanto in the modern world* (pp. 408–413). Bailieboro, Ontario: Esperanto Press.
Sherwood, B. (1983). *The educational value of Esperanto: An American view* (Esperanto documents 31–A). Rotterdam, Netherlands: Universala Esperanto-Asocio.
Shrum, J., & Glisan, E. (2000). *Teacher's handbook: Contextualized language instruction* (2nd ed.). Boston: Heinle & Heinle.

# REFERENCES

Shulman, L. (1987). Knowledge and teaching: Foundations of the new reform. *Harvard Educational Review, 57,* 1–22.
Siegelman, E. (1990). *Metaphor and reasoning in psychotherapy.* New York: Gailrand Press.
Sign language: A way to talk, but is it foreign? (1992, January 7). *The New York Times.*
Silberman, C. (1971). *Crisis in the classroom.* New York: Random House.
Simon, P. (1980). *The tongue-tied American: Confronting the foreign language crisis.* New York: Continuum.
Sinclair, H., Berthoud, I., Gerard, J., & Veneziano, E. (1985). Constructivisme et psycholinguistique génétique. [Constructivism and genetic psycholinguistics.] *Archives de Psychologie, 53,* 37–60.
Siple, P., & Fischer, S. (Eds.). (1991). *Theoretical issues in sign language research: Vol. 2, Psychology.* Chicago: University of Chicago Press.
Skutnabb-Kangas, T. (1994). Linguistic human rights: A prerequisite for bilingualism. In I. Ahlgren & K. Hyltenstam (Eds.), *Bilingualism in deaf education* (pp. 139–159). Hamburg, Germany: Signum Press.
Skutnabb-Kangas, T. (2000a). *Linguistic genocide in education—or worldwide diversity and human rights?* Mahwah, NJ: Lawrence Erlbaum Associates.
Skutnabb-Kangas, T. (2000b). Linguistic human rights and teachers of English. In J. Hall & W. Eggington (Eds.), *The sociopolitics of English language teaching* (pp. 22–44). Clevedon, UK: Multilingual Matters.
Skutnabb-Kangas, T., & Bucak, S. (1995). Killing a mother tongue: How the Kurds are deprived of linguistic human rights. In T. Skutnabb-Kangas & R. Phillipson (Eds.), *Linguistic human rights* (pp. 347–370). Berlin, Germany: deGruyter.
Skutnabb-Kangas, T., & Phillipson, R. (Eds.). (1995). *Linguistic human rights: Overcoming linguistic discrimination.* Berlin, Germany: deGruyter.
Sleeter, C. (1995). Reflections on my use of multicultural and critical pedagogy when students are white. In C. Sleeter & P. McLaren (Eds.), *Multicultural education, critical pedagogy, and the politics of difference* (pp. 415–437). Albany, NY: State University of New York Press.
Sleeter, C., & McLaren, P. (Eds.). (1995). *Multicultural education, critical pedagogy, and the politics of difference.* Albany, NY: State University of New York Press.
Smit, B. (1993). Language planning for a future South African educational system: The German language scenario—Pedagogical issues. *Journal for Language Teaching, 27,* 155–166.
Smit, B. (1996). Towards global learning in post-apartheid South Africa. *Journal for Language Teaching, 30,* 59–67.
Smit, U. (1994). Investigating language attitudes as a basis for formulating language policies: A case study. *Southern African Journal of Applied Language Studies, 3,* 23–35.
Smith, J. (1977). *On teaching classics.* London: Routledge & Kegan Paul.
Smith, N. (Ed.). (1981). *Metaphors for evaluation: Sources of new methods.* Beverly Hills, CA: Sage.
Smitherman, G. (1977). *Talkin' and testifyin': The language of black America.* Detroit, MI: Wayne State University Press.
Smitherman, G. (1981). 'What go round come round': *King* in perspective. *Harvard Educational Review, 51,* 40–56.
Smitherman, G. (1998). Ebonics, *King,* and Oakland: Some folks don't believe fat meat is greasy. *Journal of English Linguistics, 26,* 97–107.
Soder, R. (Ed.). (1996). *Democracy, education and the schools.* San Francisco, CA: Jossey-Bass.
Sparks-Langer, G., & Colton, A. (1991). Synthesis of research on teachers' reflective thinking. *Educational Leadership, 48,* 37–44.
Spivey, N. (1997). *The constructivist metaphor: Reading, writing and the making of meaning.* San Diego, CA: Academic Press.
Spolsky, B. (1989). *Conditions for second language learning.* New York: Oxford University Press.
Spring, J. (1994). *The American school, 1642–1993* (3rd ed.). New York: McGraw-Hill.

# REFERENCES

Spring, J. (2000). *The universal right to education: Justification, definition, and guidelines.* Mahwah, NJ: Lawrence Erlbaum Associates.
Srivastava, R. (1988). Societal bilingualism and bilingual education: A study of the Indian situation. In C. Paulston (Ed.), *International handbook of bilingualism and bilingual education* (pp. 247–274). New York: Greenwood.
Staples, B. (1997, January 4). The trap of ethnic identity: How Africa came to Oakland. *The New York Times,* p. A-22.
Steedman, P. (1988). Curriculum and knowledge selection. In L. Beyer & M. Apple (Eds.), *The curriculum* (pp. 119–139) Albany: State University Press of New York.
Steffe, L. (1995). Alternative epistemologies: An educator's perspective. In L. Steffe & J. Gale (Eds.), *Constructivism in education* (pp. 489–523). Hillsdale, NJ: Lawrence Erlbaum Associates.
Steffe, L., Cobb, P., & von Glasersfeld, E. (1988). *Construction of arithmetical meanings and strategies.* New York: Springer-Verlag.
Steffe, L., & Gale, J. (Eds.). (1995). *Constructivism in education.* Hillsdale, NJ: Lawrence Erlbaum Associates.
Stevenson, P. (1997). *The German-speaking world: A practical introduction to sociolinguistic issues.* London: Routledge.
Stevick, E. (1996). *Memory, meaning, and method: A view of language teaching* (2nd ed.). Boston: Heinle & Heinle.
Stewart, W. (1975). Continuity and change in American Negro dialects. In J. Dillard (Ed.), *Perspectives on Black English* (pp. 233–247). The Hague, Netherlands: Mouton.
Steyn, J. (1980). *Tuiste in eie taal.* [At home in one's language.] Cape Town, South Africa: Tafelberg.
Steyn, J. (1987). *Trouwe Afrikaners: Aspekte van Afrikaner-nasionalisme en Suid-Afrikaanse taalpolitiek, 1875–1938.* Cape Town, South Africa: Tafelberg.
Steyn, J. (1992). Die behoud van Afrikaans as ampstaal. In V. Webb (Ed.), *Afrikaans ná apartheid* (pp. 201–226). Pretoria, South Africa: J. L. van Schaik.
Steyn, J. (1998). Nuwe aktiwiteite rondom Afrikaans: Die totstandkoming van 'n 'Afrikaans oorlegplatform'. *Tydskrif vir Geesteswetenskappe, 38,* 253–264.
Stokoe, W. (Ed.). (1980). *Sign and culture: A reader for students of American Sign Language.* Silver Spring, MD: Linstok Press.
Stokoe, W. (1993). *Sign language structures.* Silver Spring, MD: Linstok Press (Original work published 1960)
Strike, K., Haller, E., & Soltis, J. (1988). *The ethics of school administration.* New York: Teacher's College Press.
Strike, K., & Soltis, J. (1992). *The ethics of teaching* (2nd ed.). New York: Teacher's College Press.
Strike, N. (1996). Talking our way out of the laager: Foreign languages in South African education. *Language Matters: Studies in the Languages of Southern Africa, 27,* 253–264.
Šušnjar, A. (2000). *Croatian-English/English-Croatian dictionary.* New York: Hippocrene.
Swanepoel, P., & Pieterse, H. (Eds.). (1993). *Perspektiewe op taalbeplanning vir Suid-Afrika/Perspectives on language planning for South Africa.* Pretoria, South Africa: University of South Africa.
Symoens, E. (1989). *The socio-political, educational and cultural roots of Esperanto.* Antwerp, Belgium: Internacia Ligo de Esperantistaj Instruistoj.
Szerdahelyi, I. (1966). Esperanto et propédeutique linguistique. [Esperanto and linguistic propedeutics.] *Langues Modernes, 60,* 255–259.
Taagepera, R. (1993). *Estonia: Return to independence.* Boulder, CO: Westview Press.
Tai, J. (1988). Bilingualism and bilingual education in the People's Republic of China. In C. Paulston (Ed.), *International handbook of bilingualism and bilingual education* (pp. 185–201). New York: Greenwood.
Tarsitani, C. (1996). Metaphors in knowledge and metaphors of knowledge: Notes on the constructivist view of learning. *Interchange, 27,* 23–40.

# REFERENCES

Taylor, W. (Ed.). (1984). *Metaphors of education*. London: Heinemann.
Teal, S., & Reagan, G. (1973). Educational goals. In J. Frymier (Ed.), *A school for tomorrow* (pp. 37–84). Berkeley, CA: McCutchan.
Thompson, L. (1985). *The political mythology of apartheid*. New Haven, CT: Yale University Press.
Tobin, K. (Ed.). (1993). *The practice of constructivism in science education*. Hillsdale, NJ: Lawrence Erlbaum Associates.
Tollefson, J. (1991). *Planning language, planning inequality: Language policy in the community*. New York: Longman.
Tollefson, J. (Ed.). (1995). *Power and inequality in language education*. Cambridge, England: Cambridge University Press.
Tollefson, J. (2000). Policy and ideology in the spread of English. In J. Hall & W. Eggington (Eds.), *The sociopolitics of English language teaching* (pp. 7–21). Clevedon, UK: Multilingual Matters.
Tonkin, H. (1977). *Esperanto and international language problems: A research bibliography* (4th ed.). Washington, DC: Esperantic Studies Foundation.
Tonkin, H. (1987). One hundred years of Esperanto: A survey. *Language Problems and Language Planning, 11*, 264–282.
Tonkin, H. (1988, April 16). Beyond the competitive edge: The peaceful uses of language study. Keynote address, Annual Conference of the California Foreign Language Teachers Association.
Tonkin, H. (1997). Introduction: Planned languages and *LPLP*. In H. Tonkin (Ed.), *Esperanto, interlinguistics, and planned language* (pp. vii–xxiii). Lanham, MD: University Press of America and Center for Research and Documentation on World Language Problems.
Tozer, S., Violas, P., & Senese, G. (1998). *School and society: Historical and contemporary perspectives* (3rd ed.). Boston: McGraw-Hill.
Trabasso, T., & Harrison, D. (1976). Introduction. In D. Harrison & T. Trabasso (Eds.), *Black English* (pp. 1–5). Hillsdale, NJ: Lawrence Erlbaum Associates.
Traugott, E. (1976). Pidgins, creoles, and the origins of vernacular Black English. In D. Harrison & T. Trabasso (Eds.), *Black English* (pp. 57–93). Hillsdale, NJ: Lawrence Erlbaum Associates.
Trudgill, P. (1995). *Sociolinguistics: An introduction to language and society* (Rev. ed.). Harmondsworth, Middlesex: Penguin.
Tutu, D. (1983). *Hope and suffering*. Grand Rapids, MI: William Eerdamans.
Uzicanin, N. (1996). *Bosnian-English/English-Bosnian compact dictionary*. New York: Hippocrene.
Valdés, G. (1981). Pedagogical implications of teaching Spanish to the Spanish-speaking in the United States. In G. Valdés, A. Lozano, & R. García-Moya (Eds.), *Teaching Spanish to the Hispanic bilingual* (pp. 3–20). New York: Teacher's College Press.
Valdés, G., Lozano, A., & García-Moya, R. (Eds.). (1981). *Teaching Spanish to the Hispanic bilingual: Issues, aims, and methods*. New York: Teacher's College Press.
Valdman, A. (2000). Comment gérer la variation dans l'enseignement du français langue étrangère aux Etats-Unis. *The French Review, 73*, 648–666.
Valli, C., & Lucas, C. (1995). *Linguistics of American Sign Language: An introduction* (2nd ed). Washington, DC: Gallaudet University Press.
van Cleve, J. (Ed.). (1993). *Deaf history unveiled: Interpretations from the new scholarship*. Washington, DC: Gallaudet University Press.
van Dijk, T. (1995). Discourse analysis as ideology analysis. In C. Schäffner & A. Wenden (Eds.), *Language and peace* (pp. 17–33). Aldershot, UK: Harwood Academic Publishers.
Van Doren, M. (1959). *Liberal education*. Boston: Beacon Press.
van Lier, L. (1995). *Introducing language awareness*. London: Penguin.
van Lier, L. (1996). *Interaction in the language curriculum: Awareness, autonomy and authenticity*. New York: Longman.

Van Manen, J. (1977). Linking ways of knowing with ways of being practical. *Curriculum Inquiry, 6,* 205–208.
van Rensburg, C. (1993). Die demokratisering van Afrikaans. In *Linguistica: Festschrift E. B. van Wyk* (pp. 141–153). Pretoria, South Africa: J. L. van Schaik.
van Rensburg, C. (Ed.). (1997). *Afrikaans in Afrika.* [Afrikaans in Africa.] Pretoria, South Africa: J. L. van Schaik.
van Uden, A. (1986). *Sign languages of deaf people and psycho-linguistics.* Lisse: Swets & Zeitlinger.
Verhoef, M. (1998a). Funksionele meertaligheid in Suid-Afrika: 'n ontereikbare ideaal? *Liberator, 19,* 35–50.
Verhoef, M. (1998b). 'n teoretiese aanloop tot taalgesindheidsbeplanning in Suid-Afrika. *South African Journal of Linguistics, 16,* 27–33.
Vihalemm, T., & Lauristin, M. (1997). Cultural adjustment to the changing societal environment: The case of Russians in Estonia. In M. Lauristin & P. Vihalemm (Eds.), *Return to the western world* (pp. 279–297). Tartu, Estonia: Tartu University Press.
Vitas, D. (1998). *Croatian.* Hauppauge, NY: Barron's Educational Series.
von Glasersfeld, E. (1984). An introduction to radical constructivism. In P. Watzlawick (Ed.), *The invented reality* (pp. 17–40). New York: Norton.
von Glasersfeld, E. (1989). Cognition, construction of knowledge, and teaching. *Synthese, 80,* 121–140.
von Glasersfeld, E. (1993). Questions and answers about radical constructivism. In K. Tobin (Ed.), *The practice of constructivism in science education* (pp. 23–38). Hillsdale, NJ: Lawrence Erlbaum Associates.
von Glasersfeld, E. (1995a). A constructivist approach to teaching. In L Steffe & J. Gale (Eds.), *Constructivism in education* (pp. 3–15). Hillsdale, NJ: Lawrence Erlbaum Associates.
von Glasersfeld, E. (1995b). *Radical constructivism: A way of knowing.* London: Falmer Press.
von Glasersfeld, E. (1996). Footnotes to 'The many faces of constructivism.' *Educational Researcher, 25,* 19.
Vygotsky, L. (1978). *Mind in society: The development of higher psychological processes.* Cambridge, MA: Harvard University Press.
Vygotsky, L. (1986). *Thought and language.* Cambridge, MA: MIT Press. (Original work published 1934)
Wagner, C. (1989). *Lengua y enseñanza: Fundamentos lingüisticos.* [Language and teaching: Linguistic fundamentals.] Santiago, Chile: Editorial Andres Bello, Universidad Austral de Chile.
Walker, G. (1989). The less commonly taught languages in the context of American pedagogy. In H. Lepke (Ed.), *Northeast conference on the teaching of foreign languages: Shaping the future* (pp. 111–137). Middlebury, VT: Northeast Conference on the Teaching of Foreign Languages.
Wallace, M. (1991). *Training foreign language teachers: A reflective approach.* Cambridge, England: Cambridge University Press.
Wallinger, L. (2000). American Sign Language instruction: Moving from protest to practice. *Northeast Conference on the Teaching of Foreign Languages Review, 48,* 27–36.
Walter, H. (1988). *Le français dans tous les sens.* Paris: Éditions Robert Laffont.
Wardhaugh, R. (1987). *Languages in competition: Dominance, diversity and decline.* Oxford, England: Basil Blackwell.
Wardhaugh, R. (1993). *Investigating language: Central problems in linguistics.* Oxford, England: Basil Blackwell.
Warren, A., & McCloskey, L. (1993). Pragmatics: Language in social context. In J. Gleason (Ed.), *The development of language* (3rd ed.; pp. 195–237). New York: Macmillan.
Webb, V. (Ed.). (1992). *Afrikaans ná apartheid.* [Afrikaans after apartheid.] Pretoria, South Africa: J. L. van Schaik.
Weinstein, B. (1980). Language planning in francophone Africa. *Language Problems and Language Planning, 4,* 55–77.

# REFERENCES

Weinstein, B. (Ed.). (1990). *Language policy and political development.* Norwood, NJ: Ablex Publishing.
Whatley, E. (1981). Language among black Americans. In C. Ferguson & S. Heath (Eds.), *Language in the U.S.A.* (pp. 92–107). Cambridge, England: Cambridge University Press.
Whiteman, M. (Ed.). (1980). *Reactions to Ann Arbor: Vernacular Black English and education.* Arlington, VA: Center for Applied Linguistics.
Wicklund, R., & Brehm, J. (1976). *Perspectives on cognitive dissonance.* Hillsdale, NJ: Lawrence Erlbaum Associates.
Widdowson, H. (1998). Skills, abilities, and contexts of reality. *Annual Review of Applied Linguistics, 18,* 323–333.
Wieczorek, J. (1994). The concept of 'French' in foreign language texts. *Foreign Language Annals, 27,* 487–497.
Wilcox, P. (2000). *Metaphor in American Sign Language.* Washington, DC: Gallaudet University Press.
Wilcox, S. (Ed.). (1989). *American deaf culture: An anthology.* Burtonsville, MD: Linstok Press.
Wilcox, S., & Wilcox, P. (1997). *Learning to see: American Sign Language as a second language* (2nd ed.). Englewood Cliffs, NJ: Prentice-Hall.
Williams, G. (1992). *Sociolinguistics: A sociological critique.* London: Routledge.
Williams, M., & Burden, R. (1997). *Psychology for language teachers: A social constructivist approach.* Cambridge, England: Cambridge University Press.
Williams, N. (1965). A language teaching experiment. *Canadian Modern Language Review, 22,* 26–28.
Winitzky, N., & Kauchak, D. (1997). Constructivism in teacher education: Applying cognitive theory to teacher learning. In V. Richardson (Ed.), *Constructivist teacher education* (pp. 59–83). London: Falmer Press.
Wink, J. (1997). *Critical pedagogy: Notes from the real world.* New York: Longman
Wink, J. (2000). *Critical pedagogy: Notes from the real world* (2nd ed.). New York: Longman.
Wolfram, W. (1979). *Speech pathology and dialect differences.* Arlington, VA: Center for Applied Linguistics.
Wolfram, W. (1998). Language, ideology and dialect: Understanding the Oakland Ebonics controversy. *Journal of English Linguistics, 26,* 108–121.
Wolfram, W., & Fasold, R. (1974). *The study of social dialects in American English.* Englewood Cliffs, NJ: Prentice-Hall.
Wong, S. (1993). Promises, pitfalls, and principles of text selection in curricular diversification: The Asian-American case. In T. Perry & J. Fraser (Eds.). *Freedom's plow* (pp. 109–120). New York: Routledge.
Wood, T., Cobb, P., & Yackel, E. (1995). Reflections of learning and teaching mathematics in elementary school. In L. Steffe & J. Gale (Eds.), *Constructivism in education* (pp. 401–422). Hillsdale, NJ: Lawrence Erlbaum Associates.
Woods, D. (1996). *Teacher cognition in language teaching: Beliefs, decision-making and classroom practice.* Cambridge, England: Cambridge University Press.
Woodward, A., Elliott, D., & Nagel, K. (Eds.). (1988). *Textbooks in school and society.* New York: Garland.
Wrigley, O. (1997). *The politics of deafness.* Washington, DC: Gallaudet University Press.
Yaguello, M. (1991). *Lunatic lovers of language: Imaginary languages and their inventors.* London: Athlone Press.
Young, D. (1988). Bilingualism and bilingual education in a divided South African society. In C. Paulston (Ed.), *International handbook of bilingualism and bilingual education* (pp. 405–428). New York: Greenwood.
Zamenhof, L. (1963). *Fundamento de Esperanto.* Marmande, France: Esperantaj Francaj Eldonoj. (Original work published 1905)
Zeichner, K., & Liston, D. (1987). Teaching student teachers to reflect. *Harvard Educational Review, 57,* 23–48.

Zeichner, K., & Liston, D. (1996). *Reflective teaching: An introduction.* Mahwah, NJ: Lawrence Erlbaum Associates.
Zietsman, A. (1996). Constructivism: Super theory for all educational ills? *South African Journal of Higher Education, 10,* 70–75.
Zotwana, S. (1991). *Xhosa in context: From novice to intermediate.* Cape Town, South Africa: Perskor.

# Author Index

## A

Achard, P., 62
Ackerman, D., 75, 76, 77
Afolayan, A., 115
African National Congress (South Africa), 121, 122, 123
Aikman, S., 102
Akinnaso, F., 115
Alexander, N., 115, 120
Alexander, R., 34
Allen, H., 33
Almond, B., 95
Altbach, P., 7, 110
Andrews, L., 138
Annamalai, E., 96
Anthonissen, C., 119
Anward, J., 64
Anyon, J., 7
Apple, M., 7, 8, 72
Applebaum, B., 140
Armstrong, N., 51
Asoko, H., 60
Augarde, T., 85, 95
Auld, W., 46

## B

Baai, Z., 126
Bahan, B., 44, 45, 103
Bailey, G., 37, 40
Baker, C., 106
Baldauf, R., 3, 95, 112
Ball, R., 51, 111
Ball, S., 50
Bamgbose, A., 126
Banjo, A., 126
Banks, J., 7

Barkhuizen, G., 118, 122, 126
Barnard, M., 122
Barnes, D., 58
Baron, D., 102, 112, 136
Barrow, R., 12
Bartlett, L., 17
Bartolomé, L., 62
Barzun, J., 1
Battison, R., 106
Baugh, J., 37, 38, 39, 40, 42
Baynton, D., 103
Beardsmore, H., 3
Beer, W., 115
Belka, R., 42
Benesch, S., 138
Bennet, J., 35
Benseler, D., 87
Benson, P., 96
Berliner, D., 24
Berthoud, I., 59
Beukes, A., 122, 124, 126
Beyer, L., 7
Bezberezhyeva, Y., 101
Biron, C., 76
Blackledge, A., 105
Blommaert, J., 118
Blyth, C., 56
Boseker, B., 102
Boulter, C., 62, 63
Bourdieu, P., 62
Bouvet, D., 103
Bowers, C., 9
Brady, J., 140
Bragg, L., 44
Braine, G., 26
Brananman, L., 3
Branson, J., 103
Brecht, R., 3

**171**

Brehm, J., 90
Breier, M., 120
Brink, A., 126
Brooks, M., 60
Brophy, J., 21
Brosh, H., 79
Brubacher, J. 22, 67, 85, 90, 94
Bucak, S., 100
Bullivant, B., 115, 121
Burde, A., 126
Burden, R., 56, 64, 67
Burling, R., 38
Burnaby, B., 96, 115
Butters, R., 40
Byrnes, D., 138

## C

California State University, 35
Campbell, G., 100
Case, C., 22, 26, 67, 85, 90, 94
Cawley, M., 128
Cenoz, J., 95
Chambers, J., 33, 36
Chambliss, J., 25
Chastain, K., 55
Chen, I., 9
Chen, P., 112
Chick, J., 122, 126
Chinn, P., 7
Chisanga, T., 122, 126
Chomsky, N., xiv, 12, 42
Christian, D., 110
Christian-Smith, L., 7
Christison, M., 20
Cioran, S., 136
Clachar, A., 100
Clandinin, D., 25
Cleary, L., 34
Cluver, A., 111, 122, 126
Clyde, J., 67
Clyne, M., 9
Cobarrubias, J., 110, 111, 114, 116
Cobb, P., 56, 59, 60
Cobern, W., 60
Cohen, H., 48
Cohen, L., 44
Collier, V., 6
Colton, A., 24, 25

Combrink, J., 126
Commins, P., 131
Condon, M., 67
Confrey, J., 60
Connelly, F., 25
Constitutional Assembly (South Africa), 122, 125
Coolahan, J., 130
Cooper, D., 55
Cooper, J., 19, 55, 135
Cooper, R., 109, 110, 111, 112
Co-ordinating Committee on the National Action Plan (South Africa), 126
Corson, D., 95, 102, 134
Coulombe, P., 97
Crabtree, C., 8
Craig, B., 9, 56, 62
Crawford, J., 102
Crookall, D., 64, 68
Crystal, D., 41, 99
Cummins, J., 6
Curriculum and Examinations Board (Ireland), 130
Curtain, H., 3

## D

Davis, R., 55
Davison, D., 76
DeFranco, T., 76, 77
Degenaar, J., 97
de Kadt, E., 126
de Klerk, V., 118
Delpit, L., 39, 41
Demos, J., 27
Department of Arts, Culture, Science and Technology (South Africa), 125, 126
Department of Education and Culture, House of Assembly (South Africa), 126
Department of National Education (South Africa), 121, 122
Desai, Z., 122, 126
de Saint Martin, M., 62
DeStefano, J., 38
Dewey, J., 13, 22, 71, 82, 85
Dicker, S., 83
di Lampedusa, G., 85

# AUTHOR INDEX

Dillard, J., 38
Djité, P., 114
Dogançay-Aktuna, S., 112
Donna, S., 32
Dorian, N., 129, 131
Dowling, T., 136
Driver, R., 60
Duffy, T., 58
Dunn, R., 8

## E

Eastman, C., 111, 113
Eco, U., 54
Edmondson, W., 43
Edwards, J., xi, 46, 95, 115, 127, 128, 129, 130, 131, 133
Elgin, S., xiv, 12, 41, 69, 137, 142
Elliott, D., 7
Ellis, Y., 51
Emenanjo, E., 112
Emmorey, K., 43
Erting, C., 103
Everson, M., 3

## F

Fairclough, N., 62, 126, 135
Faltis, C., 62
Fantini, A., 47
Fasold, R., 37
Fensham, P., 55
Fernandez, S., 9
Fettes, M., 102
Finchilescu, G., 125
Fischer, R., 44
Fischer, S., 43
Fishman, J., 110, 128, 131
Fitzgibbons, R., 21
Flinders, D., 9
Fodor, I., 113
Forman, G., 58
Forster, P., 46, 48
Fosnot, C., 26, 55, 58, 59, 65
Foucault, M., 50
Frank, H., 47
Franklin, P., 19
Frawley, W., 60
Fredericks, M., 56, 57
Freire, P., 28, 73, 80, 93

Frishberg, N., 45
Fromkin, V., 63

## G

Gaganakis, M., 126
Gale, J., 58
García-Moya, R., 9
Gardner, H., 20
Gardner, R., 64
Gee, J., 10
Gehlker, M., 76
Genesee, F., 95, 115
Gerard, J., 59
Gergen, K., 59
Gerwin, D., 78
Giroux, H., 28, 79, 91
Glenny, M., 33
Glisan, E., 76
Glossop, R., 47
González, R., 102
Goodlad, J., 13, 28, 32
Goodman, N., 77
Goodman, T., 47
Gollnick, D., 7
Gomes de Matos, F., 96
Goswami, D., 25
Gough, D., 122, 126
Gozzi, M., 76
Green, T., 57
Gregor, D., 47
Gregory, S., 44
Grennon Brooks, J., 56, 58, 60, 61
Grenoble, L., 99
Gruenais, M., 128
Grundy, P., 96
Guérard, A., 54
Gunnarsson, B., 62
Gunstone, R., 55
Guntermann, G., 19
Gutman, A., 13, 28
Guyton, E., 67

## H

Hadley, A., 3
Hagège, C., 113
Hale, T., 51
Haller, E., 32
Hamel, E., 102

Hamm, C., 12, 21
Harries, L., 112
Harrison, D., 37
Hartley, G., 44
Hartshorne, K., 120
Hashimoto, R., 56
Haugen, E., 112
Hawkesworth, C., 33
Heath, S., 10, 39
Hechter, M., 129
Henning, E., 67
Hernandez, R., 35, 36.
Hernández-Chávez, E., 102
Herriman, M., 96
Heugh, K., 120, 121, 122, 125, 126
Hindley, R., 112, 127, 128, 131, 133
Hinnebusch, T., 113
Hirst, P., 12
Hitler, A., 13
Hoffmeister, R., 43, 44, 103
Holborow, M., 126
Holmes, S., 35
Hornberger, N., 102
Hovda, R., 67
Howard, G., 140
Hudson, R., 33
Hudson-Edwards, A., 129
Humphries, T., 44
Hymes, D., 5, 10

# I

Irwin, J., 21, 24, 25, 86
Itakura, H., 96
Ivanič, R., 126

# J

Jacob, J., 115
Jacobowitz, E., 45
Jacobs, H., 76
Jacobs, R., 42
Jacobvitz, R., 140
Janks, H., 126
Janton, P., 46, 47
Jarvis, D., 87
Jarvis, G., 4, 5
Jernudd, B., 109, 111, 117
Johnson, M., 56, 69

Johnson, R., 51, 103
Jonassen, D., 58
Jordan, D., 47
Joseph, J., 114

# K

Kafai, Y., 58
Kagan, O., 87
Kamii, C., 55
Kamwangamalu, N., 121, 122, 126, 127
Kanpol, B., 140
Kaplan, R., 95, 112
Karlsson, F., 43
Kaschula, R., 119
Kashoki, M., 122
Kauchak, D., 61, 62
Kaufman, D., 56, 58, 60, 61
Keane, M., 128
Keeskes, I., 4
Keiny, S., 67
Kelly, G., 7
Kennedy, C., 110, 111
Kerr, D., 117
Kerth, T., 44
Khubchandani, L., 115
Kiger, G., 138
Killion, J., 22, 23
Kincheloe, J., 72
King, K., 102, 112
King, M., 126
Klee, C., 51
Kloss, H., 125
Knowlson, J., 54
Kochman, T., 38
Kramer, C., 53
Kramsch, C., 78
Krashen, S., 69
Kriel, M., 126
Krishnaswamy, N., 126
Kroll, S., 53
Kumaravadivelu, B., 56
Kyle, D., 67
Kyle, J., 43

# L

Labov, W., 37, 38, 39
Ladwig, J., 85

# AUTHOR INDEX

Lakoff, G., 56, 69
Lakoff, R., 35, 36
Lambert, R., 111, 134
Lampe, J., 33, 53
Lane, H., 42, 43, 44, 103, 106
Lanehart, S., 37, 54
Language Plan Task Group (South Africa), 107, 124
Lanier, J., 26
Lantolf, J., 60
Large, A., 47, 54
Larson, C., 140
Laurence, D, 19
Lauristin, M., 100, 102
Leach, J., 60
Lee, G., 27
Lee, P., 41
Lemmer, E., 120
Leonard, P., 28
Leon-Smith, G., 47
Lessow-Hurley, J., 77
Lewis, E., 131
Liddell, S., 103
Lillo-Martin, D., 43
Linell, P., 62
Ling, D., 48, 49
Linn, M., 33, 34
Lins, U., 47
Lippi-Green, R., 51, 54, 83
Lipton, G., 3
Liskin-Gasparro, J., 3
Liston, D., 25, 26, 67
Littlewood, W., 55
Lockhart, C., 67
Lodge, R., 51
Lohnes, W., 87
Lomas, C., 12
Lonning, R., 76, 77
Louw, J., 115, 125
Louw-Potgieter, J., 125
Low, W., 45
Lowenberg, P., 126
Lozano, A., 9
Lubensky, S., 87
Lucas, C., 43
Luelsdorff, P., 38
Luke, A., 7
Lyons, N., 140

## M

Maartens, J., 126
Macedo, D., 102
MacMillan, M., 97
Macnamara, J., 128
MacPherson, L., 46
Magadla, L., 59
Magner, T., 88
Maguire, G., 128
Maher, C., 55
Malan, C., 122
Mamdani, M., 126
Mancing, H., 43, 44
Manning, G., 55
Manning, M., 55, 138
Mansoor, S., 126
Mansour, G., 120
Marinova-Todd, S., 15
Marivate, C., 120
Markarian, R., 47
Mar-Molinero, C., 51, 112
Marr, T., 102
Marshall, D. , 15
Martel, A., 71
Martin-Jones, M., 6
Matras, Y., 99, 100
Mawasha, A., 126
Maxwell, B., 36
Maxwell, D., 46
Maynor, N., 40
Mazrui, Alamin, 110, 127
Mazrui, Ali, 110, 127
McCloskey, L., 39
McKay, S., 117
McKeon, D., 6, 15
McLaren, P., 28, 91, 140
McRae, K., 97
McWhorter, J., 35, 36, 37, 38
Measures, E., 62
Melis, I., 102
Merrill, M., 58
Methany, D., 76
Metzger, M., 43
Miller, D., 103
Miller, K., 76
Miller, S., 56, 57
Mintzes, J., 55

Miskel, C., 26
Mokoena, A., 136
Moll, L., 60
Moore, J., 46
Moores, D., 103
Morris, R., 125
Mortimer, E., 60
Msimang, C., 126
Mtintsilana, P., 125
Mtuze, M., 118
Mufwene, S., 37, 38, 39, 40
Munnik, A., 136
Muñoz, J., 140
Musker, P., 126
Mutasa, D., 126

## N

Nagel, K., 7
Nahir, M., 111, 112, 113
Nash, G., 8
National Council of Teachers of Mathematics, 76
National Education Policy Investigation (South Africa), 120, 123
National Standards in Foreign Language Education Project, 8, 75, 76
Natsis, J., 51
Nattinger, J., 57
Ndebele, N., 120, 126
Neisser, A., 49, 106
Nelson, K., 55, 63, 64
Nettle, D., 16, 99
Nicaise, M., 58
Nieto, S., 7
Noddings, N., 55, 59
Nollendorfs, V., 87
Nordberg, B., 62
Norlander-Case, K., 22
Norris, D., 33
Novak, J., 55
Nover, S., 103
Ntshoe, I., 120
Nuessel, F., 46, 47, 57
Nwachukwu, P., 112
Nxumalo, T., 136
Nyawose, G., 125
Nyikos, M., 56

## O

Ó Baoill, D., 129
O'Cinneide, M., 128
Ó Domhnalláin, T., 128
Ó Dubhghaill, A., 128
Office of the Deputy President (T. M. Mbeki) (South Africa), 125
Ogunbiyi, I., 115
Ó Huallacháin, C., 128
Okrand, M., 52
Okumus, E., 100
Olivier, P., 96
Olszewski, L., 35
Ó Riagáin, P., 112, 128
O'Rourke, T., 103
Orr, E., 41, 42
Ortony, A., 69
Osborn, T., xiii, 2, 8, 16, 29, 30, 72, 76, 78, 79, 87, 89, 137, 142
Ó Siadhail, M., 128
Osora, A., 12
Ovando, C., 138, 140
Overfield, D., 76
Oxford, R., 64, 68
Ozolins, U., 100, 101

## P

Padden, C., 44
Papp, T., 4
Parker, S., 67
Partridge, M., 33
Passeron, J., 62.
Paulston, C., 128, 129
Payne, J., 100
Peeters, Y., 122
Péguy, C., 95
Peirce, B., 126
Penn, C., 124
Pennycook, A., 47, 97, 117, 127, 135, 138
Perry, T., 39, 41
Pesola, C., 3
Peters, C., 45
Peters, R., 12
Petrie, H., 7
Phillips, J., 66

# AUTHOR INDEX

Phillipson, R., 47, 96, 97, 110, 114, 117, 126, 127
Piaget, J., 59
Pieterse, H., 122
Pinnock, P., 136
Piron, C., 127
Plüddemann, P., 126
Ponayi, M., 23
Posner, R., 34
Preskill, S., 140
Pretorius, F., 120
Prillwitz, S., 43
Prinsloo, K., 122
Prinsloo, M., 120
Pufall, P., 58
Pullum, G., 54

## Q

Quell, C., 62
Quick, M., 47

## R

Rahman, T., 126
Rainer, J., 67
Ramanathan, V., 126
Rannut, M., 96, 101, 102
Reagan, G., 25
Reagan, T., xiii, 2, 8, 22, 44, 45, 47, 50, 54, 62, 67, 78, 79, 85, 89, 90, 94, 102, 103, 106, 110, 115, 116, 118, 120, 121, 122, 124, 126, 127, 138
Rée, J., 43
Reid, J., 20
Reilly, J., 43
Resnick, M., 58
Rhodes, N., 3
Ricento, T., 115
Richards, J., 19, 67
Richardson, D., 46, 67
Richardson, V., 58, 59
Richmond, I., 47
Rickford, J., 37, 38, 39, 40, 42
Rickford, R., 42
Ridge, S., 122
Rifkin, B., 87
Robinson, C., 126

Rodman, R., 63
Romaine, S., 6, 99, 129, 132, 133
Rouchdy, A., 88
Rubin, J., 109, 117, 128
Ruíz, R., 9
Rutherford, S., 45
Ryazanova-Clarke, L., 113

## S

Sáenz-Badillos, A., 112
Safford, E., 103
Safford, P., 103
Samway, K., 6, 15
Sarason, S., 29
Sarinjeive, D., 126
Scheffer, I., 57
Schein, J., 44
Schiffman, H., 110, 126
Schlyter, B., 100
Schmied, J., 126
Schmitt, N., 19
Schneider, E., 37, 38
Schön, D., 22
Schorr, J., 35
Schmitt, N., 19
Schuring, G., 122, 126
Schwandt, T., 58
Scott, J., 42
Scott, P., 60
Scott, R., 92
Senese, G., 27
Shanahan, D., 77
Shapiro, J., 104, 107
Shapiro, M., 111
Shelton, J., 51
Sherwood, B., 47
Shrum, J., 76
Shulman, L., 18, 19, 20
Siegelman, E., 57
Siegrühn, A., 126
Silberman, C., 21
Simon, P., 5
Sinclair, H., 59
Siple, S., 43
Skutnabb-Kangas, T., 16, 96, 97, 98, 99, 100, 103, 126, 127, 135
Slattery, P., 72
Sleeter, C., 140, 141

# AUTHOR INDEX

Smit, B., 126
Smit, U., 126
Smith, J., 141, 143.
Smith, N., 69
Smitherman, G., 36, 38
Snow, C., 15
Soder, R., 13
Soltis, J., 32, 90
Sparks-Langer, G., 24, 25
Spivey, N., 56
Spolsky, B., 6
Spring, J., 27, 95, 98
Srivastava, R., 115
Staples, B., 35
Steedman, P., 7
Steffe, L., 7, 56, 58
Steinberg, S., 72
Stevenson, P., 51, 112
Stevick, E., 56
Stewart, W., 37
Steyn, J., 120, 125
Stillman, P., 25
Stokoe, W., 42, 106
Strike, K., 32, 90
Strike, N., 126
Summo-O'Connell, R., 9
Šušnjar, A., 53
Swanepoel, P., 122
Symoens, E., 47
Szerdahelyi, I., 47

## T

Taagepera, R., 100, 101
Tai, J., 112
Tarsitani, C., 56
Taylor, T., 114
Taylor, W., 69
Teal, S., 25
Terrell, T., 69
Thomas, A., 126
Thompson, L., 120
Tobin, K., 56
Todd, L., 40
Todnem, G., 22, 23
Tollefson, J., 97, 104, 109, 111, 112, 117, 126, 135
Tonkin, H., xii, 47
Tozer, S., 27

Trabasso, T., 37
Traugott, E., 40
Trudgill, P., 33, 38. 40
Turi, J., 122
Tutu, D., 49

## U

Uzicanin, N., 51

## V

Valdés, G., 9
Valdman, A., 51
Valli, C., 43
van Cleve, J., 44
van den Berg, O., 126
van Dijk, T., 117
Van Doren, M., 17
van Lier, L., 62, 138
Van Manen, J., 23
van Rensburg, C., 122, 126
van Uden, A., 42
Veneziano, E., 59
Verhoef, M., 122, 125, 126
Vihalemm, T., 100, 102
Violas, P., 27
Vitas, D., 51
Vollhaber, T., 43
von Glasersfeld, E., 56, 58, 59, 60, 61, 68
Vygotsky, L., 60

## W

Wade, R., 122, 126
Wade, T., 113
Wagner, C., 95
Walker, G., 3
Wallace, M., 19, 26
Wallinger, L., 42
Walter, H., 51
Walton, A., 3
Walworth, M., 103
Wandersee, J., 55
Wardhaugh, R., 55, 128, 129, 132
Warren, A., 39
Webb, V., 126
Weinland, T., 76, 77
Weinreich, M., 33, 53

# AUTHOR INDEX

Weinstein, B., 110, 114
Weis, L., 7
Welles, E., 19
Wells, G., 62
Whaley, L., 99
Whatley, E., 38
White, R., 55
Whiteman, M., 36
Wicklund, R., 90
Widdowson, H., 66
Wieczorek, J., 79
Wilcox, P., 42, 45
Wilcox, S., 42, 44, 106
Williams, G., 111
Williams, M., 56, 64, 67
Williams, N., 47
Winitzky, N., 61, 62
Wink, J., 73, 86
Wolfram, W., 36, 37, 39, 41
Woll, B., 43
Wong, S., 79

Wood, T., 56
Woods, D., 62
Woods, R., 12
Woodward, A., 7
Wrigley, O., 104

## Y

Yackel, E., 56
Yaguello, M., 54
Young, D., 115

## Z

Zahirovič, D., 53
Zamenhof, L., 47
Zeichner, K., 25, 26, 67
Zeller, I., 76
Zietsman, A., 67
Zotwana, S., 136

# Subject Index

## A

academic freedom, 86
Aelfric of Eynsham, 143
Africa,
    anglophone, 115
    francophone, 114–115
African American Vernacular English
    (AAVE), xii, 35–42, 46, 48–50,
    52, 54
African National Congress (ANC),
    121–123, 125
Afrikaans, 119–122, 125–127, 140
American Sign Language (ASL), xii,
    35–36, 42–46, 48–49, 52,
    102–103, 140
Anglo-Normans, 128
Anglo-Saxon, 140, 143
apartheid, 118–120, 122, 126
Arabic, 3, 5, 88, 115, 119
assessment, authentic, 80
audiolingual method, 1, 55

## B

*Bantu Education Act,* 120
basic interpersonal communicative skills
    (BICS), 6, 14
behaviorism, 55, 59
bilingualism, xi, xii, 4, 14, 69, 119–120,
    122, 126, 129, 139
bilingual education, 5–6, 10, 15
Black English, *see* African American
    Vernacular English
Black English Vernacular (BEV), *see* African American Vernacular English
Bosnian, 34, 53

## C

California State University, 35
Canada, 102, 115
chauvinism,
    bicultural, 4
    linguistic, xii
China, People's Republic, 112
Chinese, 3, 112
code switching, 10, 139
    official, 10
cognitive academic language proficiency
    (CALP), 6, 12
colonialism, 110, 120
communicative approach, 1, 77, 138
constructivism, xii, 55–56, 58–62, 64–65,
    67
    radical, 59–60
    social, 60, 62
corpus planning, 111–112, 124–125
critical
    activism, 91, 93
    language awareness, xii, 12, 81, 105,
        134–135, 139
    language education, 72
    multiculturalism, 91
    pedagogy, 27–32, 86, 92, 137
Croatian, 34, 53
culture, 78, 80–81, 95, 139
    dominant, 28
    dominated, 28, 47, 107
    genocide, 102–103
    teaching, 77, 79–80, 138
curricular nullification, 87–91, 93–94,
    140
    additive, 89–90, 93
    consequential, 89

dissonantal, 89–90, 93
ethical, 89–91, 93
harmonious, 89, 91
intentional, 89, 91
subtractive, 89, 94
unethical, 89–90, 94
curriculum,
bias, 7, 142–143
critical approach, 71, 75
critical language, 72–73, 79–80, 82
development, 71–73, 76
foreign language, 71, 76, 79–80, 82
formal, 7–8, 142
hidden, 7, 142
integration, 75
interdisciplinary, 75–78, 80–83
national, 72
Curriculum and Examinations Board, 130

## D

Danish, 33, 140
Deaf, 44–45, 102–106
deafness,
medical/pathological view, 103, 106
sociocultural view, 103, 106–107
decision–making, 29
*Declaration of Indigenous Peoples Human Rights,* 98
decreolist theory, 40
democracy, xii, 13, 27–28, 71, 118, 125, 142
desirability test, 117
dialect, 33–35, 50, 53; *see also* language variety
discourse, xii, 91–92, 104
classroom, 10
educational, 34, 41, 57
human rights, 95–96
public, 57
scientific, 62
dissonance, cognitive, 90–91
Dutch, 140

## E

Ebonics, *see* African American Vernacular English
educated person, xii, 12, 137

education,
democratic, 13, 29
liberal, 20
matter, 21
manner, 21
means, 95
moral dimensions, 32
mother-tongue, 125–127; *see also* bilingual education, *moedertaalonderwys*
multicultural, 78
outcomes, 21, 95
policy, 95, 110, 120–122, 130, 136
process goals 25
product goals, 25
vocational, 20
effectiveness test, 118
Egypt, 115
*Engleutsch,* 112
English, xi, 5–6, 10–11, 15, 26, 33, 35, 37, 43, 45, 47–49, 63, 75, 78, 102, 112, 115, 119, 120–122, 126–127, 129, 132–133, 138, 143
American, 37–38, 40, 42, 52
Black, *see* African American Vernacular English
mainstream, 37, 42
non-standard, 35
standard, 40
epistemology, 7, 55–56, 58, 64–65, 67, 78
genetic, 59
Eskimo, 54
Esperanto, xii, 35–36, 46–49, 52, 140
Estonia, 100–102, 105
Estonian, 101–102
ethics, professional, 26, 32
European Union (EU), 132

## F

Finland, 101
foreign language,
cognitive arguments, 4, 12
cultural arguments, 4, 12
pragmatic arguments, 4–5, 12
"foreignness," 87, 93
*Franglais,* 111–112

# SUBJECT INDEX

French, xi, 1, 3–5, 9, 13, 45–46, 51, 111–112, 115, 141

## G

Gaelic, Scots, 128
Gaeltacht, 129, 131, 133
German, xi, 1, 3–4, 33, 45–46, 51, 68, 87, 112, 140
grammar-translation approach, 1, 137
Greek, 45, 143
Guam, 114

## H

Hebrew, 112, 115, 119
Hopi, 45

## I

Ibo, 112
ideological hegemony, 7, 92
ideology, 51, 54, 79, 87, 92, 95, 97, 104, 110–111,113–116, 120, 126, 139
ideology of language policy, 113–116
India, 115
indigenous people(s), 98, 102
intelligence(s),
    bodily-kinesthetic, 20
    interpersonal, 20
    intrapersonal, 20
    logical-mathematical, 20
    multiple, 20
    musical, 20
    naturalistic, 20
    spatial-visual, 20
    verbal-linguistic, 20
Interagency Language Roundtable Scale (ILR), 3
internationalization, 114–116
Iran, 99
Iraq, 99
Ireland, 118, 128–133
Irish, 112, 118, 127–133, 135
Isle of Man, 128
Israel, 112, 115
Italian, 141

## J

Japanese, 3, 5, 47

justness test, 118

## K

*King v. Ann Arbor*, 36
Kiunguja *see* Swahili
Klingon, 52
knowledge,
    construction, 69, 81
    content, 18–19
    curriculum, 18–19
    misconstruction, 66, 69, 94
    of educational contexts, 18, 20
    of educational ends, 18, 20
    of learners, 18, 20
    pedagogical, 18–19
    pedagogical content, 18, 20
    school, 85
    scientific, 60
    tacit, 23
Kurdish, 99–100
Kurds, 99

## L

language(s), 33, 50, 53
    acquisition, 6, 46, 64, 69, 139
    African, 119, 124–127, 136
    attitude planning, 124
    attitudes, xii, 105, 133, 137, 139
    auxiliary, 46
    awareness, 73
    Celtic, 128
    change, 139
    classical, 141–142
    deficit, 40–41, 103, 107
    difference, 41, 125, 139
    diversity, 52, 78, 99, 110, 115, 119, 127, 139
    ecology, 139
    equity, 119
    European, 127
    families, 139
    Germanic, 44
    heritage, 10, 26–27
    human, xiv, 8, 12, 39, 46, 54
    Indian, 115
    indigenous, 45
    idiolect, 63

integration, 119
international, 46
modernization, 111–113, 136
morphology, 19
non-human, xiii
pathology, 139
phonology, 19, 38–39
planning, xiii, 109–111, 113–114, 116–127, 133–136, 139
policy, xii, xiii, 97, 102–127, 130, 135–136, 139
purification, 111
purism, 139
reform, 112
responsibilities, 105, 139
revitalization, 111–112
rights, xii, 49, 95–99, 102–106, 115, 119, 122, 124, 126–127, 139
Romance, 34
sign, 16, 43, 107
Slavic, 44
standardization, 111–112
struggle (taalstryd), 120
syntax, 39
toleration, 127
variety, 36–38, 46, 50, 54
variation, 33, 51, 139
language of wider communication (LWC), xi, 47, 115, 119, 132
Language Plan Task Group (LANGTAG), 124
Latin, 4, 112, 128, 141–143
Latin America, 102
Latvia, 100
learning, second language, 11, 15, 139
learning theory, 55–56, 58, 67
less commonly taught languages, 10
linguistic assimilation, 114–116, 136
linguistic genocide, 102–103
linguistic imperialism, 97, 103
linguistic legitimacy, xii, 8, 33–36, 49–50, 102, 139
linguistic pluralism, 114–115, 136
linguistic prescriptivism, 38
linguistic relativity, *see* Sapir–Whorf hypothesis
linguistic universals, 12
literacy, 28, 119–120, 139
literature, 79, 137
literary genres, 45

Lithuania, 100

## M

Macedonian, 53
macrocontextualization, 72
Manx, 128
metalinguistics, xiii, 138–140, 142
metaphors, 56–58
*moedertaalonderwys*, 120–121
monolingualism, xi, 5, 14, 104, 114–115, 137
Morocco, 115
multilingualism, xi, xii, 14, 95, 110, 115, 118–119, 121–122, 125–127
mutual intelligibility, 33

## N

National Education Policy Investigation, 123
native speaker, 10, 26–27, 30–31, 53, 93–94, 140
Navajo, 43
Nigeria, 112, 115
Norman-French, 129
Norwegian, 33, 112

## P

paradigm, incommensurable, 104
Pedi, 125
Peru, 115
Philippines, 114–115
Plato, 25
pluralist dilemma, 121
*Policy Framework for Education and Training*, 122
portfolios, 140
positivism, 29
praxis, 73, 91, 140
problem posing, 73–74, 82
Puerto Rico, 114

## Q

Quechua, 115

## R

racism, 7
reading, *see* literacy

# SUBJECT INDEX

*Reconstruction and Development Programme,* 121
reflection, 22
   cognitive element, 24–25
   critical, 24, 27, 85–86, 91, 140
   critical element, 24
   for-practice, 22–23, 26
   in-practice, 22–23, 26
   levels/hierarchy, 23
   narrative element, 24–25
   on-practice, 22–23, 26
reflective inquiry, 17
reflective practice, 17, 22, 25–26, 32, 85
religion, 27
rights, 135
   human, 95–99, 102, 105
   language, xii, 49, 95–99, 102–106, 115, 119, 122, 124, 126–127, 139
   linguistic human, 99
Russian, 3, 45, 87, 101, 113, 140

## S

Sanskrit, 119
Sapir-Whorf hypothesis, 41, 54
Saxonist movement, 112
schemata, 24
Scotland, 128
Serbian, 34, 53, 141
Serbo-Croatian, 33, 53
Sesotho, 125, 136
sexism, 7
*Sign Language Structures,* 42
social expectation of failure, 6
South Africa, 49, 103, 107, 115, 118–120, 123–125, 127, 135–136
South African Sign Language (SASL), 103, 107, 124–125
Southern Sotho, *see* Sesotho
Soviet Union, *see* Union of Soviet Socialist Republics
Spanish, xi, 1, 3–4, 8–9, 19, 46, 51, 111, 141
*Standards for Foreign Language Learning,* 76
standards, national, 8, 75
*Star Trek,* 52
status planning, 111, 124–125
Swahili, 88, 112, 115, 125
Swedish, 33, 101
Swedish Sign Language, 103

Syria, 99, 115

## T

*taalstryd, see* language struggle
Tagalog, 115
Tanzania, 112, 115
teaching,
   as art, 17, 21
   as science, 17, 21
   knowledge base, 18, 21, 30–32
textbook(s), 7–8, 77, 94, 115, 117, 142
tolerability test, 118
translation, machine, 14
Tsonga, 125
Turkey, 99, 100

## U

Union of Soviet Socialist Republics (USSR), 100, 113
UNESCO, 43
*United Nations Declaration on the Rights of Persons Belonging to National or Ethnic, Religious and Linguistic Minorities,* 97–98, 103
United States, 102–103, 135–137, 140
U.S. English Movement, 102, 106
*Universal Declaration of Human Rights,* 97–98

## V

validity, connective, 78–79
Vernacular Black English (VBE), *see* African American Vernacular English
vernacularization, 114–115

## W

writing, *see* literacy

## X

Xhosa, 136, 141

## Y

Yugoslavia, 33

## Z

Zulu, 125, 141